MOONLIGHTING

148 Great Ways to Make Money on the Side

MOONLIGHTING

148 Great Ways to Make Money on the Side

CARL HAUSMAN

— and —

The Philip Lief Group

Produced by The Philip Lief Group

AVON BOOKS ◆ NEW YORK

MOONLIGHTING: 148 GREAT WAYS TO MAKE MONEY ON THE SIDE is an original publication of Avon Books. This work has never before appeared in book form.

AVON BOOKS
A division of
The Hearst Corporation
105 Madison Avenue
New York, New York 10016

First Avon Books Trade Printing: February 1989

AVON TRADEMARK REG. U.S. PAT. OFF. AND IN OTHER COUNTRIES, MARCA REGIS-TRADA, HECHO EN U.S.A.

Printed in the U.S.A.

OPM 10 9 8 7 6 5 4

CONTENTS _____

Contents

INTRODUCTION

For Steve Jobs and Steve Wozniak, the dream to build a better home computer began as a part-time venture in a garage. As any computer folklorist knows, their garage-based workshop grew to become Apple Computer.

Not all successful home-based business grow so grandly, of course. A Boston-area arts administrator who started a moonlighting janitorial firm saw the business grow into a full-time venture. The business is no Apple Computer, but it does gross about $60,000 a year.

Of course, not everyone wants to supplant his or her full-time job. Many moonlighters just want some extra cash and, perhaps more important, the satisfaction of owning a part-time enterprise that is all their own, a business dependent solely on their abilities and perseverance. Across the nation, people who moonlight as writers, cabinetmakers, interior decorators, even errand runners use their ingenuity to invent new approaches and solve old problems.

THE MOONLIGHTING REVOLUTION

Just a few years ago, "moonlighting" brought to mind late-night drudgery performed by people who just couldn't meet their expenses with their day-job salary alone. But all that has changed—dramatically. Today, moonlighting is considered a respectable, if not always glamorous, way to earn extra cash, develop new skills, and satisfy deep-seated creative urges.

It's also a growing trend. According to the U.S. Bureau of Labor Statistics, approximately four million Americans hold two jobs, and of those four million about half are white-collar professionals. An interesting aside to this figure is that an increasing number of moonlighters are self-employed; about one and a half million people are self-employed at least part-time.

One other very important statistic for people with an entrepreneurial

1

bent: the home is becoming an increasingly important center of business activity. It's estimated that there are about ten million Americans who market their talents and skills from their home either full- or part-time.

But what do the numbers mean? Quite simply, they translate to opportunities for freedom and fulfillment. The era of the home-based moonlighter is dawning. No less an authority than John Naisbitt, author of *Megatrends,* has predicted that home-based entrepreneurs will become an increasingly crucial part of the nation's economic framework. Futurist Alvin Toffler concurs, and asserts that the increased ease of transmitting information will give birth to a rising number of "electronic cottages," home-based workstations linked by computer to information-processing centers. And every economic indicator available heralds the continuing growth of service industries—low-investment businesses ideal for the home-based entrepreneur.

THE BEST OF ALL POSSIBLE WORLDS

If you're considering a home-based moonlighting venture, the odds are on your side, and they're better than ever before. Now is the time to take stock of your abilities and interests and make a comprehensive assessment of the opportunities available. That, of course, is exactly what we'll be doing in this book.

But first, a fundamental question needs to be asked: Why think about home-based moonlighting in the first place? There are several very good answers, and some of them may surprise you a bit. Home-based moonlighting offers:

- Diversity and a cushion against the shocks of the full-time job market. The arts administrator/janitorial service owner mentioned earlier enjoyed a great deal of autonomy in his work because he wasn't completely dependent on his day job. When push came to shove, it was the day job that got shoved in favor of the higher paying moonlighting business. But it's not always a matter of substituting one job for another. Many moonlighters find that their second career can actually help advance them in their regular job. New skills picked up from a part-time sales position, for example, enabled one technician to make the step from repairman to highly paid manufacturer's representative. Similar growth-oriented success stories have revolved around moonlighting-inspired computer skills, writing abilities, and management capabilities.
- The benefits of entrepreneurship without many of the costs. An outside office can be stunningly expensive, not only because of rent but because of the myriad hidden costs: utilities, extra insurance, transportation to and from the office, and the need to purchase duplicate items already available in the home. Cost control is in itself a source of con-

siderable income, and no one is in a better position to control those costs than the moonlighter who uses the basement for an office and a card table for a desk.

- Flexibility. Presumably you've already got someone setting your schedule from nine to five, so the last thing you need is a rigid requirement that you be behind the bar at The Four Aces Grill from six to eleven. The costs of this rigidity are deeper than you might at first suspect. For one thing, you may have an infrequent overflow of work from your day job; if that work can't be done at night, your primary source of income will be compromised. Also, if you're a parent, you know you can't always predict what will happen on a given day. You need to be able to adjust your schedule to meet the ordinary and not so ordinary demands of family life. And don't forget the exhaustion principle: you can't do your best work on those days when you're feeling physically and mentally beat up. Most home-based moonlighting jobs allow for some flexibility and therefore let you do your best work.

- A virtually uncapped second income. One moonlighting writer made $20,000 from a how-to book that involved six months' worth of writing evenings and weekends. You might not make that much from writing a book (or starting a cleaning business, or establishing a practice as a financial planner, or selling insurance), but, then again, you might. As many home-based businesspeople point out, the thrill of the business is the possibility of grabbing that brass ring. The main job provides the steady income; the moonlighting job offers the promise.

- An opportunity to play and win at your own game. During the day you play by someone else's rules and are largely under the control of external factors. Without a specific academic degree or the requisite political contacts, you might be dead-ended in your present job or field. Moonlighting, though, gives you a chance to corner a piece of the market and make it your own. An expert part-time cake decorator or instructional video producer can learn the business inside out and succeed on personal initiative, not degrees or contacts. While a home-based entrepreneur will always be subject to external factors (competition being the most important), he or she can avoid such roadblocks as office politics or the boss's nephew.

TIME-SHIFTING AND THE MOONLIGHTER

A major factor in the success profiles of home-based moonlighting businesses is the shift in working times brought about by changes in technology and the nature of service-oriented businesses. In simpler terms, there are many more businesses today that can be run successfully during evening and weekend hours. A part-time research firm (an excellent prospect, by the way) can do literally all of its work during evenings and weekends because computer databases function 24 hours a day. In fact, the cost of using the database is typically far less during evenings and weekends.

A part-time service industry today often will find nights and weekends to be the times of peak demand. As examples, consider the astounding growth of entertainment-related service industries, such as disc jockeys with mobile sound-playback equipment who are cashing in on the growing demand for after-hours entertainment. Also, examine the phenomenal growth of financial planning services, which, by their nature, are offered during other people's non-working hours.

But if you have a primary job that allows you freedom during typical business hours (or you don't have a primary job), so much the better. You'll be able to capitalize on services offered to people who can't find the time to get things done during the day. Also, you will be able to meet and interact with businesspeople more conveniently.

Either way, you *can* start a home-based business as long as you meet two basic criteria:

1. You must have the potential and temperament to be a home-based moonlighter.
2. There must be a market for your product or service.

ANALYZING YOUR POTENTIAL

First, give some serious thought to whether you really want to work at home. While there are many pleasant aspects to home work and entrepreneurship in general, there are problems as well. It's wise to consider them honestly now. Also, give some thought to whether you are cut out to be an entrepreneur—whether you have the capacity for risk and almost unending hard work.

If you foresee a major problem in either area, maybe home-based moonlighting is not for you. Ask yourself these two questions:

Question #1: Can I Tolerate Working at Home?

"I feel like I don't really have an office and I don't really have a home," notes one rather unhappy home-based consultant. "During the day, when I want to be working, there are always home-related chores that need attention. My wife thinks nothing of having a repairman stop by at noon because she knows I'll be there to let him in. But dealing with a repairman can take most of the afternoon—nothing's ever simple, and they always need you to make a dozen decisions.

"Now at night, I'd like to put things aside and maybe watch a football game. But the work is always down there [in the basement office] waiting to be done, and sometimes I can't put it out of my mind."

A home-based moonlighter has to be able to handle this tug-of-war over his or her living quarters and available time. Experts advise that you set minimum and maximum hours on your home-based business. Too few hours will lead to failure, for obvious reasons. Too many hours spent on your part-time business will detract from your regular job and your family life. In addition, you'll probably find that by capping your time commitment you impose deadlines on yourself, and people who work under deadlines usually get more done in less time than those who allow the task at hand to expand and consume them.

You also need self-discipline. However you do it, you must abandon the mind-set and start *working* during your scheduled hours. Some people put a sign up on the home office door telling family members, in no uncertain terms, that they are not to be bothered. At least one other home-based entrepreneur takes a walk around the block, leaving his "home" and returning to his "office."

Question #2: Do I Have an Entrepreneurial Personality?

According to the U.S. Small Business Administration, research indicates that successful entrepreneurs generally share certain characteristics. You can find out if you possess these attributes by taking the following quiz. Fill in a Y if you feel that the entry describes you. Write N if it does not. Enter U if you can't decide.

Entrepreneurial Trait Indicator

_____ I have a strong desire to be my own boss.

_____ Win, lose, or draw, I want to be master of my own financial destiny.

_____ I have significant specialized business ability based on both my education and my experience.

_____ I have an ability to conceptualize the whole of a business—not just individual parts, but also how they relate to each other.

_____ I believe I would intuitively sense what is "right" for my business and have the courage to pursue it.

_____ One or both of my parents were entrepreneurs; calculated risk-taking runs in the family.

_____ My life is characterized by a willingness and a capacity to persevere.

_____ I possess a high level of energy, sustainable over long hours to make the business successful.

While the test is not infallible, and not every successful home-based entrepreneur will answer yes to every question, you may wish to reevaluate your plans if you answered *U* or *N* to three or four questions.

ANALYZING THE POTENTIAL OF THE BUSINESS _____

No matter how great your prowess as an entrepreneur, you'll need a product or service that will sell and produce a decent income. In addition, your business should be especially adaptable for success as a part-time home-based operation.

What types of businesses fit that description? Dr. Geoffrey Kessler, a Los Angeles-based consultant who specializes in entrepreneurship, maintains that the home-based moonlighter will do best in "simple businesses in which the customer's needs occur at the times when you can meet them." A simple business gives you the advantage of learning the process of running a business while not being overburdened with technical complexities. The advantages of being available when customers need you are obvious; should they find you not available, it is far too easy for them to take their business elsewhere.

Finding a simple business that allows you to do the work when it's needed really isn't so difficult; this book contains 148 such prospects and there are assuredly thousands more, including many you may think of while reading this book. The difficult part is matching your skills and ambitions with the demand for your product or service. Remember, there really must be a match. You may have a terrific skill, but it won't produce a dime of profit if there's no demand for it. Conversely, your career in a high-demand business may be short-lived if you passionately hate the work.

Should you already have a business identified and the market scoped out, fine. But if you're still weighing the options, now's the time to take a realistic inventory. You can start by filling out the following self-evaluation form adapted from business guidelines supplied by the SBA. These are ideas that have proven workable for others. There's also room for your own ideas. Be sure to include them because it's important to examine as many of your interests as possible.

Rate your interests and strengths on a scale of 0 for no interest or strength, to 10 for a great deal of interest or strength. Do the same with your best approximation of the market strength (demand) for your product or service. Then total your points in the right-hand column.

Interest / Aptitude Gauge				
	Level of Interest	Personal Strength	Market Strength	Total Points
Personal Services				
Housecleaning				
Babysitting				
Tutoring				
Secretarial				
Catering				
Business Services				
Office cleaning				
Computer services				
Public relations				
Research				
Handiwork				
Woodworking				
Crafts				
Upholstery				
Artistic Work				
Painting				
Photography				
Decorating				
Calligraphy				
Graphics				
Repair Services				
TV				
Motors				
Clothing				
Furniture				
Instruction Skills				
Languages				
Arts				
Music				
Sales Skills				
Home products				
Real estate				
Advertising				
Environmental / Outdoor Work				
Beekeeper				
Lawn service				
Christmas tree grower				
Mail Order				
Product sales				
Written material				
Import / export				
Writing Skills				
Creative				
Journalistic				
Your Own Ideas				
_____				
_____				
_____				

Now, evaluate the likelihood of success for each category.

0–10	Sorry, almost a sure loser
11–15	Maybe, but proceed with caution
16–20	Some potential; worth further study
21–25	Probably a winner—if you answered the questions correctly
26–30	A winner

Something else to think about when evaluating ideas: Be sure that, in addition to being simple and realistic for a moonlighter's working hours, your business is not going to be handicapped by being in your home. If your business will depend on drop-in traffic and you live out in the suburbs, forget it. If the nature of your enterprise necessitates businesspeople making frequent trips to your home office, you may be pursuing the wrong line of business. While it may not be fair or reasonable, many businesspeople judge others by their office (note the relationship to the word *official*) surroundings and will mistrust someone operating from his or her home. To their minds, it's just not very businesslike.

Do you plan to be a consultant whose work is primarily done by telephone and mail? Then the home office is no problem and actually is an asset to the cost-conscious start-up operation. Are your sights set on manufacturing handicrafts and selling them to local gift shops? If so, you'll be traveling to your customers, and your base of operations will not matter.

What does matter at this point is that you get the home business started properly without running afoul of any local ordinances.

THERE'S NO PLACE LIKE HOME IF... ─────────

Home can be the ideal work environment, but you've got to carefully evaluate certain considerations before start-up. Of particular interest are zoning regulations and home-work laws.

Zoning

Zoning ordinances are, at best, a cumbersome hodgepodge of regulations that suffer from spotty enforcement. Most are undeniably well intentioned, but the rather archaic nature of many of the laws and their hit-or-miss enforcement can pose a nettling problem to the home-based businessperson.

Basically, zoning ordinances govern the use of the land and what structures may be placed on that land. Agricultural areas commonly have no zoning restrictions, but suburban and urban areas typically are divided into industrial, commercial, and residential zones. Industrial zones often are graded as to the different kinds of industry permitted within them; some zones, for instance, allow for light but not heavy industry.

The only way for you to know whether your business will meet zoning ordinances is to read the regulations, which are available at your city or town hall. Now, it may be that your particular business is permitted specifically by the language of the regulation—a "professional practice, such as an accountant, artist...," in which case, you're home free. More often, though, you'll have to do a bit of interpretation as to whether your enterprise qualifies under the ordinances.

If you have a question don't be reluctant to call the powers that be. In most communities those powers are embodied as the zoning board, which sets policy, and the board of appeals, which rules on specific cases and can grant variances. (Often the two boards are staffed by the same people.) The zoning officer can give you some guidance as to what probably will or won't cause a problem in your community. Zoning officials aren't ogres, by the way; they're usually volunteers who are concerned about keeping the community attractive and maintaining property values. There are good reasons for zoning regulations—something you'll appreciate if you've ever lived in a place where gas stations popped up on both sides of your ranch house.

Zoning regulations will vary considerably depending on your location, but there are some basic zoning facts of life that remain relatively constant:

1. Zoning regulations are usually enforced only when somebody complains. That "somebody" is usually a neighbor who gets tired of having cars parked up and down the street.
2. Remember that people, as well as cars, will attract unflattering attention to your home-based business. Neighbors typically do not like a parade of strangers next door, and with good reason. The aforementioned parking problems also cause legitimate concern.
3. Signs are usually the biggest bones of contention encountered in zoning hassles. After all, nobody cares what you do in your basement, but somebody will probably care very much if you put a six-foot flashing neon sign in your front yard advertising your homemade waffle irons. Your zoning regulations may allow a small sign for professional practices, or they may not. Never exceed the permitted size for the sign, and if your business is questionable (in terms of zoning), go without a sign if at all possible.
4. Zoning codes cannot spell out every possible contingency; as a result,

the interpretation of those laws frequently hinges on what is reasonable for the character of the neighborhood and the precedent established by businesses that have operated in the area. So make it your business to keep track of what goes on with other neighborhood businesses. If your neighbor the accountant has a small sign and has cars parked in front of his house—and operates unfettered by the zoning officer—that's ammunition you can use if the legality of your home computer consulting practice is challenged.

Home-Work Laws

Laws governing what kinds of business can and cannot be carried on from the home vary from state to state, and there are also some federal regulations. It's in your best interest to check these before making a substantial investment of time and money.

You'll find that many home-work laws pertain to sewing and knitting. As is the case with many laws that seem absurdly restrictive today, there were good intentions behind their inception. Many home-work laws date from the 1940s, when the government cracked down on home sweatshops, where women were paid absurdly low wages for sewing and knitting piecework. (Garment firms doled out piecework to circumvent the new minimum wage laws.)

Today, the laws seem outmoded and are enforced only on occasion. One celebrated case in 1981 saw the Labor Department lift some restrictions on home-produced knitted outerwear (hats, scarves, etc.), but a strange network of laws relating to home-produced garments still exists. You'll also find some odd home-work restrictions in individual states; Missouri, for instance, singles out the manufacture of artificial flowers in its list of restrictions.

You can find out about home-work restrictions by checking with government agencies; the easiest place to begin is with the office of your state's secretary of state. Many offices have toll-free numbers and take public information very seriously. Although the agency might not have the information you need, it will steer you to the right source.

HOME SWEET OFFICE

Working at home can be environmentally pleasing, but your immediate goal is not to replicate the plush surroundings of a Fortune 500 executive suite. At the same time, you do need a comfortable and workable environment.

Planning the Environment

Here's a three-point plan for designing an office that won't break your back or your bank account:

1. Buy *task furniture*, not executive furniture. Task furniture, as it's
   known in the trade, is designed for people who actually do the work.
   Take, for example, the secretarial chair: it's functional, designed to
   give support in all the right places, and not very attractive. You don't
   have to impress anybody, but you do have to sit in your chair and
   crank out the work hour after hour. So pass up the shiny, impressive,
   and superexpensive executive chairs and desks in favor of task furniture.
2. Shop for office furniture at used goods outlets. And when you're
   shopping, make an effort to integrate what you already own into the
   office scheme. If you don't mind an eclectic touch, improvise some of
   the furnishings. A door set across two filing cabinets makes an absolutely superb desk, and plywood and bricks can be used to construct
   inexpensive but highly efficient shelving.
3. Give some thought to ergonomics. Table height is a good example.
   Many home offices center on the computer, but that computer often
   winds up on a desk that is simply too high for a comfortable sitting
   position. Check it out for yourself: typing stands are usually 26 inches
   high, but desks and tables are usually 29 inches. A typing stand
   usually will be too small to hold a computer, but if you put the computer on a desk or table you'll be forcing yourself into years of dis-
   comfort in the "sit-up-and-beg" posture. It's wise to improvise more
   appropriately sized computer furniture or else to invest in an inexpensive task-oriented computer desk. (But be sure your computer will fit
   into the desk: some designs won't accommodate certain computer systems.)

   Along the same lines, pay attention to your furniture arrangement.
   Furniture in the center of the room can create narrow and complex
   traffic patterns, which in turn create accidents and frustration. Put office furniture against the walls and leave the center of the room open
   for circulation.

How Much to Spend?

The figures may vary, of course, but here's a basic guide:

Desks. You can probably pick up a good used metal desk for under $150.
A new task-oriented desk can cost $300 and up. Fancy wooden desks
can cost you thousands.

Chairs. Cut costs anywhere but your chair. You'll be spending most of
your time there, and a bad chair can make life exceedingly uncomfort-
able. An adjustable secretary's chair may set you back about $100, but
it's worth it. If you have back problems, investigate the new generation
of backless chairs, in which you rest your knees on pads. In any case,

be sure to get a chair with wheels because you'll need to move frequently when looking for files or answering the phone. You don't need a high-backed, high-priced executive's chair.

Answering machine. Figure $100 to $200 for a decent model. Some of the new voice- or code-activated remote units, which allow you to listen to your messages from a remote location by triggering playback with your voice or by dialing a code, are excellent for people who travel during the day or who want to check calls while they're at their day job. Give some serious thought to spending a little extra on a remote-control machine; the convenience may prove to be well worth the added cost.

Telephone. If you can make do with your residential phone, by all means do so. A business line costs a lot of money. For starters, you'll have to pay an installation fee, which in some parts of the country can cost as much as $200 (almost twice the cost of a residential installation). If you've never had business service before, you'll have to give the phone company an up-front deposit in many cases. Basic business service can be expensive, too. At the time of this writing, in New York City, for example, you pay $12.87 per month plus 8.1 cents for each call (dropping to 1.1 cents per call after the first five minutes). You must have a business phone if you plan to take out a Yellow Page ad.

Unless you've got some compelling reason, forget about fancy high-tech phones. They're expensive to buy or rent, they provide features you just won't need right away, and they break down more often than simple phones. You can save a lot by getting a standard phone in basic black.

Filing cabinets. Buy them used; they usually work just as well as the shiny new ones, and you can live with a dent or a sticky drawer for the kind of money you'll save. A new four-drawer model can set you back $300 or more. You can buy a similar used model for $75. A coat of black spray paint will make it look like new.

Photocopiers. The new generation of personal photocopiers, such as those by Canon, work beautifully and reliably. They're not suited for turning out hundreds of copies in a hurry, but you probably don't need heavy office capacity anyway. You do need to make copies of correspondence, contracts, and other documents, and you don't need the hassle and interruption of running out to the photocopy shop five times a day. While cost cutting is critical to any start-up operation, a photocopier just might be worth the expense. You can pick up an excellent model starting for about $650.

Computers. There's a great deal of variability here. You can spend anywhere from under $1,000 for a basic word-processing unit, printer and all, to $10,000 for a complete desktop publishing center.

Hint: look for a computer system that bundles the software you need in the package. Also, it's a good idea to buy your computer, printer, and software in the same place. That way, you'll know that the items are compatible and you won't get caught up in finger-pointing if something doesn't work (e.g., the guy who sold you the software tells you it's a hardware problem, and the gent who pushed the $2,000 computer on you tells you you're suffering software failure).

THE BUSINESS OF BEING IN BUSINESS

There are many complexities involved in running your own business, and before going any further you'll want to

1. draw up a business plan,
2. draft a financial plan, and
3. —shudder—calculate tax consequences.

The Business Plan

Put your business plan on paper, even if you're the only one who will ever see it. It's important to collect your thoughts in one place, think through potential problems, and have a ready reference to guide your expansion. Your business plan should include these features:

Name of the business and its purpose. Should you decide to incorporate (see below), the name is a real issue, since you can't incorporate if another business has the same name. This won't be much of a problem if your enterprise is Joe Zigliewicz and Son Drain Cleaning, but more generic names may cause trouble. Think of three possible names for the firm (in some states, you have to submit three choices for the business name when you incorporate).

Form of the business. Your basic choices are sole proprietorship, partnership, and corporation. There are various incarnations of partnerships and corporations.

The advantage of a sole proprietorship is its simplicity; you usually only need to file a couple of forms (check with your town or city clerk to find out what's required in your area). The prime disadvantage is that you have unlimited personal liability for costs incurred by the business.

A partnership is also relatively simple to create. Most two or three-person businesses are of the type known as an unlimited partnership. The problem with this type of business is that you have unlimited liability for the actions of your partner. Should he or she run up a huge bill and skip to Brazil, you'll be the one who has to explain to the collection agency and possibly even cover the costs.

A corporation forms a new legal entity, a new "person," if you will. This legal entity has many of the rights and obligations of a flesh-and-blood person, and also offers some protection to its officers and share-holders. For instance, if you're sued, you only stand to lose the corporations' assets, not your house, car, etc. But you can wind up paying much more in taxes, and it costs money to establish and run a corporation, even a so-called S corporation, which is taxed as a part-nership rather than a corporation if it meets strict IRS guidelines. Count on spending $500 to $1,500 for filing and legal fees.

Function of the business. Write out what you plan to do and how you plan to do it. Be as specific as possible. Include a list of your own capabilities and strengths, as well as the types of jobs and responsibilities you'll have to farm out.

Marketing plan. Identify your potential customers and to the best of your ability estimate how many of them there are. Do research to answer the following questions: How large is the market in terms of geographic areas? What is the impact of competition? Can you offer better service or lower prices than your competitors? How will you advertise? What are the costs of advertising in the various media in your area?

The Financial Plan

It's wise to make a table of profit projections. Granted, this is going to encompass a lot of guesswork, but at least you'll have something down on paper and will have a mechanism for keeping a running record of ex-penses and income.

Keep a tally of your expenditures. Don't forget to include such items as office supplies, deposits for utilities, and legal fees. Now, estimate your income and to the best of your ability determine if you're going to be able to cover all your bills. A simplified way of projecting this cash flow is the cash forecast shown on page 15.

Remember, this is a forecast to be filled out in advance and followed as closely as possible (at least in terms of expenses; no one complains about additional unexpected income). If you stick to your spending forecast, you can eliminate much of the uncertainty—and some of the ulcers—that start-up entrepreneurs typically encounter.

Estimated Cash Forecast

	Jan.	Feb.	Mar.	April	May	June	July	Aug.	Sept.	Oct.	Nov.	Dec.
(1) Cash in Bank (Start of Month)												
(2) Petty Cash (Start of Month)												
(3) Total Cash (add 1 and 2)												
(4) Expected Cash Sales												
(5) Expected Collections												
(6) Other Money Expected												
(7) Total Receipts (add 4, 5 and 6)												
(8) Total Cash and Receipts (add 3 and 7)												
(9) All Disbursements (for month)												
*(10) Cash Balance at End of Month in Bank Account and Petty Cash (subtract 9 from 8)												

*This balance is your starting cash balance for the next month.

The Balance Sheet

This is nothing more than a listing of what you own and what you owe. Assets include property, money in the bank, receivables, and inventories. Debts include accounts and notes payable, and taxes owed. Defining the exact scope of assets and liabilities involves some technicalities (such as depreciation) best addressed by an accountant.

That, incidentally, raises two final points related to your financial plan. One is that the balance sheet is an essential tool should you ever plan to borrow money from a bank. Now, most home-based businesses are small in scope and won't involve taking out a loan. And frankly, if you're so precariously perched that you do not have $2,000 to $3,000 available, perhaps a small business start-up is not a realistic option right now. However, you may reach a point at which some cash is needed to tide you over until some expected profit rolls in, or you may need to make an unplanned expansion; if so, the balance sheet and financial projection must be in order for the perusal of the bank officer. This is particularly important if you do intend to borrow money up front (before any profit is made) for a capital-intensive business such as a word-processing firm.

The second point involves the accountant and, to an extent, the lawyer. Accountants and lawyers are not cheap, but in many cases they are worth every penny. Suppose you do intend to borrow money; you'll have very tough sledding indeed without the services of a lawyer and/or accountant. Remember that accountants and lawyers who specialize in new business start-ups deal with bankers all the time. They know the bankers personally and furnish much of the business that keeps the bank alive. So give some serious thought to engaging an accountant and lawyer should your business involve borrowing money or any other difficult start-up situation.

Look for professionals who specialize in small business. Your family lawyer may be great for fighting speeding tickets, but he might know little or nothing about business planning and liability insurance needs. Ask around; talk to other small business owners about their lawyers. Do the same with accountants. Remember, the fellow who can help you project growth for the firm is not necessarily the same guy who does such a neat job with your taxes.

Tax Consequences

To an extent, Uncle Sam is on your side when it comes to setting up a business. He allows you to deduct the cost of running a business from your home. New tax laws will enable you to deduct up to $10,000 in capital costs as expenses in the year in which they occurred, but you can no longer claim an investment tax credit. This differs from the old laws, under which you were forced to depreciate all capital costs over a period of several years. You still must depreciate so-called intangibles such as computer software; generally, the period of depreciation is three years under the new law.

Never, never forget to keep records of all your deductible business expenses. It's simply astounding how many home businesspeople fail to add in costs such as insurance, telephone bills, and postage. All these are legitimate expenses, and you're entitled to them. Don't cheat yourself.

Now, about deducting the home office itself. Have a heart-to-heart with your accountant before doing this (in fact, be absolutely sure to grill your accountant about all tax liabilities, because the tax codes are in a state of flux). There have been cases where people who have claimed part of their homes as a business deduction were socked with a huge tax bill when they sold the house and found that the portion of the home they deducted as a business was taxed as though it were a business which had been sold. Having 10 percent (or whatever) of your home sale price taxed in this manner can bring about some ticklish consequences.

ONWARD

So that's the basic story on working from your home. There are many details to work out according to your individual situation; and you can locate more information on general business practice and management by thumbing through the brief bibliography at the end of this book.

Now we'll move on to the 148 moonlighting ideas you can start and run from your home. A few words of introduction:

- Businesses are as different as people. The way businesses are represented in this book is not the only way they can be established and run. In fact, many businesses operate with considerable overlap into other types of ventures. A home word-processing business (page 306), for example, can also accommodate an addressing service (page 19) or a desktop publishing enterprise (page 101) and can even serve as an excellent adjunct to the business of a freelance magazine article writer (page 127). As a result, an effort has been made to cross-reference related and complementary entries whenever possible.
- Estimates of start-up costs and hours per week are just that—estimates. There's no precise way to determine these factors. For one thing, it's reasonable to assume that many people contemplating going into a particular business would already have some of the tools and equipment required. When such is the case, the entry will say so explicitly (e.g., "about $500 above the cost of the delivery truck"). Start-up costs generally reflect what you can start the business for if you look for bargains in equipment and services. They do not include costs of office furniture

or general filing fees that are required of everyone. The costs of special permits, however, are factored in.

Estimated hours are expressed as a range. The lower end is an approximation of the minimum number of hours you can invest in a particular business in order to get any return at all. The upper range reflects the amount of time the *busiest* moonlighters find themselves investing in their particular business.

- Most entries contain a *Resources* section which often contains books and periodicals dealing with that particular subject. A word about locating these books: You can order almost any book in print through a bookstore as long as you know the title and the author; that information, along with the name of the publisher, is provided in the entries. Just ask the store clerk to order it for you. And be assertive with the clerks; if they say they can't find a listing for the book, ask them again. Many times they haven't been adequately trained in ordering.

At some point certain books listed will go out of print, meaning that they are no longer actively distributed by the publisher. If the clerk tells you the book is out of print, you can go to a shop that specializes in out-of-print books or simply visit your local library. Any good-sized library will probably have most of the books mentioned here on its shelves, and if not, the book can be secured through interlibrary loan. You can get virtually any book in existence through interlibrary loan, no matter where you live.

So let's start examining some home-based business opportunities. These ideas have worked for others, and they can work for you, too. All you need is stamina, guts, and a dream.

ADDRESSING SERVICE _____

☐ Start-up costs: If computerized, minimum of $1,000.
☐ Estimated hours per week: 5 to 10
☐ Number of staffers needed for start-up (including founder): 1

There's a healthy traffic in mail today. Anyone who's unloaded a mailbox knows that junk mail is a big business. But there's more to mailing than junk advertisements—people and businesses of all types need mail addressed and sent to clients and potential clients. They also require a service that helps them keep their mailing lists organized and up-to-date.

WHO BUYS THIS SERVICE? _____

Take, for example, the local auto repair shop that wants to send a newsletter to current customers. Since the newsletter is a relatively simple affair—a one-page typed update of what's happening at the shop and what special bargains will be offered—having it printed up is no big deal. But how on earth will the owner mail it to his customers? Go through all the old receipts and write down each name and address? Probably not. If he has any sense of the worth of his own time, he'll hire a professional, possibly a moonlighting professional, possibly *you*.

WHAT'S INVOLVED _____

Most addressing services use a computer, although there are some that still do the work with a typewriter and three-by-five index cards. There are very sophisticated pieces of machinery designed for fully professional addressing and direct-mail firms, but you don't need to get into that type of hardware. Instead, here's what you can do:

- Use a personal computer with a database and a word-processing/merging program to store and organize the information. A database will allow you to access and sort information on a variety of variables. For instance, the auto repair shop owner might want a mailing only to customers living right in the city, or to a certain zip code in the city, or to all owners of cars four years old or older. A database allows you to pull out such information if you've keyed it in correctly. Thus you can call up a list and command your word-processing/merging program to spit out the addresses.

- Help the client organize his or her lists. You might suggest to the repair shop owner that he construct a list of current customers, prior customers whose business he might like to recapture, people who might be interested in a special on winterizing, etc. If you're advising a public relations counselor, you could help him or her create various lists of local media (i.e., radio stations, newspapers, etc.).

- Physically address the pieces. Your computer can be set up to print addresses one by one. In that event, simply place the mailing piece in the printer and command the computer to print the address in the appropriate location on the piece. Even better is to buy special adhesive label sheets at an office supply house and print out the whole list on the sheets; the labels are detachable. This is sometimes difficult, though, because often the computer printer can't be made to precisely print within the individual label borders. An easy solution: print out all the addresses on plain paper. Cut the paper into individual labels (a ruler and a razor blade does this faster than scissors). Then use rubber cement to daub the back of the labels before you affix them to your mailing pieces.

GETTING THE BUSINESS

Send out letters to prospective clients. Likely candidates include businesses that depend on return clients and that require many promotional pieces. For starters, try: public relations counselors, local political candidates, electronics stores, any store or office that generates repeat business —don't forget vets, dentists, etc. Also, contact the local firms that send you junk mail and see if you can undercut the price they now pay for the service.

FEES AND CHARGES

Be careful of offering per-piece rates because some jobs will take longer than others. Also, remember that you'll have to build in a fair price for list development—a job which can involve looking up hundreds of zip codes and hours and hours of keying in information. You'll have to use your judgment to determine how many hours the job will take, and then charge your hourly rate for the whole package. To determine the hourly rate, be sure to figure in the cost of operating your computer, which usually can be computed by using the annual depreciation figure as you compute it on your income tax plus the annual repair and/or service contract costs. Divide the annual cost by the estimated number of hours per year you use the gear. Then add your desired hourly profit figure to the hourly equipment use figure to determine the correct rate.

ADVERTISING: COLLATERAL DESIGNER _____

☐ Start-up costs: Usually under $500, since much of the work is farmed out; but you'll need funds to cover bills for contractors, which will vary from project to project.
☐ Estimated hours per week: 5 to 15
☐ Number of staffers needed for start-up (including founder): 1, but several subcontractors will usually be necessary periodically.

The term *collateral* was an obscure and technical word up until a few years ago. It worked its way into popular usage when people skilled in communication decided there was a ton of money to be made in the field and they needed something to call that particular kind of work. In the broadest sense of the word, collateral refers to anything that has to do with advertising other than placing the ad. Practically, collateral usually refers to brochures.

And are there brochures! Almost every business in existence today has one or more brochures. They may range from full-color travel pieces to highly technical guides for the customers of a particular manufacturer.

Designing collateral is an important function of an ad agency, but you don't have to set yourself up as an agency to do it. Should you have a flair for design, persuasive writing, and dealing with businesspeople, collateral design offers a world of relatively hassle-free opportunity. Essentially, you'll design the brochure yourself, pulling together all the specialists—writers, artists, printers—who are involved in the process. You can also do any part of that work yourself, such as writing the brochure copy.

CASHING IN

From a moonlighter's standpoint, the important thing to remember is that big ad agencies hate to do collateral. They just can't charge enough to make the job profitable. An enterprising freelancer, though, can capitalize on low overhead by offering an attractive price (while still making a decent profit, of course).

Should you have talents and abilities in the brochure production area, you can market your services by

- Approaching existing advertising agencies and offering to take some of the work off their hands. Some agencies farm out collateral work in return for a piece of the action. This is an ideal way to start because you'll have some support from professionals.
- Writing or calling the marketing departments of local firms. Try heavy industry; they have to sell their goods to someone (such as buyers for secondary manufacturing firms), and they need extensive documentation of their products and/or services.

In either case, samples of your work are a must. If you have nothing on hand now, volunteer to create a brochure for a local charitable or church organization. (Don't pay for the printing; just offer your services for free.) You'll probably find many willing takers.

THE BUSINESS OF COLLATERAL

You won't be able to do all the work yourself. Instead, you'll have to rely on printers and probably freelance artists and photographers. Dealing with many different vendors can be nettlesome, but don't despair because that's how you can make money. It is perfectly acceptable—standard practice, in fact—to mark up the costs of the services so that you make a commission. Approximately 15 percent is about right for starters.

An ad agency customarily takes a 15 percent commission. For example, if you buy a $1,000 ad on behalf of a client, and since you're an agency you get a 15 percent discount on the $1,000 gross, you pocket about $150. The same theory applies to marking up collateral, except that you will have to figure your 15 percent commission on the *net* price of goods and services. So if you run up an $850 printing bill (your net) on behalf of a client, mark up the $850 by 15 percent. In this case, 15 percent comes out to $127.50, so your total charge is $977.50, which you can round off to either $980 or $1000 at your discretion.

ADVERTISING: COPYWRITER_____

- ☐ Start-up costs: Nothing above standard office supplies and equipment.
- ☐ Estimated hours per week: 2 to 10
- ☐ Number of staffers needed for start-up (including founder): 1

"Don't tell people how good you make the goods; tell them how good your goods make them."

> —Advertising agency owner Leo Burnett, whose agency created the Jolly Green Giant, Tony the Tiger, and the Pillsbury Dough Boy

Can you sell benefits? Can you convince a reader that a certain product will make him or her more beautiful, more successful, more popular? If so, you have the right writing stuff to tap into the highly profitable world of advertising copywriting.

SELLING THE SIZZLE _____

It's a widely accepted axiom that a copywriter "sells the sizzle, not the steak." Concise, punchy copy must tout the benefits of the product and do so in such a way that the words translate to results.

Advertising agencies, which prepare and place advertising for businesses, always have in-house copywriters but usually have more work than the staff can handle. Initially, a freelancer will at least get an interview at most ad agencies, and in agencies where a big project has just been landed there's a good chance you could walk into an immediate assignment.

Copywriting, by the way, isn't limited to the words in advertisements. Ad agencies also need writers to create copy for brochures and press releases. And above all, they need *expertise*. If you can provide the commodity, you're in business.

THE MOONLIGHTING EXPERT

Simply stated, the formula for breaking in at your local agencies is to make yourself an expert (or at least be able to pass as one) in one or more of the following areas:

- high tech
- manufacturing
- finance and investment
- banking
- personnel recruitment
- medical or pharmaceutical practice

Perhaps you already have some specialized knowledge. An accountant, for example, will have had a broad exposure to finance. A factory worker knows more about manufacturing than do a dozen ad agency executives. Whatever you do, find a niche and exploit it. (If you have a definite and demonstrable writing skill, you can always take on general assignments, but be aware that you'll be competing against full-time professional commercial writers for those jobs.)

Ad agencies hunger for specialized writers because of the sheer volume of technical assignments they're given and because it's very difficult for even experienced writers to learn enough about a business to write convincing copy at a moment's notice. You'll have a head start if you contact an agency director with a letter that reads:

Dear Mr. Smith:

I'm a frustrated English major who has spent the last ten years working in a pharmaceutical industry. I know the market very well and believe I could write copy which would . . .

or

Dear Mr. Smith:

In my work as a computer programmer, I deal with many purchasers of software and hardware and believe I know exactly what motivates them to buy—as well as what turns them off. I would like to do some freelance ad copywriting in the high-tech field and wonder if . . .

or even

Dear Mr. Smith:

I have two hobbies: writing and investing. I know the investment market inside out, and believe I can write better direct-response copy than the stuff I get in the mail every day. Could I meet with you and . . .

Get the idea? Use a hook like one of these to get you into the office of the agency executive in charge of copy. Show him or her some of your writing samples, such as a brochure you put together or a press release for your organization. If you have nothing to show, offer to take an assignment on speculation ("on spec," in the industry parlance), in which case, you won't get paid unless the piece is used. (You might consider writing some sample copy for a fictitious advertisement, but dummying up an ad is very difficult; better to show actual copy.)

RESOURCES

An advantage of ad copywriting is that there are outstanding resources for learning about the craft. For one thing, you can study and dissect the advertising copy you see every day. Also, consider subscribing to publications such as *Business Marketing* (Crain Communications, 740 Rush St., Chicago, IL 60611). *Business Marketing* has a monthly feature titled "Copy Chasers," in which ads and ad copy are critically analyzed—an invaluable learning tool. *Adweek,* which publishes regionally tailored issues from major cities gives an informative overview of advertising. You can find *Adweek* on newsstands or in the periodical section of your library. Stanley M. Ulanoff's *Advertising in America: An Introduction to Persuasive Communication* (Hastings House), a textbook widely available in libraries, contains sound advice on writing copy. You might also try *Advertising Freelancers* by Sue Fulton and Ed Buxton, Executive Comm., 1985.

To find the names of advertising agencies and the types of accounts they handle, visit your public library and ask for the advertising Red Book.

ADVERTISING:
HOME AD AGENCY _____

☐ Start-up costs: Usually under $1,000, but it's important to have a cash cushion to tide you over while waiting for reimbursement from clients for costs you have incurred.
☐ Estimated hours per week: 10 to 15
☐ Number of staffers needed for start-up (including founder): 1

There are scores of people who have a message they want to get across, and they are often willing to pay for the services of an expert who can communicate that message to the buying public. While the profession of advertising crosses into many other areas, the heart of the business is the ad agency.

WHAT DOES AN AD AGENCY DO? _____

An agency designs and places advertising for customers and takes a commission on the price of the advertising. In addition, a typical agency may be called upon to handle a variety of other chores, including public relations, graphic presentations, and brochures. Items such as brochures are known in the trade as *collateral,* and are such an important part of the communications business that they have become, for many, a business unto themselves. (See *Advertising: Collateral Designer* page 21.)

The various production duties in the communications business can be handled by any type of firm or freelancer, but for all practical purposes only an agency places advertising. A graphic arts house might design an advertisement, but the ad agency places it in a magazine. Collateral production houses design and print many of the same types of promotional pieces that come from an ad agency, but they don't deal with the media in the purchase of column inches or airtime.

HOW AN AGENCY WORKS _____

Generally, agencies go about placing advertising in the media by

- Meeting with clients to determine their needs.
- Developing ad campaigns, and writing copy designing art, etc.
- Securing the most effective and cost-efficient vehicles for their clients' ads.

OPPORTUNITIES

The ad agency business is notoriously tough to crack, and the moonlighter faces a clear-cut challenge. However, moonlighters can and do get clients because they can keep their overhead low. Overhead in the traditional ad agency can be frighteningly high; as a result, many agencies simply don't want small clients. In fact, larger agencies need major accounts just to make their weekly salaries and rent.

A small operator won't ever get the big glamour accounts, but he or she can bring in a substantial second income through smaller accounts. Here's the basic procedure: after working with the client to design an ad strategy, contact the publications or broadcast/cable outlets through which you wish to place your client's message. You can find all the information you need in a database called *Standard Rate and Data Services,* known in the trade as SRDS. SRDS is also published in a volume. Look for the book in your local library; you may want to purchase your own issues later, but since SRDS is expensive you're better off making frequent trips to the reference room.

The ad agency is entitled to a commission of 15 percent on the gross amount of advertising purchased. If you buy $1,000 of advertising for a client, you make $150. You get this commission because media offer a discount to ad agencies, ostensibly because they want to work with ad professionals but also because the discount/commission system encourages ad agencies to place as many ads as possible.

The catch is that media offer the discount only to a "recognized" advertising agency, which is often undefined. Because this regulation is primarily intended to protect media from bad credit risks, you can circumvent the whole issue by paying your bill up front. For example, if you buy a page of advertising for your client for $1,000, send a check from your agency for $850 and clearly indicate it is "for payment of advertisement _____, minus $150 agency commission." You simply collect $1,000 from your client later. Paying the media up front leaves you with a cash flow deficit—since you have to recover the funds from the client—but solves the problems you'll undoubtedly have trying to establish an agency credit account with a newspaper, magazine, or broadcast outlet.

RESOURCES _____

Your library will have many good books on advertising practice, but you can't go wrong with *Ogilvy on Advertising* (Crown), an insightful book by advertising executive (and virtual folk hero) David Ogilvy.

AEROBICS INSTRUCTOR _____

☐ Start-up costs: None, provided you freelance for established studios or spas.
☐ Estimated hours per week: 5 to 15
☐ Number of staffers needed for start-up (including founder): 1

The aerobics craze shows no sign of peaking. Each year, more and more women—and, increasingly, men—lace up their workout shoes and begin the ritual of bouncing and stretching. You can capitalize on this trend by filling the growing demand for aerobics instructors.

THE FREELANCER IN THE AEROBICS BUSINESS _____

Although you'll be working at other people's studios, you'll be working as a freelancer. Today, you can work for more than one studio; there used to be something of a bias against freelancers, but in most places that's no longer true. You'll find yourself in particularly high demand should you be able to lead classes at odd hours, such as midday or early morning.

The students in an aerobics class see an instructor lead the group through a half hour or hour of exercises; what they don't see is the amount of time the instructor puts in at home choreographing the routines.

Your job is to learn the routines that are currently popular and that are favored by local spas, and lead the class through the dances and exercises.

MARKETING YOURSELF

An aerobics instructor will be most marketable if he or she is certified by one of the national aerobics associations and knows cardiopulmonary resuscitation (CPR). The national associations offer tests and/or classes for instructors; you can find a full smorgasbord of such associations in the ads carried by magazines such as *Shape* and *American Health,* both of which are available at newsstands. CPR instruction is offered in many locations; call your local Red Cross chapter for details.

Aerobics looks like fun—and most of the time it is—but an instructor also has a lot of responsibility. You are responsible for monitoring the physical well-being of the people in the class, as well as for motivating them to get through the rigorous routine. That can be difficult; many instructors burn out emotionally before they tire physically. And remember, too, that you'll have to be in great shape to teach several classes each day.

Market yourself as a freelance instructor by calling area health clubs, schools, YMCAs, and YWCAs. You'll be better off financially if you market yourself on the basis of teaching individual classes rather than taking on a part-time job at a club. You'll probably be able to average $10 per hour-long class at a small private studio; some pay as much as $18 for quality instructors. If you take a regular part-time job at a large club, you might wind up making substantially less per hour.

RESOURCES

You can investigate the training programs advertised in the aforementioned magazines. Also, take a lot of aerobics classes; if you're good, the instructor or owner may recruit you as an apprentice. There are many books on aerobic dancing, including *Jackie Sorenson's Aerobic Lifestyle Book* (Simon & Schuster) and Beth Kuntzleman's *The Complete Guide to Aerobic Dancing* (Fawcett).

ANTIQUES DEALER _____

☐ Start-up costs: $1,000 to $5,000, depending on whether you are starting with or without inventory—someone now interested in antiques already may have collected a considerable inventory
☐ Estimated hours per week: 3 to 10, more for a home-based retail shop.
☐ Number of staffers needed for start-up (including founder): 1

Anyone involved in the antiques business will confirm the fact that people love old and beautiful objects. More to the point, people are quite willing to pay dearly for them. You can profit from this by buying and selling antiques, using your home as a base. There's always the possibility that the business could develop into a part- or full-time retail shop on the premises, should your temperament and the local zoning laws allow. One drawback of the retail shop on premises is that you'll have people frequently visiting your home. Many people involved in antiques prefer to use their home solely for storage and office headquarters, rather than as a retail facility.

LEARNING THE ROPES _____

Any antiques dealer starts by immersing himself or herself in the sometimes complex and arcane world of old and valuable objects. Attend every flea market you can; go to auctions; quiz other dealers about their buying and business practices. (Most antiques enthusiasts are surprisingly willing to share their expertise.)

It's important to understand from the beginning that the purpose of antique dealing is to buy low and sell high, with supply and demand as the governing principle. A dealer exploits this principle in a number of ways:

- Buying from someone who doesn't know the true value of the object. If you've done your homework, you'll know that the sad-looking table selling for $20 at the local flea market is really a valuable piece of Victorian oak.
- Selling in areas of high demand. That Victorian oak piece might fetch a fair price in New England, but it's sure to command a fortune in Texas. If you can take your wares on the road (or sell by mail order), you can reap a substantial profit. Incidentally, the tactic works both ways: branding irons might sell cheaply in Texas, but they'll move for a high price in Boston.
- Anticipating rising value. Collectors get to know the trends. If they see that the price of a certain type of collectible is rising, they'll buy up as much as available, hold on to it, and resell later when its value has peaked.

MONEY MATTERS

Because of the buy-and-sell nature of the business, it takes money to make money in antiques. Most people get into the business by buying a few items and gradually building up their inventory. Should you choose to have a home-based shop, though, it's important to have a good inventory on hand. Many experts recommend at least a $2,500 to $5,000 investment, usually in a fairly broad inventory of smaller items.

In order to succeed, it's essential to turn over inventory quickly. A study published in a regional antiques magazine noted that successful dealerships turned over their total inventory one and a half times in a given year and averaged a markup of 64 percent. Less successful businesses turned over about three-quarters of their inventory in a year and averaged a 50 percent markup.

EXPANDING THE BUSINESS

The itinerant dealer can expand his or her business simply by attending more shows and auctions. Start by buying space at small shows, maybe for $40 a day. You'll probably make some money (you certainly don't stand to lose much) and will gain valuable experience. Keep buying low, selling high, and turning over the stock. Pretty soon you can move into big shows; the investment—sometimes as much as $100 a day for a table—will probably pay off if you have a large and profitable inventory.

When your business starts to roll, print up some brochures and hand them out to other dealers and to the administrators of antiques shows. You can make good contacts and will probably get yourself invited back to future shows.

RESOURCES

Pick up a copy of Bruce Johnson's *How to Make Up to Twenty-Thousand Dollars a Year in Antiques-and-Collectibles* (Rawson) as well as *How to Be Successful in the Antique Business* by Ronald Barlow (Scribners). There are also various associations you might query, such as the National Association of Dealers in Antiques, 7080 Old River Rd., RR6, Rockford, IL 61103. Be sure to keep up with antique magazines, such as *Antiques* (Old Mill Rd., P.O. Box 1975, Marion, OH 43306), which carries listings of major shows in its column "What's Where When." *The Antique Trader* (P.O. Box 1050, Dubuque, IA 52001) is an exhaustive price guide to antiques and collector's items.

ART BROKER

☐ Start-up costs: About $100 for basic promotional material, considerably more for more sophisticated materials such as brochures and slides.
☐ Estimated hours per week: 5 to 10, higher if out-of-town travel is involved.
☐ Number of staffers needed for start-up (including founder): 1

Art is rarely created for art's sake today. The simple fact is that artists have to eat, too. But artists are often not very good businesspeople, and that's where you, the broker, come in.

THE BUSINESS OF THE ART WORLD

A broker represents an artist and tries to sell the artist's work to galleries. The broker works on a commission basis, which can vary considerably.

Be forewarned that selling art requires some specialized knowledge. Not only do you have to know if the prospective client's work is good, but you must also be aware of whether the client's work is reflective of whatever current trend is sweeping the art community. If you can't sell it, you can't make money. That's why most art brokers have had extensive experience in the field, often as gallery owners or artists themselves.

WHAT'S INVOLVED

An art broker typically

- Calls on galleries and tries to sell his or her client's work. This usually involves showing slides of the works or in some cases bringing in prints of the artist's paintings. Brochures are usually a necessity.
- Advises the artist on promotion. One art broker noted that her clients are typically terrible self-promoters. She has to convince them to design a brochure touting their work. In today's market, a brochure is the primary selling tool. Usually, artists bear the brochure costs themselves, although the broker sometimes prints up brochures featuring one or more clients.
- Gives guidance on art trends and marketing techniques. For example, a broker may take charge of framing the work in the manner that will make it most salable.

STARTING UP

Brokers usually contact an artist whose work they know and admire. If the artist is not already represented, and if the artist sees any value in working through a broker, a formal or informal deal will be struck. Often the broker will take a commission of 5 to 10 percent. However, if an enormous amount of promotion and sales work is involved, that figure can rise as high as 20 percent.

The brokerage business, incidentally, is getting better because of the recent trend of artists selling printed editions. Prints give you additional sales opportunities because you can sell the original painting and the prints.

RESOURCES

Galleries are listed in the phone book, and a magazine called *Decor* (408 Olive St., St. Louis, MO 63102) carries listings of galleries and shows. You'll also want to read fine art magazines on a regular basis to keep up with trends. As one broker noted, "Trends are everything, and if you stand still, you're falling behind."

ARTIST _____

☐ Start-up costs: Variable, usually $200 and up for supplies.
☐ Estimated hours per week: 10 to 25
☐ Number of staffers needed for start-up (including founder): 1

Talented people can make money through their artistic abilities, but the road isn't easy, especially in the area of fine arts. There are, of course, many kinds of art other than what we usually consider fine arts. Crafts (page 91), for example, usually can be sold more readily than paintings or sculpture. In addition to painting or sculpture, an artist may also work in such areas as graphic arts (page 141) or woodworking (page 304).

OPPORTUNITIES IN ART _____

Given the right amount of talent and luck, practitioners of the fine arts can make some extra income at their work. In one respect, art is the ideal moonlighting job. You can work on a piece of art anytime, and since there's no deadline involved you can work at your own pace.

You also won't have any trouble doing the work at home. Unless your tastes run to gigantic works or welded sculpture, there's usually nothing that can't be handled in a well-lit, reasonably large room with good ventilation.

WHERE TO SELL YOUR WORK _____

There are many strategies for selling artwork. Assuming you have the talent, you can

- Do on-site portraits. Contact local shopping malls to find out how much they charge for renting space within the mall. A simple charcoal portrait can fetch between $10 and $25, and if you really cook along you can finish 10 a day.

- Sell in mall kiosks. Again, find out what the going rental rate is; if the numbers add up right (if you think you can make a profit), set up your paintings. You'll have to take less than you would earn from a gallery show, of course, but paintings usually can be moved quickly in a mall.
- Include your work in community art shows, which are usually quite receptive to local artists. Check *American Artist* magazine (1 Color Court, Marion, OH 43305) for listings of community shows and juried shows (described below).
- Enter juried art shows. A juried show is one in which works must pass initial scrutiny by a committee before being placed on sale. Some juried shows are very hard to crack, but many admit about half of the entrants.
- Sell your work to galleries. Today, most galleries prefer to buy work outright rather than sell on consignment. You can deal directly with gallery owners or work through a broker.
- Give art classes. You can turn a nice profit teaching 10 students who are each paying $5 an hour.

PRICING YOUR WORK

How much to charge? That's a question you'll have to answer for yourself, since there are no hard and fast rules on pricing. Obviously, an artist's work commands a higher price if he or she is well known, which is a difficult status to achieve, or deceased (which is not worth the trouble if you're thinking about it just for the sake of marketing). Advice from experienced pros: start low and concentrate on moving the paintings. Go on to the next work, and don't get into the habit of thinking that every one of your pieces is pure gold.

AUCTIONEER

☐ Start-up costs: Basic business expenses, plus fees to attend an auctioneer's school if you elect to go that route. Such schools can cost upwards of $750, including travel and lodging.
☐ Estimated hours per week: 3 to 18
☐ Number of staffers needed for start-up (including founder): 1

Going once ... going twice ... SOLD to the lady in the green hat! The auctioneer's chant and the frenetic pace of the auction are definitely a big part of the scene, but there's a great deal of action you don't see. An auctioneer must be adept at appraising, advertising, and marketing. If you've entertained the notion of becoming an auctioneer, bear in mind that it's probably harder than you thought—but according to folks in the field, it's a lot more interesting than you may have imagined, too.

ABOUT AUCTIONS AND AUCTIONEERS

An auctioneer sells all sorts of property, anything from distressed merchandise to tractors; from lumber to fish. Regardless of what you sell, you need to know the goods and you need to know the laws relating to selling property. In some states you'll need a license to be an auctioneer, and in some jurisdictions you'll need to complete continuing education credits. Some local laws will also require you to serve an apprenticeship. Be sure to check out state and local requirements.

Some auctioneers specialize in a certain type of goods, such as farm machinery. However, there aren't that many specialized markets, so the majority of auctioneers sell a variety of items.

THE JOB ITSELF

Individual auctioneers are hired by administrators and executors of an estate, by local governments, and by auction houses. Some auctioneers generate business by advertising in trade journals and in general-interest newspapers.

In general, you work on a commission basis, although sometimes you'll have flat fee jobs, often in the case where there's a small amount of merchandise that has to be auctioned and the commission would not be large enough to attract an auctioneer. Commissions vary widely according to locale and type of goods being sold; real estate, or an estate sale, as examples, might fetch a commission of five to seven percent of total sales, but the auctioneer may have to spring for his or her own advertising budget out of the commission.

A great deal of preparation is involved in some auctions, such as sales of artwork. The auctioneer has to appraise the value of the goods or have the value appraised by an outside expert—not an easy job in the sophisticated world of art. Livestock auctions, though, may involve little or no preparation; you just show up and sell.

RESOURCES

You can learn about auctioneering as a profession and get a listing of auctioneering schools by writing to the National Auctioneers Association

(8880 Ballentine, Overland Park, KS 66214). A good book about the field is *Auctions and Auctioneering* by Ralph Cassaday, Jr. (University of California Press).

AUDIOVISUAL SERVICE

☐ Start-up costs: Usually upwards of $5,000, but the cost varies depending on the kind of jobs you'll be tackling.
☐ Estimated hours per week: 10 to 12
☐ Number of staffers needed for start-up (including founder): 1, but 2 or more may be more realistic.

Audiovisual support is needed for a variety of modern functions, including speeches, seminars, and sales meetings. Demand is so great that many hotels have created their own in-house media departments. In addition, moonlighters take up some of the slack when the opportunity presents itself. You can take advantage of that demand, if you know the ins and outs of audiovisual equipment and presentations.

WHAT IS AN AUDIOVISUAL SERVICE?

AV support can take many forms, but in many cases it involves

- Providing equipment for slide presentations.
- Furnishing video gear for recording or playback.
- Recording audio from presentations.
- Setting up microphones and speaker systems for events.

EQUIPMENT

If your setup is nothing more than a microphone and a speaker, you could be in business for under $100. Slide projectors are more expensive. A good projector will cost upwards of $300, while control units (for fading between projectors at preprogrammed times) can cost several thousand dollars. Video gear costs in the thousands.

SERVICES

How you use the equipment is limited only by your imagination and personal enterprise. Some people who are adept at organizing slides can make a very good part-time income from producing and presenting slide shows. An expert with mikes and loudspeakers can do a good part-time business at country fairs and other events. Should you own a VCR and a high-quality monitor—and don't mind carting them around—you can sell your services to small hotels and other facilities that play host to meetings.

INCOME

People who operate equipment-intensive business typically charge a high rate for services, and with good reason. Audiovisual equipment frequently wears out and needs repair. You must calculate the depreciation, repair expenses, and replacement expenses of the gear plus transportation costs, then add on your expected hourly fee. Remember, too, that you are fully justified in charging a door-to-door rate if you pick up and deliver equipment.

MARKETING

A Yellow Pages ad under "Audiovisual Services" is often effective. Ads in newspapers, in the experience of some AV moonlighters, have been less useful.

In addition to cold-calling on hotels and meeting centers, as well as public relation agencies and PR offices of local firms and institutions, don't forget to market your services to other, larger AV agencies. They often have an overflow and may take you on as a private contractor.

RESOURCES

TAB Books publishes a series that deals in part with much of the equipment you will use in an audiovisual service. Of particular interest: *Designing, Building and Testing Your Own Speaker System with Projects* by David B. Weems, *Buyer's Guide to Component TV* by Carl Giles and Barbara Giles, and *Video Cassette Recorders: Buying, Using and Maintaining* by Bill Pasternak.

BABYSITTING SERVICE_____

☐ Start-up costs: Variable, but start-up is possible for a couple of hundred dollars for incidental costs.
☐ Estimated hours per week: 10 to 20, possibly more if you do a great deal of the sitting yourself.
☐ Number of staffers needed for start-up (including founder): This could be done as a one-person operation, but most babysitting services act as agencies, employing a number of sitters.

The rise of the two-job marriage has given birth, so to speak, to a difficult problem: what to do with the kids when Mom and Dad are at work. One solution is the babysitting service—a new version of an old business.

NANNIES FOR HIRE _____

Modern-day nannies may find their own clients or they may be part of a placement service. In either case, they provide child-care in the clients' homes. Babysitting services provide trained, carefully screened babysitters, and many offer their employees monthly contracts. According to a recent article in the *New York Times,* about a thousand nannies in New York City alone work under contracts that pay up to $1,400 a month, plus benefits.

STARTING OUT _____

You probably can't start on a large scale or offer big contracts at first, but your foremost consideration will be finding trustworthy people. If you act as a placement agency, it's imperative that you do a thorough interview with prospective sitters. In some states, you and/or your sitters will have to be bonded.

WHAT YOU'LL DO

It's probably best to start out small with a trusted group of friends. Offer your services to other friends and acquaintances. Should the business catch on, you can then advertise for clients and for sitters. Ideally, you want sitters with a background in working with children; teachers and nurses are ideal.

PRICES

Babysitters usually do not draw high incomes. $4 to $6 an hour is typical for dependable adults. If you act as an agency, you will, of course, keep a percentage of the billings, probably in the neighborhood of 20 percent.

PITFALLS

Since babysitting services are relatively new, you may find yourself in the situation of being neither fish nor fowl when dealing with the government. One successfully franchised service originally ran into some problems because the government considered it an employment agency and wanted to tax it accordingly. So thoroughly check out the laws and restrictions in your area before starting this type of venture.

BED AND BREAKFAST___

☐ Start-up costs: If no major improvements or modifications are needed on your property, only a few hundred dollars for supplies and promotion.
☐ Estimated hours per week: 5 to 15 of actual contact time, food preparation, room maintenance.
☐ Number of staffers needed for start-up (including founder): 1

Bed and breakfast accommodations have been popular in Europe for many years, but have just begun to catch on in the U.S. According to author and bed and breakfast expert Bernice Chester, there are about 10,000 B & B's in the nation, four times the total of five years ago. As the trend increases, so do opportunities for a moonlighting B & B owner to supplement his or her income.

WHAT YOU'LL NEED _____

The first thing you need to consider is your home's location. If you are not in or very near an area that attracts tourists and vacationers, it may be difficult to draw enough business.

A bed and breakfast—which basically translates to a room rented in a private home, complete with breakfast—can be started in almost any home as long as there's a reasonably secluded room for the guests and some way to ensure privacy for your own family, such as a TV room reserved for family members. In addition, a separate bathroom for guests is highly desirable. You usually are expected to have air conditioning, and you must have a reasonably large closet in the guest's room. Obviously, the house will have to be attractive or quaint-looking or you'll have few takers.

Basically, you provide homey surroundings at a reasonable price, along with a substantial breakfast. Usually, B & B owners take pains to come up with an unusual and fairly elegant meal.

HOW TO FIND GUESTS

The most effective way to attract guests is through a reservation organization, a service that refers guests to you in return for a commission, usually 20 to 30 percent of the total bill. In addition, some guests will seek you out on their own, usually after reading about your B & B in a listing such as *Bed and Breakfast, USA* (R.D. 2, Box 355A, Greentown, PA 18426); you can get a listing in this publication by joining the Tourist House Association of America (same address). At the time of this writing, yearly membership was $15.

START-UP CONSIDERATIONS

Because B & B's are relatively new to this country, zoning laws are often unclear. B & B owner and author Beverly Mathews suggests that you get advice from a trusted advisor who knows your community, such as a local lawyer or insurance agent, to find out where you stand.

You should print up some brochures. Also, give some consideration to advertising in your local newspaper during periods when out-of-town guests will be attending major local events.

How much to charge? That will depend on the economic climate in your area in general, and specifically on the volume of the tourist trade. Your rates will also be related to what local hotels are charging, to some degree. A room with a double bed and a private bath might go for $35 a night in some areas, but would bring in substantially more in an area where the tourist trade is very brisk or the accommodations are quite elegant.

RESOURCES

Two widely available books tell you just about everything you need to know about running a bed and breakfast. Jan Stankus' *How to Open & Operate a Bed & Breakfast Home* (Globe Pequot) contains extensive information about the business. Mary Zander's *How to Start Your Own Bed and Breakfast* (Golden Hill Press) is also complete and helpful.

BEEKEEPER _____

☐ Start-up costs: One hive can be set up for under $100, but for a revenue-producing part-time commercial operation a $1,000 investment would be more realistic.

☐ Estimated hours per week: 10 during peak honey harvesting seasons, considerably less during other times of the year.

☐ Number of staffers needed for start-up (including founder): 1

Quick, here's a word association test: What do you think of when you hear the word *bee*? If you think of honey, keep reading. If your initial reaction was sting, flip to the next entry.

That's a quick test proposed by beekeeper and author John F. Adams. He and other experienced beekeepers note that mental suitability is half the battle in pursuing a fascinating hobby that can provide a part-time income.

WHY EVERYBODY'S BUZZING ABOUT BEES _____

Almost 200,000 people keep bees in the United States—about five million colonies of bees. Beekeepers sell honey, rent their hives to farmers for crop pollination, and also make a profit from the sale of beeswax and the bees themselves.

You can keep bees almost anywhere with little risk to you or your neighbors. There are colonies kept on rooftops in New York City, as well as in the harsh environs of the Canadian Rockies. Bees are hardy and generally don't bother people, except that they do need quite a bit of water in the summer. They can make a nuisance of themselves at nearby swimming pools if they don't have a handy water supply. Some localities do have ordinances against keeping bees (Washington, DC, is one example), but such rules are rare.

Handling bees is actually quite safe. You'll wear full protective gear, and when you open the hives to retrieve the honey, you will tranquilize the bees with smoke, which makes them very docile. Some adult education programs offer courses in beekeeping, in which you'll learn about handling procedures and be reassured of the safety of the hobby.

You should be aware though, that bees are susceptible to a number of bee diseases and parasites, which can wipe out entire hives.

WHAT YOU'LL NEED TO START

A beekeeper needs a movable-frame hive, gloves, a veil, a smoker to calm the colony when honey is collected, and, of course, some bees. You can buy most of the aforementioned by mail order (even the bees), but you can almost always find a local supplier. Check with a nearby farm extension agency for information on supplies and resources.

Hives wind up costing about $50 each by the time they're equipped with residents, but the cost can be amortized among large colonies. (Truly intrepid beekeepers often don't buy their bees—they capture them from a hive in the woods.) If you're planning to mount a reasonably large commercial operation, you may want as many as 40 or 50 hives. You'll need a reasonably good area for beekeeping, meaning a region where the bees can gather a great deal of pollen. Hives near (though not necessarily on) dairy farms are excellent.

PUTTING YOUR BEES TO WORK

A one-pound jar of honey can fetch about $1.40 in some areas if you sell it yourself although prices vary widely throughout the country; local beekeepers' organizations can give you information on prices and methods of selling. If you buy the jars in quantity, each one will cost about six cents. You will also have to get some labels printed up, but the cost is almost negligible. (A word of advice from a veteran: Don't put a picture of a bee on your label. Most people regard bees as pests and don't like to be reminded of where the honey came from.) Some home-sellers set up unattended "conscience stands"; you'll have to be the judge of the honesty of passersby in your area.

Another option is to sell your honey to wholesalers. However, they usually pay considerably less than you would make selling directly to customers. You'll probably only make about 50 cents a pound, but there's no messy bottling—a tank truck simply pulls up and sucks up your honey.

RESOURCES

One advantage of beekeeping as a hobby and part-time job is that there are so many good books written on the subject. Beekeeping seems to attract highly literate people. Some of the best works available are *The Complete Guide to Beekeeping* by Roger A. Morse (Dutton) and Diane Sammataro and Alphonse Avitabile's *Beekeeper's Handbook* (Scribners). Be sure to investigate local beekeeping classes; beekeepers love teaching as much as they love their bees.

BOAT CHARTER_____

☐ Start-up costs: Widely variable, depending on the cost of the boat. Note that boats do not come cheaply, and most require a great deal of upkeep.
☐ Estimated hours per week: 10 to 25
☐ Number of staffers needed for start-up (including founder): 1

Understand from the beginning that owning and renting a boat is not a terrific way to make money. Even the major charter companies with fleets of boats and expert staffers sometimes have a difficult time keeping . . . well, afloat. But if you already have a big power boat or sailboat (or plan to buy a boat because you want one for your own recreation), you can, given the right circumstances, generate some part-time income from it.

ECONOMICS OF BOAT CHARTERING _____

While renting out your boat won't make you rich, it can ease the pain of the high costs of boat ownership. According to marine consultant Jim Turner, the owner of a new boat might need to charter it 24 days out of the month just to cover bank payments, maintenance, and insurance, and guarantee a reasonable profit.

Keeping your boat chartered most of the time isn't easy. And while you probably won't go into chartering just for profit, you can cover many of your costs and possibly develop an interesting part-time business.

THE BOAT BUSINESS

Speaking of costs, take a deep breath and flip through the latest boating catalog. You'll find that a 39-foot sportfishing boat, complete with diesels, radar, and a fighting chair, costs somewhere in the vicinity of $180,000. Now, should you own this boat, you can reasonably expect to rent it out for more than $1,000 a week without a crew (known as renting out a "bareboat"). With a crew, you could possibly earn twice that amount, but most of the extra money would go toward paying the crew.

Prices for sailboats are equally breathtaking, both on the purchase and rental end. But if you keep in mind the high cost of insurance, maintenance, and boat financing, you'll realize why rentals are so high and why even with a high rental fee you might not make your monthly target if you operate the boat strictly as an income producer.

OPTIONS

There are ways to make money with a boat, though. If you happen to live in or near the Florida Keys, for instance, you'll find a brisk trade in old six-passenger boats, which you can pick up for under $50,000. If you know where the fish run in those parts, you can take fishermen out on weekends and during your free time and probably make a decent profit.

That assumes, of course, that you're handy or can partner with someone who is. Old boats (the only kind we mortals can afford) *do* need maintenance. And on the subject of old boats, a handyman who can fix up a sailboat and has an attractive locale can sometimes sell out "sunset cruises" or similar short trips. These are especially profitable when you provide meals; you can easily charge $25 a head (and more, depending on the area and the food and drink you provide) for dinner on the river, or whatever you choose to call it.

RESOURCES

Boat ownership is not something you want to rush into. Take your time and learn everything you can about boats; the salespeople at marinas are usually quite knowledgeable and will include a generous dose of information along with their sales pitch. You'll also want to inquire at the local Coast Guard headquarters about restrictions governing rental of boats. There are hundreds of books on boats lining the shelves of libraries and bookstores, and any of them will be useful depending on your particular interest. A very helpful magazine on the technical and business aspects of boating is *Motor Boating and Sailing* (P.O. Box 10075, Des Moines, IA 50350), which is widely available at newsstands.

BOOKBINDER _____

☐ Start-up costs: Usually over $1,500, sometimes quite a bit more if you have high-quality equipment. But start-up costs can be held to a reasonable level if you improvise and subcontract some of the work.
☐ Estimated hours per week: 5 to 20
☐ Number of staffers needed for start-up (including founder): 1

Bookbinding is not particularly easy or profitable, but it can be intensely satisfying, which is why so many people do it as a hobby. Choose bookbinding as a part-time endeavor if your first love is books.

THE ART OF BOOKBINDING _____

Bookbinders place pages into a book, cover the book, and stamp the cover with the title and author's name. In addition, many bookbinders conserve and repair the pages of older volumes. The basic tool of the trade is a press, which can cost several hundred dollars but can sometimes be improvised by using boards and woodworker's clamps. A page cutter is very expensive—as much as $2,500—but you can sometimes pick up a used one for a fraction of that. Stamping machines (the devices that imprint the title on the cover) can be even more expensive, so it's wise to hold off on that purchase initially; you can always subcontract the stamping to a professional bindery.

WHO HIRES BOOKBINDERS? _____

In some cases, people hire bookbinders to repair a precious book, such as a family Bible. This is much more complicated than it might at first seem. The job could easily take 50 to 100 hours, and you would have to charge between $200 and $500 for the work. Clients usually pick a binder for this type of job from a telephone book ad or newspaper classified.

Page repair takes some experience and patience. Most bookbinders charge between $3 and $4 per page.

Libraries are a good source of income for a bookbinder. Colleges will contract for binding of dissertations and theses, for example, usually at the rate of $18 to $20 each. You can contact librarians by telephone or letter and let them know of your service.

RESOURCES

If you're intrigued by bookbinding, check out *The Craft of Bookbinding* by Eric Burdett (David & Charles) and *Bookbinding and Conservation by Hand: A Working Guide* by Laura S. Young (Bowker), which give you some basic instruction and list sources of supplies and information.

BOOK PUBLISHING

☐ Start-up costs: About $5,000, although you could easily spend more.
☐ Estimated hours per week: 10 to 20
☐ Number of staffers needed for start-up (including founder): 1

Books are big business, and nowadays small publishers are getting an increasingly large chunk of the publishing pie. You can start a small publishing house, possibly for under $5,000, if you can come up with specialty books that you believe will sell well to a certain identifiable audience.

WHY PUBLISH YOURSELF?

For one thing, it's difficult to get a limited-appeal book published through regular channels. It's estimated that over 350,000 book-length manuscripts are written each year, but less than a tenth are actually printed. And that figure doesn't count the hundreds of thousands of proposals sent to publishers each year.

The reason for this trend is that commercial publishing houses have enormous overhead; they usually must generate large, wide-scale sales to meet the bottom line. This means that some perfectly workable and potentially profitable books are overlooked because they only appeal to a small audience. But a small, loyal audience willing to spend money can produce a good profit for a small publisher.

So if you have a book idea you think could make a profit, give some thought to self-publishing.

WHAT YOU'LL DO

For starters, you need to come up with a manuscript, probably one you've written yourself. How-to books are usually the best bet. Next, you must have the work typeset and put into book form. Check the phone book for typesetters and book printers. Publications such as *Writer's Digest* carry ads for printers in this line of work, but check locally first.

Remember that printers are different from subsidy publishers. Subsidy publishers claim that they offer the full range of publishers' services, including promotion and editorial assistance. They will typically charge you large fees for this type of "support." Self-publishing is a much better idea.

It's a judgment call as to how many books to print, but be aware that your per-unit cost drops dramatically when you have a larger print run. Printing 5,000 copies instead of 500 typically will halve the per-unit cost. However, unless you are able to sell the books, you may end up with 3,000 copies sitting in your garage.

Do quite a bit of investigating, because various methods of production make a big difference in cost. New hot-melt binding techniques do a good job for a reasonable price. Desktop publishing (page 101) may create a virtual revolution in the self-publishing industry.

MARKETING

How do you sell books? Mail order (page 181) is a good option. According to self-publisher Dan Poynter, more books are sold through the mail than through stores. You can also try to sell books through retail outlets, but a retailer typically wants a 40 percent discount, so your profit in this area gets sliced pretty thin. You can market to libraries, and in some cases, you can sell directly to a wholesaler.

RESOURCES

You can start by checking out a comprehensive work titled *The Book Market: How to Write, Publish and Market Your Book* by Aron M. Mathieu (Andover Press). An excellent step-by-step guide is *The Self-Publishing Manual: How to Write, Print, and Sell Your Own Book* by Dan Poynter (Para Publishing). Para Publishing (P.O. Box 4232-P, Santa Barbara, CA 93140-4232) offers a wide variety of related materials; write to them for a free catalog.

BROADCAST SALES ____

☐ Start-up costs: None
☐ Estimated hours per week: 7 to 15
☐ Number of staffers needed for start-up (including founder): 1

Here's an excellent opportunity, particularly for people who live in medium-size cities and small towns. Give some thought to selling radio airtime to local merchants and businesspeople. The rewards can be high and the service is interesting. There's also a touch of glamour in broadcast sales that you won't get selling cosmetics or brushes door to door.

THE RADIO SALES BUSINESS ____

Radio stations have a staff of full-time salespeople who sell commercials to clients. The salespeople usually have a hand in writing commercials and in developing ideas for a series of ads. They work from a list of established clients and also call on potential clients. But it's the repeat business, especially from advertising agencies, that keeps them in business; "prospecting" for new clients is not a highly appealing task.

If you don't mind prospecting, and if you have some contacts in the local business community, you could turn a neat profit as a freelance, home-based radio salesperson.

WHAT YOU'LL DO ____

You'll work as an independent contractor, meaning that you're not paid anything except for commissions. (Staff salespeople usually draw a minimum salary and earn commissions.) While this means that you won't have any salary cushion, it also means that you may be able to negotiate a higher commission rate than that given the staff. In a small- or medium-size market you might be able to get from 10 to 20 percent of the commercial selling price. Commission percentages in major markets will be smaller because the amount of money involved will be significantly higher. There's also less opportunity for freelance work in major markets.

WHY YOU'LL BE IN DEMAND

"It's a good opportunity for qualified persons," notes Tim Cushman, sales manager of WHEB radio in Portsmouth, New Hampshire. "Stations are always looking to boost sales, and with a freelancer working on a straight commission basis nobody has anything to lose."

You'll have a better chance of success if you can tap into a market you know well. Do you have contacts in the business community? Do you work in banking? You might be able to exploit those contacts and sell to new prospects.

One thing to remember: A broadcast salesperson typically acts as his own collection agent and is paid commission only on what he collects.

GETTING STARTED

Contact the local sales managers at area radio stations and see who would be interested in making a deal. It's not kosher to sell for more than one station at a time, so go with the station that offers the best plan.

RESOURCES

You'll need some special knowledge of broadcast economics and sales. A good guide is Charles Warner's *Broadcast and Cable Selling* (Wadsworth). Tim Cushman, through his agency, Sound Results, offers a good training manual for radio salespeople. For more information, write to Sound Results, Chesley Drive, Barrington, NH 03825.

CAKE DECORATOR _____

☐ Start-up costs: About $300 for basic supplies and equipment.
☐ Estimated hours per week: 5 to 8
☐ Number of staffers needed for start-up (including founder): 1

Cake decorating is an ideal home-based business because you can do other things while the cake is in the oven; in addition, you'll be able to feed your mistakes to the family. And there *will* be mistakes—even the most experienced cake decorators note that the business is one of trial and error.

WHAT YOU'LL BE DOING _____

Cake decorators supply cakes to functions such as weddings and parties and often operate out of their home. Before starting your home-based business, be sure to check local health laws to make sure you're not in technical violation of an ordinance. (For a fuller discussion, see *Caterer*, page 62.)

The business, say the pros, is almost entirely based on word of mouth. Prospective customers usually recall seeing a cake they admired and inquire as to the decorator of that masterpiece. While you won't need to do extensive advertising, it is a good idea to have some business cards printed up. You can leave them with the host of the affair which features your cake, or in some cases leave them on the table near the cake.

TOOLS OF THE TRADE _____

You probably have some of the equipment on hand already. Do a quick inventory to see if you have the following:

- A heavy-duty mixer, preferably more than one.
- Cake pans in various sizes.
- Decorating equipment, including parchment tubes and tips for making leaves, roses, borders, etc.

Almost all moonlighting cake decorators are expected to supply the cake as well as do the decorating, so you'll have to be an experienced baker to turn a decent profit. Or you can buy the cakes you decorate but the profit margin will be sliced more thinly and the taste may not be as good.

OTHER CONSIDERATIONS

Before doing anything, heed the words of experienced cake decorators: This job can be anything but fun, especially during the summer months. Also, be aware that delivering cakes to the scene of the event is a hassle. If you have to deliver, be sure you build a fair compensation into your fee. And don't forget to take an emergency cake repair kit with you, because accidents can and do happen.

As a rule of thumb, some cake decorators figure out their charge by tripling the cost of the ingredients. You can add quite a bit more for highly elaborate jobs.

RESOURCES

Two widely available books can get you started: *Creative Cake Decorating,* edited by Jill Burmeister (Better Homes and Gardens), and *Betty Crocker's Cake Decorating With Cake Recipes for Any Occasion,* which takes you on a step-by-step illustrated journey through various facets of cake baking and design.

CALLIGRAPHER _____

☐ Start-up costs: Under $100 for the basics.
☐ Estimated hours per week: 4 to 8, but occasionally more time for big projects.
☐ Number of staffers needed for start-up (including founder): 1

Calligraphy, the art of ornamental hand lettering, is not difficult to learn, although you will probably want to take a class to learn the basics. Those with an artistic flair can—with practice—whip up wonderful creations.

WHAT YOU'LL NEED _____

The equipment is simple and comparatively inexpensive. You can get started by buying

- one pen holder
- two Speedball nibs (one calligrapher recommends a C-2 and C-4 for right-handers an LC-2 and an LC-4 for lefties)
- graph paper and tracing paper

The only other immediate need is a table on which you can work and a well-lighted desk surface.

HOW CALLIGRAPHY WORKS _____

You use interchangeable pen nibs to produce lines of different widths and shapes. A squarish nib produces Old English letters, while an oval-shaped nib can be used for flowing script. Calligraphy guides (more on these in a minute) show you how to form the letters.

HOW CALLIGRAPHY MAKES A PROFIT _____

Many individuals and firms have some occasional need for calligraphy. Restaurants are prime examples. Those fancy, flowing menus are often designed and executed by calligraphers. While typesetters and printers can reproduce some of the effect of calligraphy, the personal touch—that special effect so coveted by specialty restaurants—only comes from a human hand.

Envelope addressing and invitations are part of the calligrapher's business, so weddings, bar mitzvahs, and other formal occasions are good opportunities. Organizations presenting scrolls or awards also will frequently retain a calligrapher. And some especially expert calligraphers, such as Barry Craig Morentz, president of the Society of Scribes, create custom-made books.

BUSINESS BASICS _____

A competent calligrapher usually can earn between $15 to $25 an hour. You can stir up business by sending xeroxed samples to restaurants and by developing a working relationship with local typesetters. Printers will probably tolerate you because they'll be able to steer their customers to a service (and therefore print up more invitations or menus).

RESOURCES _____

If you're interested in this low-risk business, you can find many books and manuals in your local library. *Getting Started in Calligraphy* by Nancy Baron (Sterling) is a good choice. In addition, the manuals supplied with beginners' calligraphy sets are quite helpful.

CANDLEMAKER _____

☐ Start-up costs: You can get into the business for under $500.
☐ Estimated hours per week: 6 to 15, more if you get large orders.
☐ Number of staffers needed for start-up (including founder): 1

Candles can be beautiful works of art, but fortunately you don't have to be an artist to make them. Modern molds and waxes allow even a beginner to achieve some breathtaking effects, and you can often sell your candles at a substantial profit.

THE BASICS

Candlemakers need a supply of wax, usually sold in ten-pound slabs, some candle molds, and a way to melt the wax. A coffeepot can serve as a melter, but a secondhand deep fryer does the job a little more efficiently. Many candlemakers use a finishing bath, which usually is nothing more than a plastic wastebasket filled with water. You can buy candlemaking materials in craft stores; check the Yellow Pages under "Crafts."

The kitchen is an ideal place to make candles, but be sure to wear an apron or overalls and put down some papers because wax can and does make a terrible mess if you spill it.

THE ARTISTIC TOUCH

Of course, no one will pay you for a standard, run-of-the-mill candle; even if they did, you couldn't possibly beat the competition of the large-scale factories. Your artistic touches are what will make the candle attractive, unique, and marketable. Some of the personal touches you can add include

- Dyeing the candles in vivid colors. New dyes allow quick and easy coloration. Various dyes can be combined in one candle.
- Creating different shapes. By using wax with a very high melting point, you can learn to make a so-called hurricane candle, a large ornately designed candle, sections of which may appear to be braided, curled etc. Conversely, you can use a low-melting-point wax simply poured into a decorative textured jar to produce a unique container candle.
- Using decorations. Some candlemakers attach metal decorations, such as stamped snowflakes, to spruce up their efforts.
- Adding scent.

SELLING YOUR WORK

There are a number of options. Mail order is one, but be sure to send some of your candles to friends in distant cities first to test how well your packing protects your creation. Better yet, you can sell to craft or specialty stores in your area. While there's no set formula for determining price, you can research the competition and determine what the market will bear. Retailers generally mark up candles 40 to 50 percent. Sometimes, you'll have no alternative but to sell on consignment, but be wary of this because candles get broken in stores. After a few consignment sales, you'll probably be able to convince the retailer to buy a stock.

Some people set up candle galleries in their homes. Be sure to check on zoning restrictions before you try this.

MOVING UP

You can expand your operations considerably should demand prove high. Buying more molds and greater quantities of wax is the first step, but in addition you'll have to do some careful calculation to determine the most efficient way to mass-produce the candles.

RESOURCES

There are many good candlemaking books to guide you, including Ruth Monroe's *Kitchen Candlecrafting* (Barnes). Candlemaking is also a popular course in craft centers and adult education programs.

CARICATURIST

☐ Start-up costs: Under $100 for basic materials.
☐ Estimated hours per week: 5 to 10
☐ Number of staffers needed for start-up (including founder): 1

Caricature comes from the Italian word *caricare*, "to load." It is the "loading" of exaggerated features. Big heads become huge heads; long noses become enormous noses.

If you can artistically express this sort of exaggeration, you might be able to develop an interesting sideline doing in-person sketches. And if your drawing talents lend themselves to the humor of the printed page, you may be able to market your skills as a cartoonist (page 60).

DRAWING CARICATURES

Some caricature artists simply set up an easel in a public place and advertise for clients. This is made a bit easier if you can display some of your previous works; your own caricature is a good advertising display since potential customers can get an idea of how your work reflects what you had to start with.

Other caricaturists reject setting up in public, maintaining that it's far more productive to isolate a good potential group of clients and hone in on them. One example is your local college. One successful caricature artist places posters featuring his work on college bulletin boards. The advertising copy is simple and to the point:

Caricatures
Student Lounge
Monday 3:30–6:30
$3

You might be able to charge more, possibly significantly more, than $3. But that's not a bad rate if you can turn up clients in volume, which is what you'll do if you set up your easel in a busy student lounge. (By the way, you will probably have to get some sort of approval to advertise and sell your service on a college campus. Start by asking the student affairs office. Usually, such approval is easy to obtain.)

OTHER OPPORTUNITIES

Another marketing strategy: Do free caricatures of bartenders and/or bar owners. They are fond of hanging their likenesses in their establishments, and once customers start noticing your work, they may want a similar piece for themselves. Play your cards right and you might get the use of the bar to practice your craft.

Advertising agencies sometimes use caricature, so send samples to local agencies.

RESOURCES

Caricature is art with a difference: you have to develop a flair for capturing your model's (or victim's) odd points and blowing them out of proportion. A fine book on caricature is *How To Draw Caricatures* by Lenn Redman (Contemporary).

CARPET-CLEANING SERVICE _____

☐ Start-up costs: $1,000
☐ Estimated hours per week: 10 to 15
☐ Number of staffers needed for start-up (including founder): 1

Carpet cleaning is something that most ordinary homeowners don't like to attempt. It takes quite a bit of effort and some specialized equipment that is often difficult for the homeowner to rent and use. Many moonlighters take advantage of this and operate a successful part-time carpet-cleaning service with a minimum investment.

WHAT YOU'LL NEED TO GET STARTED _____

There are two types of carpet cleaners: steam extractors and rotary shampooers. Each has its adherents, but many carpet-cleaning professionals feel that the rotary shampooer does a more thorough job of cleaning deep-seated dirt. In addition, the rotary machine can be used for other jobs, such as polishing floors.

In addition to a carpet-cleaning machine, you'll need a good vacuum cleaner and a variety of spotting agents and other cleaning fluids. A van is helpful, but almost all carpet cleaners will fit into a large station wagon.

Carpet-cleaning machines cost about $700 for the low-end variety and up to $2,500 for a high-power industrial model.

DOING THE JOB AND FIGURING THE BILL _____

You'll learn a lot about cleaning carpets through experience (and you might want to get that experience by moonlighting for someone else before starting your own business). Among the tricks you'll pick up are how to maneuver the cleaner—not an easy job at first—and use the spotting agents to eradicate the most difficult stains. You'll also learn which jobs are hopeless and shouldn't be taken on.

Billing is relatively simple. Most carpet cleaners charge between 15 and 20 cents per square foot of carpet to be cleaned. Each additional room might be done for a flat fee—say, $39.95.

MARKETING

Ads in weekly papers work well. Fliers and word of mouth also produce a lot of business. Remember that carpet cleaning is, or at least should be, a regular job. Keep a calendar; call your clients back in six months and ask if they want another cleaning.

RESOURCES

As mentioned, the best way to learn this business is while on someone else's payroll. Also, don't hesitate to ask janitorial supply people for their advice. They know a lot about the proper cleaning agents and techniques and, of course, have a vested interest in keeping you in business.

CARTOONIST

☐ Start-up costs: Supplies usually can be purchased for under $50, but allow a generous amount for postage.
☐ Estimated hours per week: 5 to 15
☐ Number of staffers needed for start-up (including founder): 1

A cartoonist has to do more than draw. He or she must express an idea, convey a satirical dig, and, above all, make people laugh. If you have these abilities, consider cartooning, which offers an opportunity for self-expression as well as added income.

THE BASICS OF CARTOONING _____

Most cartoons with which you're familiar are syndicated, that is, they're distributed to a variety of publications through a central source. This means that the cost is dramatically amortized among the purchasers. Unfortunately, this also means that publications are unlikely to buy locally produced cartoons because they would cost as much or more per panel as the big-name features.

However, this doesn't automatically mean that there's no market for your work. You can often find lucrative markets in specialty publications, and local publications can and do buy cartoons of particular local interest. Like the caricaturist (page 57), you can find an outlet for your talents at small advertising agencies.

MARKETING YOUR WORK _____

You'll want to send your work to art editors at newspapers and magazines. There is some difference of opinion as to what to send—the original, a rough, or a photocopy—but the essential point is that you offer an amusing idea with a *new slant*. That slant, the personal point of view, is what sells cartoons.

Always send a stamped, self-addressed envelope with your submission. Otherwise, you may not get the cartoon back. Incidentally, don't forget to back your cartoon with a stiff piece of cardboard to keep it from being mutilated in the mail.

MAKING SALES _____

Keep the cartoons in the mail because you can't sell them if they're in your bureau drawer. And be aware from the start that the odds are against you, even in smaller specialty publications. The art editor of *Medical Economics* magazine, for example, reported that he sees over 12,000 roughs and gag lines a year but uses only one or two percent of those submissions.

There seems to be a higher success ratio in the advertising business. Advertisers do not use a great deal of cartooning talent, but when they do the pay is usually pretty good and the artist may be called back when another cartoon is needed.

If you're working on commission from an ad agency, you can usually get upwards of $20 an hour for your work. When dealing with publications, the work is sold on a per-piece basis, and the scale varies considerably. A local paper might pay only $10. A full-page spread in a national publication can fetch you more than $500.

RESOURCES _____

There are many good books on cartooning. For starters, try *Drawing Comic Strips* by Jack Markow (Putnam). Roy Paul Nelson's *Humorous Illustration and Cartooning* (Prentice-Hall) offers excellent instruction and advice. For information on how to sell your cartoons, consult *Artist's Handbook,* a directory of potential clients published annually by Writer's Digest Books.

CATERER _____

- ☐ Start-up costs: Highly variable. Even if all equipment is rented or borrowed, allow a cushion of $1,000 to cover initial costs and purchases.
- ☐ Estimated hours per week: 8 to 15
- ☐ Number of staffers needed for start-up (including founder): 1, but additional help employed on a per-job basis is almost always needed at some point.

An Atlanta caterer, who wishes to remain anonymous, has some strong words of advice for prospective caterers: "If you don't know a lot about food, stay out of catering. I was an expert cook, but when I started catering I made some dreadful mistakes. Don't just walk into a catering job, because you can really screw up and maybe even poison somebody."

While she and other caterers warn that the business is difficult for novices, people in the profession unanimously agree that the field offers excellent opportunities for part-time income because most catering jobs are at night and on weekends.

STARTING OUT _____

Catering is about 50 percent food skills and 50 percent social skills. You *must* make contacts in order to attract clients. Selection of caterers is heavily dependent on word of mouth from satisfied clients and contacts among networks of friends and acquaintances.

Here are suggestions on how to make contacts:

- To learn about the business firsthand, get a job in a local restaurant that does a lot of catering work. Quite often a restaurant will farm out small jobs to ambitious staffers on a freelance basis.
- Volunteer to cater charitable events for free. Donate your services, charging only for the cost of the food. Or offer to cater a friend's party. If all goes well, they'll recommend you to others. You'll meet many prospective clients this way, gain some experience, and help some people who need it.
- Give cooking classes. You'll meet other people involved in culinary trades and will almost certainly gain a couple of clients from among your students.

BUSINESS BASICS

You may run into problems with local health department laws if you cater from your home kitchen. In most localities, you're required to meet certain facility codes that could be prohibitively expensive for a part-timer. For example, you may be required to have a professional stove, a sink with a certain number of washing compartments, special tiles on the floor, and so forth.

People do work out of their kitchens, though, often in violation of health ordinances. Many caterers avoid any possibility of trouble by renting a professional kitchen and preparing the food there. Check out churches and social halls in your area that may rent kitchen facilities. Another option is to prepare all the food in the client's kitchen; you give the meal a homey touch and stay on the right side of the law at the same time.

Generally, you'll serve the food on the client's dishes, although this is not always the case. Check on whether your client has an adequate supply of plates, cups, silverware, tablecloths, and other items. If not, you can supply these items or obtain them from a rental supply house. (Many places that rent lawn tillers and carpet cleaners also usually carry party supplies such as dishes and tableware; you can also go directly to a specialized party supply house.)

How do you determine prices? Many caterers simply charge triple the cost of the food purchased. Don't forget to record *all* the food and food products used, by the way. Write down how much salt you use, how many spices, and if you can, factor in the costs of the energy used. For projects such as puffed pastry that demand a great deal of skill, you can charge four or five times the cost of materials.

MAKING THE BUSINESS GROW

Special touches and good service will spread your reputation and eventually fill your calendar. One caterer reported astounding success from a very simple gimmick: During a Christmas party, she presented guests with bread wreaths adorned with her business card. Six calls resulted from that personalized touch.

Be scrupulous about not taking a job you are not sure you can handle. The results can be ugly and the word of mouth will work against you. Another problem encountered by caterers who take on too-large jobs is storage. If you don't have adequate refrigeration space, for example, the food can become stale or even go bad. Dishes that are highly sensitive to spoilage, such as mayonnaise-based salads, could actually make people sick. That, of course, is publicity you don't need.

RESOURCES

You can increase your knowledge of the business by collecting a good supply of relevant cookbooks. In addition, get a copy of Marjorie P. Blanchard's *Cater from Your Kitchen* (Bobbs-Merrill). Also, you can pick up some valuable hints from Manfred Ketterer's *How to Manage a Successful Catering Business* (Williams).

CHILDREN'S PARTY PLANNER

- ☐ Start-up costs: About $500 to cover initial advertising and other first-time costs.
- ☐ Estimated hours per week: 5 to 15
- ☐ Number of staffers needed for start-up (including founder): 1

Planning and pulling off a party for children is quite a bit different from doing the same for adults (see page 200). You'll have to provide different types of food and entertainment, and proceed with an essentially different goal: keeping everybody entertained while at the same time avoiding disaster.

KNOW YOUR TERRITORY

One woman started a successful party-planning business by limiting it to girls of a certain age. When her associates questioned her ("I mean, couldn't you do boys . . . or older girls . . . or . . ."), she responded that of course she *could,* but she was able to do a much better job by specializing.

There's wisdom in those words. The needs and wants of partying toddlers are profoundly different from those of teenagers, and if those desires are not met, the party could be a 14-carat disaster. So understanding the nature of a certain age group is crucial.

Before starting, you'll need to know these basic principles:

- Waste is always a big problem with any children's party. Most of the food ends up in the trash, since children tend to take more on their plates than you'd expect. Experienced party planners know to provide more food than children can possibly eat because children for some reason at least want the food on their plates before they throw it away. And of course, knowing what (and what not) to serve to each age group is critical.
- Entertainment must be provided for younger children. You can have a professional clown or magician, or you can simply lead them in sing-alongs or pin the tail on the donkey. But you'll have to have some activity planned, or the children will become extremely restless.
- Parties should be short. Two hours is about the max for most youngsters. Things really begin to drag after that.
- Be aware of spillage problems with younger kids. Don't put your client's house in jeopardy by serving grape juice, and never use plastic cups if you can avoid it. Use bottom-heavy mugs.

MARKETING

Finding clients is relatively simple after you get the first few; experienced children's party planners say that the network of satisfied customers expands quickly. Just be sure that you leave a supply of your business cards with each client. They'll refer other mothers to you. Give some thought to rubber-stamping your name and phone number on the party favors the children will take home with them. For starters, of course, you can always place an ad in the local paper serving your neighborhood.

PRICING

What you charge depends primarily on what you provide. Most children's party planners bring food, favors, and everything else, such as supplies for any games or activities planned. In that case, you probably will charge about $10 per child.

RESOURCES

There are a number of cookbooks that feature food for youngsters' parties. One of the best all-around guides to children's parties is *Parties for Home & School: A Piece of Cake* by Sandra Lanb & Dena Bellows (Good Apple). Another useful source is *The Pennywhistle Party Planner* by Meredith Brokow and Annie Gilbar (Weidenfeld & Nicolson).

CHIMNEY SWEEP

☐ Start-up costs: $3,000
☐ Estimated hours per week: 12 to 30
☐ Number of staffers needed for start-up (including founder): 1

First, the bad news: There were over 100,000 chimney-related home fires last year, most of them breaking out when a buildup of creosote burst into flames. Now, the good news: You can help prevent these potential tragedies—and make a profit at the same time—by becoming a part-time chimney sweep.

WHAT A SWEEP DOES

First of all, a sweep gets dirty. He or she must climb up on roofs to lower in brushes and chains, and also climb into the fireplace to work on the bottom of the chimney. It's a dusty, grimy job, no doubt about it.

In addition to cleaning, chimney sweeps often install wood-heating equipment, repoint (fix mortar between bricks on) chimneys, and install chimney caps to keep out rain. On occasion, a sweep will install a steel liner in a brick chimney.

EQUIPMENT NEEDED FOR START-UP

You'll need a powerful vacuum, one which moves about 700 cubic feet of air per minute. Brushes will be a considerable expense, too, because you'll need about 20 of them. Houses have widely varying flue openings (square, rectangular, and round) and you need brushes to fit each. Fiberglass poles are essential, as are a set of chains, some goggles, masonry concrete and ladders. Some sweeps have a sophisticated tool called an insert puller, which allows easy removal of a fireplace insert. That will set you back about $300.

Don't forget that you'll need an insurance policy, too.

FEES

A chimney sweep usually charges between $50 and $80 to clean a chimney, a job which takes about an hour and a half. You'll also do some consulting with the owner about maintenance and safety procedures following the cleaning, so figure the whole job will take about two hours.

MARKETING

A Yellow Pages ad is important for a chimney sweep. Also ads in local shoppers traditionally do an excellent job for sweeps. Other advertising vehicles have been tried with varying success; one sweep, for example, reported very poor results from a series of radio ads.

RESOURCES

This is a business you can't rush into; you need to know what you're doing or you're courting disaster. The National Chimney Sweep Guild (18115 Georgia Avenue, P.O. Box 503, Olney, MD 20832) offers certification and support materials for chimney sweeps. In addition, read *Residential Fireplace and Chimney Handbook,* 4th ed by J. E. Amrhein (Masonry Institute of America).

CHRISTMAS TREE GROWER _____

- [ ] Start-up costs: Aside from the land, you'll need a chain saw and brush cutter, which can be purchased for around $600 for both, as a low-end estimate. Seedlings can cost as little as $20 per hundred.
- [ ] Estimated hours per week: 2 to 5, but higher in pruning and harvesting seasons.
- [ ] Number of staffers needed for start-up (including founder): 1

Raising and selling Christmas trees can be a highly profitable business, but it's also quite risky. A brush fire, insects, or fast-spreading diseases can wipe out your crop overnight. However, the financial investment can be very low, so if you can stand to risk some hard work there may be a profit ahead.

PATIENCE FOR PROFIT _____

And by "ahead," we mean years ahead. It takes about eight years to grow a standard-size Christmas tree. But keep in mind that the tree can sell for as much as $30 in some parts of the country—a fair profit from a 20-cent seed sapling.

To harvest the best crops each year, you'll want to plant in rotation; that is, put in a hundred or so trees each year. (Believe it or not, a single acre can support almost 1,100 trees, so you don't need the Ponderosa to start your tree farm.) Using the rotation method of planting, you'll have a harvestable crop each year once the first batch of trees reaches maturity.

MAINTAINING THE FARM

The only real work involves planting, harvesting, and pruning the trees. Pruning, by the way, is a lot of work; each year you'll have to remove about half the tree's growth in order to induce it to thicken properly. Also, brush must be cut back in order to keep the trees from being choked out by undergrowth.

Disease and insects are real problems. Gary Power, a power company executive who moonlights in Christmas tree farming, suggests you invoke the eggs-in-several-baskets theory and plant different varieties of trees—for example, Norway spruce and Scotch pine—because each is resistant to particular diseases and insects that might wipe out the others.

MARKETING

There are a number of different strategies. Assuming you have a good crop of attractive trees, you can:

1. Have a tag-and-cut program: people visit in the fall and pick out a tree they'd like to cut when they return in December. You supply them with a hand saw (not a chain saw) when they return, and they do the harvesting for you.
2. Hire the services of your local Boy Scout troop. Let them harvest the trees on a wholesale basis. That is, they cut trees and buy them from you at $20 each, then market the trees elsewhere for $30 apiece.
3. Cut the trees and sell them yourself. You can rent a parking lot or abandoned gas station, but many people have just as good results by selling from their front yards.

START-UP

A good place to buy saplings is from your local soil conservation service. If you have trouble tracking down such an agency, check with your local extension service or with an area office of the Department of Agriculture. Extension agents can give all sorts of advice.

You'll have to find some land, of course, if you don't already own a plot. Just about any fertile land will do as long as it gets full sunlight. Check with local horticulturalists about soil requirements for the types of evergreens that grow well in your area. Also, be sure that the type of tree you plant is marketable as a Christmas tree in your area.

RESOURCES

If you want some technical guidelines, check out James M. Vardaman's *Tree Farm Business Management* (Wiley).

CLIPPING SERVICE _____

☐ Start-up costs: Minimal
☐ Estimated hours per week: 10 to 12
☐ Number of staffers needed for start-up (including founder): 1

Major clipping services read virtually all major national and international publications. They clip articles which mention clients and forward them to those clients. National clipping services are employed by a variety of firms, but public relations offices and agencies are major customers; they want an accurate record of just how often their client or organization was in the national press, and what kind of mention was given.

This, of course, is a service you cannot hope to duplicate in scale or thoroughness. However, an enterprising entrepreneur can establish a part-time, local clipping service and turn a fair profit.

AN IDEA FOR AN EASY, INTERESTING SERVICE _____

Running a clipping service is an ideal moonlighting job because the work can usually be done at your convenience. If you work during the day, all you need is a nearby library with evening hours. (You'll find it far more cost-effective to photocopy the publication from a library stock rather than subscribing and cutting up your copy. This strategy also allows you to service multiple clients without buying additional copies of the periodicals.)

HOW IT'S DONE _____

Contact public affairs offices of local businesses. If a firm doesn't have a department by that name, ask for the public relations or marketing department. You might also approach the CEO's executive assistant.

Ask if the firm is interested in a clipping service. Explain that you can provide a variety of services related to clipping (detailed below) and ascertain which, if any, interest the prospective client.

WHAT YOU WILL PROVIDE

You can offer two levels of services:

- Clips of all mentions of the company in local and specialized media. There is probably someone assigned to this job in-house, but it's a time-consuming job and one of the first ones they'd probably like to farm out. Specialized media include publications specific to the business's main and secondary fields of interest. For example, a forging firm would be interested primarily in clips from journals focusing on the forging industry itself, and might also want you to scan secondary publications such as mechanical engineering and metallurgy journals.
- Clips of stories that may not mention the firm but have an impact on its business. That same forging firm might be very interested in reading anything and everything about the aluminum industry or the aircraft industry. This borders on a reading service (page 228), which can work in perfect tandem with a home-based clipping service.

CHARGING FOR YOUR SERVICES

It's a good idea to avoid being paid by the clip. After all, it's not your fault that the company isn't in the news, and you'll spend just as much (or more) time scanning publications when there is no mention of the firm. Try negotiating an hourly rate and approximating the hours needed for the job; the public relations director for the firm might be able to help you come up with a realistic approximation. If it turns out that you're way off, you can renegotiate later—once the firm sees how valuable your service really is.

RESOURCES

Your best friend will be the librarian in charge of periodicals. He or she will show you how to use periodical indexes. Also, check the research hints in the section on *Reading Service Specialist* (page 228).

COLLEGE APPLICATION COUNSELOR _____

☐ Start-up costs: About $100 for basic reference materials, more if you purchase a personal computer for use in the business. Advertising may cost several hundred dollars and will probably be a recurring expense.
☐ Estimated hours per week: 6 to 12
☐ Number of staffers needed for start-up (including founder): 1

The bachelor's degree has come to have approximately the same meaning as the high school diploma did a generation ago; it's the basic credential for entry into the job market. As more and more people go to college, the number of support services offered to those college-bound people needs to increase, too. One such service is application counseling. If you have a background in higher education and/or a good feel for the college marketplace, you may be able to generate a healthy part-time income by helping others further their education.

FUNDAMENTALS _____

The fact that college is now required of people who in the past probably would not have sought higher education has a direct bearing on the job of a freelance, home-based application counselor. Many people who know very little about colleges are faced with the prospect of helping their son or daughter choose the right one. Very often, neither they nor the student really understand what they need to know and how they can find out more.

Many high schools have excellent guidance departments which give detailed assistance to the college-bound student, but some schools offer only token assistance at best.

Where do you fit into this situation? You can step in as the finder and purveyor of relevant information, translating it for the college-bound student and his or her parents.

WHAT YOU'LL DO

Basically, you help students identify colleges that will fit their needs and for which they qualify academically, and you help them with the application process. The former task is really the most important; getting into a school is dependent upon many factors that simply can't be remedied at the time of the application, but choosing the right school to begin with merits great attention.

As an application counselor, you will

- Help students choose schools with features well suited to their aptitudes and ambitions. Does the student want to major in art therapy? You'll locate the schools that offer such a major and group them according to price and competitiveness. (There are several sources for this information, detailed at the end of this entry.)
- Give students a realistic assessment of their options. The student with a combined SAT score of 850 needn't waste postage on an application to a top Ivy League school, but many students do just that. On the other hand, some students and parents sell themselves short in the applications process; you'll be able to make sure that doesn't happen. Also, a student doesn't necessarily have to spend a lot of money for a good education; as an application counselor, you can suggest good alternatives to expensive private colleges from among respected public schools and inexpensive private schools. This service meshes well with a grant and scholarship research service (page 249).
- Expedite the application materials. You'll make sure that the material is in good shape and sent out at the proper time.

WHAT YOU CAN EARN

Since this is a field without a great deal of competition, you can pretty much set your own fees and determine the range of services you'll provide. Keep an open mind, because there are many types of services that could be marketable. For example, a Santa Rosa, California, firm called Degree Consulting Services provides a written evaluation and limitless telephone follow-up counseling for $40.

That service is geared primarily for the rapidly growing segment of adults returning to school, and is a good example of how one firm focused on a particular segment of the market. You might consider specializing, too. Is there a need for information for handicapped students in your area?

How about students whose second language is English? Budding engineers? The opportunities are limited only by your imagination and the needs of your market.

MARKETING

Ads in local newspapers may be your best initial option, particularly a small display ad in the education section. (While some papers don't have an education section per se, they probably do have a segment of the Sunday newspaper where education-related stories and advertisements are grouped.)

RESOURCES

There's a largely undiscovered goldmine of information available in your local bookstore. Peterson's *National College Data Bank* and Barron's *Index of College Majors* are good for starters. Then, of course, there are the many standard guidebooks that objectively and subjectively rate colleges. Also, look over some of the more specialized publications, such as Peterson's *Competitive Colleges,* and *Graduate and Professional Programs,* also published by Peterson.

Anyone can use these excellent references, but many parents and students just don't realize the quality application resources that exist. Also, they may not be willing to expend the effort necessary to digest and correlate the contents.

But, of course, you are willing to make the effort—and that's why you might be able to establish a highly successful part-time business in this field.

COLOR CONSULTANT

☐ Start-up costs: $1,200 to $4,000
☐ Estimated hours per week: 15
☐ Number of staffers needed for start-up (including founder): 1

Did you ever notice how someone can look stunning in one color but appear washed out when wearing a different shade? If you notice how clothing color affects a person's total appearance, color consulting may be a good part-time opportunity for you. A color consultant analyzes a client's skin tone, hair shade, and eye color and recommends a group of optimal colors for clothing and accessories.

WHAT YOU'LL DO

A color consultant earns a fee either from giving a workshop for a group or by doing a personalized analysis. The analysis is done via a large collection of fabric swatches which test the mix of person and fabric color. For instance, one color analysis system prescribes colors based on the individual's "season"—that is, whether that person projects the characteristics the analyst classifies as summer, fall, winter, or spring.

THE COLOR CONSULTANT

The best-known organization in color consulting today is Carole Jackson's company, *Color Me Beautiful*. Her book, published by Ballantine, carries the same name. People who enter this organization undergo a six-day training program (which costs $1,150) at various sites across the country. They learn about color theory, how to analyze people in terms of the best colors and styles for their wardrobes, and how to use and recommend skin care products.

Marketing information is also part of the package. You'll learn how to give workshops, and how to approach the media with ideas about color and color consulting.

IS IT FOR YOU?

If color consulting appeals to you, you can apply to Color Me Beautiful, 2721-A Merrilee Dr., Fairfax, VA 22031. A company spokesperson says that applicants must be accepted into the program, and must prove— and this seems quite reasonable—that they can distinguish fine gradations of color. (Some people just can't tell colors apart very well.) There are a number of other color analysis systems, so you will want to check your bookstore and other sources for further possibilities.

THE COLOR OF MONEY

A graduate of the above program can earn $35 to $75 per analysis, and an analysis takes about 45 minutes to an hour. Rates for speaking to groups vary. Your clients primarily will be individual women; but some men are now using such services, too, and many firms and organizations are hiring consultants to advise employees on their best colors.

In some cases, you can make additional money by selling the firm's line of cosmetics. Discounts are offered to consultants on a sliding scale adjusted by volume ordered; you sell them for the full retail price and keep the difference.

RESOURCES

You may want to look at the following to learn more about the various color systems available:

Color Me Beautiful, Carole Jackson (Ballantine), *Color Me a Season: How to Find & Use Your Most Flattering Colors* (Alchemy Books), and *Color 1-Derful* by Joanne Nicholson & Judy Lewis-Conn (Bantam).

COMMERCIAL ACTOR

☐ Start-up costs: About $200 for photos, resumes, and tapes.
☐ Estimated hours per week: 4 to 10
☐ Number of staffers needed for start-up (including founder): 1

Carol, a 34-year-old secretary from Springfield, Massachusetts, recently made $150 by sitting on a couch for two hours. Mike, a real estate salesman in New York, earned several thousand dollars for saying one sentence.

Carol and Mike are two of the thousands of people who bring in respectable part-time incomes by acting in television commercials. While both are reasonably good-looking, they're never mistaken for movie stars. In fact, it's their *average* appearance that makes them bankable commodities in the world of commercial production.

WHAT IT TAKES

What sets these average people apart is their ability simply to be themselves, to project a comfortable persona that makes other "average" people feel comfortable with them. Carol, for example, played a working mother concerned with getting the best-quality furniture for her money—not a difficult job for a woman who really does have to feed, clothe, and house four children. A beer company wanted a friendly fellow who could communicate the warm feelings that develop after a beer with the boys. Mike, who had downed a few brews in his day (and shows the results around his waistline) fit the bill perfectly.

You can cash in on commercials, too, if you can fulfill one basic requirement: "We look for people who can project a *type*," says Vangie Hayes, casting director of the J. Walter Thompson advertising agency. She notes that, depending on the particular commercial, they might need someone who fits the image of a young mother, a tough cab driver, or a hard-driving businessman.

Could you project a type? Think about what people say to you and about you. Do your friends say you have an honest face? Do they accuse you of acting like "the perfect little homemaker"? Or do they half-jokingly imply that you look like a mean traffic cop after a hard day on the streets? If so, remember that the world of advertising needs honest spokespersons, tidy homemakers, even testy traffic cops.

WHAT YOU'LL NEED

You'll want some photos, resumes, and probably a tape to solicit advertisers.

- Photos should be 8-by-10-inch black-and-white glossies showing you from the top of the shoulders up. Not surprisingly, this type of photo is known as a head shot. Don't assume that you can get by with your old high school yearbook picture. Your head shots must have some life to them, showing different poses and reflecting your type. If you're a tough cab driver, you'll growl a little, while happy homemakers will beam with all the sunniness in their systems. Be sure to affix your name and phone number to the back of each picture. Shop around for a photographer who specializes in actors' photos or at least understands what you need; such a photographer is also likely to offer excellent deals on bulk printings of a hundred or so head shots.
- Your resume should indicate your acting experience and training, if any. While your head shots will show the image you can project, your resume should also indicate the type that best fits you. Almost everyone

has something to list on a resume; if nothing else, list high school public-speaking classes. If you were in a play in school or college, be sure to list the play and the character you portrayed.

You probably won't need a tape right away, but if you can, it's useful to make an audiocassette demonstrating how you read a commercial. (Try copying over the lines from a commercial you now hear on the radio.) You can make the tape on a good-quality home system. Before spending $100 or so at a professional recording studio, shop your homemade tape around first.

HOW TO START

To get started, send your resumes and photos to local television stations. Many advertisers ask the local station to produce their ads, so this is a good place to start. Then you can graduate to cable stations, television production houses, and advertising agencies. It's a good idea to call in advance to see if they are interested in receiving a photo and resume, and to make a follow-up call later. If you live in a major advertising center, such as New York or Los Angeles, you can contact talent agents. Be aware, however, that agents handle many high-earning professionals (for a percentage of the actor's fee) and won't be likely to turn handsprings over the arrival of an unknown newcomer.

Ironically, residents of smaller cities usually have a better chance of generating moonlighting income through commercials because the competition from professional actors is not so keen and because local commercial producers and agencies are more acutely in need of the right types. Note that even in small markets a good, reliable actor can usually make a minimum of $25 an hour. As your reputation spreads, you can escalate prices to whatever the market will bear.

RESOURCES

Consider taking an acting class at a local college or adult education center. Modeling schools and specialized private schools offer courses in commercial acting, but evaluate those options carefully because such schools can be very expensive. Watch commercials on television and practice doing what the actors do. Rehearse in front of a mirror and say your lines to a tape recorder.

Two excellent guides to commercial acting are Vangie Hayes and Gloria Hainline's *How to Get into Commercials* (Harper and Row), and James Peacock's *How to Audition for Television Commercials and Get Them* (Contemporary).

COMPUTER PROGRAMMING CONSULTANT _____

☐ Start-up costs: Minimal, assuming you already have a computer.
☐ Estimated hours per week: 10 to 15
☐ Number of staffers needed for start-up (including founder): 1

Computer experts can make big money in a variety of ways, including such fields as computer training (page 83). But perhaps the most profitable market, if you can crack it, is freelance programming consulting.

THE COMPUTER CONSULTING BUSINESS _____

First, a quick lesson in the way computer consultants work. In many cases, individual consultants seek out contracts and then hunt among other consultants for experts to help with the details. So step one in setting yourself up as a programming consultant is to get in touch with others in the field. You can do this by attending computer group meetings, sending your resume to other consultants you locate in the phone book, and watching the want ads in large metro papers. There are frequently ads for freelance consultants; send a resume and follow up with a phone call. Even if you don't get the job initially, you'll make a contact and you might get called back the next time.

WHAT DOES A PROGRAMMER DO? _____

Computer programmers do a variety of tasks, but those who operate on a freelance basis typically focus on designing applications for existing software. For example:

- Tailoring a database for industry. A database can be a very detailed and complicated software system, but a good programmer can take that database and make many of its functions specific and understandable for the particular business. For example, one popular database uses a dot as a prompt for entering data. This, of course, can be quite intimidating for the non-expert user. A computer consultant/programmer could tailor this database to a trucking company by figuring out how to make the prompt read, "Enter gross tonnage of today's cargo."

- Tailor the software to make it user-friendly. The trucking-company example above is one such application. Others include adding English-speaking prompts to spreadsheets (often among the least user-friendly of all programs).

- In some cases, designing entire programs for a business. Payroll programs are just about the hottest ticket going today. If you can design and implement such a program, your services will probably be in great demand.

RESOURCES

Establish a network of people who might use your services, either as consulting partners or clients. A good guide to making contacts and building a clientele is *Inside the Technical Consulting Business* by Harvey Kay (Wiley). Also, keep up on the vastly expanding store of literature on various software programs; most chain bookstores have extensive sections on programming and applications.

COMPUTER SOFTWARE DOCUMENTATION AND REVIEW WRITER_____

☐ Start-up costs: None
☐ Estimated hours per week: 5 to 20, but heavy during peak development periods.
☐ Number of staffers needed for start-up (including founder): 1

Software documentation—instructions on how to use software—is typically provided by the manufacturer, although there are freelance opportunities. Sometimes there are also opportunities to write editorial reviews of existing software packages. Either way, a computer-savvy freelancer who can communicate in crisp, clear English can earn a good moonlighting income.

WHO WRITES SOFTWARE DOCUMENTATION? _____

Usually the documentation is prepared as the software is being developed, which is one reason why the assignments generally aren't sent out of house. But on occasion they are given to freelancers. You have a better chance of generating some income by working at a local software company's headquarters during periods of peak demand. Or perhaps you could hook up your computer via modem to the company's headquarters, and enjoy the benefits of working at home while being connected to the office.

People who specialize in software documentation are more often expert writers who know something about computers rather than computer experts who do some writing (which was the case until quite recently). Software companies want someone who can communicate to the widest possible audience. If you have programming experience, so much the better.

On the other end of the software industry, there's a demand for people with essentially the same qualifications (clear writing ability, an understanding of software functions, possibly some programming experience) to evaluate software and its documentation. Computer magazines run dozens of software reviews, and you can sometimes make several hundred dollars writing such items.

Computer firms need all sorts of written communications. Over and above software documentation, they need advertising copy, documentation for hardware, and training material. So, when you make calls offering your services as a writer of software instructions, keep these other tasks in mind if the voice on the other end is not enthusiastic.

HOW MUCH TO CHARGE

A full-time documentation writer usually makes between $30,000 and $40,000 a year, so you'll want a comparable hourly charge for whatever writing you do. High-tech firms are less reluctant to part with money than are some other industries, but you may have trouble getting top dollar from firms on shaky ground (and that includes quite a few software developers). Aim for upwards of $20 an hour for any type of high-tech writing. If you're writing reviews, you'll be paid according to the editorial payment schedule of the magazine.

MARKETING

You probably already know the major computer firms in your area. Send each a resume, outlining your qualifications and experience; be sure to stress—if it's indeed the case—that you can devote large blocks of time on short-term contract work. If your interests run toward reviewing software, check the listings in *Writer's Market* (Writer's Digest Books).

COMPUTER TRAINER____

☐ Start-up costs: Negligible, assuming you are not investing in equipment for training purposes.
☐ Estimated hours per week: 10 to 15
☐ Number of staffers needed for start-up (including founder): 1

Independent consultants who have some expertise in computers make second incomes in a variety of ways. One increasingly attractive option is to train others in the use of hardware and software. There are many people who are not computer literate—and who in fact may be computer phobic—who need to know how to interact with modern technology.

FIRST ENTRY

You can start a computer-training business by giving seminars at local colleges. If you have a degree (especially an advanced degree) in a computer-related field, you probably will have little problem securing a part-time faculty position at a nearby college. Doing seminars for students in so-called computer camps is another option. These camps, often sponsored by local school systems or organizations such as YMCAs or YWCAs, aim to introduce young people to computers. You can probably find such opportunities in your area, and if you're ambitious you might even promote such an event yourself.

WORKING WITH BUSINESS

Another, perhaps more profitable, sideline is making your services available on a consulting basis to area firms that are using new computers and software. Your services just might be in great demand. One federal employee, for example, noted that knowledgeable computer people often vastly overestimate the amount of computer savvy organizations have in-house. The federal employee in question, for example, wanted to automate the huge letter-writing process in his office but had no one on staff who could handle the job. Despite his best efforts to find someone to help select software and train his staff to use it, he could not find a *competent advisor who would work for a reasonable fee*.

Mark those words well, because a part-time trainer who is competent and reasonable can find a market.

REACHING PROSPECTS

But HOW do you find that market? One method is to get established in some sort of teaching position, be it at a kids' camp, local adult education, or a nearby college. Your network of students will provide many contacts; the "friend to friend" system reaches thousands of people.

Second, network with other computer consultants. Especially in large cities, there are legions of independent consultants who often take on large projects and farm out specific jobs to other consultants. Remember, they need other consultants as badly as other consultants need them. It's a game of contacts and loosely knit associations thrown together to do a particular job.

Finally, market yourself. Send letters to firms you think may be in need of training and highlight your qualifications. Finding firms in need of your services won't be too difficult: concentrate on businesses that deal with

- A great deal of word processing (law firms, insurance companies, etc.)
- Large inventory control (supermarket and department store chains)
- Computer training itself (schools, vocational training centers, and even newly established computer-training organizations)

RESOURCES

Keep up the networking. Join local computer groups and make your availability as a consultant known. Ask satisfied customers for referrals. Also, be on the lookout for other computer-related jobs that might translate into future training opportunities. William Trego's *How to Profit from Your Computer: Starting in Year One* (Blackman Kallick) has some good ideas.

CONCIERGE SERVICE __

☐ Start-up costs: A few hundred dollars for basic promotion, although your costs will vary considerably according to the services you offer.
☐ Estimated hours per week: 8 to 16
☐ Number of staffers needed for start-up (including founder): 1

Here's a business limited only by your imagination; there are no set rules, no standard operating procedures—just a demand waiting to be filled in whatever way will be profitable in your community.

THE NUTS AND BOLTS _____

In a major hotel, the concierge is the one who makes arrangements for guests. Originally the concept of a concierge was to man the entry to the hotel, but don't let that deter you. (As long as we're talking about history, don't be daunted by the original meaning of the word *concierge*, either, because it basically meant "slave.") You don't have to work in a hotel, but you do have to make the typical kinds of arrangements a guest would like:

Where to eat
Where to shop
How to get around

A concierge is usually more of an advisor than an appointments secretary (or slave), but you can operate the business on any level you wish. The important thing is that you know your city inside out and can offer your clients specific, useful advice.

ADVICE IN ACTION

For example, a New York concierge service called Manhattan Passport handles an infinite number of details for visiting guests. "We do just what the concierge in a hotel does," says founder Ina Lee Selden, "except we don't have a hotel. You've heard of 'minister without portfolio'? We're 'concierge without hotel.'"

Ms. Selden says that her firm can arrange just about anything. "Some of the arrangements are unusual, and some are mundane. Of course, in New York even the mundane is difficult." Some of the tasks she's handled include finding opera and theater tickets, locating babysitters, getting visitors together with a tour guide, and even finding visiting businesspeople an apartment for two months (and if you know New York, you know that finding an apartment short-term is about as simple as leading elephants across the Alps).

Manhattan Passport does no advertising whatsoever; instead, it relies on press coverage, which has been generous because the firm is so unusual.

The going rate is $50 an hour, which is quite reasonable because a knowledgeable concierge can make arrangements in a hurry. Because your fee is not connected to how much money the client spends, you can also recommend many free or moderately priced attractions which your clients will appreciate.

YOUR OPPORTUNITY

There aren't many services like this in the United States, so perhaps your city is ready for a concierge business. If you really know your city, its nightlife, and its attractions this could be a profitable sideline business.

You might start by contacting local businesses that have a number of visiting executives. Also, see if an area hotel is interested in promoting your service; many hotels don't have a concierge per se, and they may be interested in steering their guests to a new and interesting service.

CONSULTANT _____

☐ Start-up costs: Above standard costs for a desk, filing cabinet, etc., budget about $300 for stationery and initial mailing expenses.
☐ Estimated hours per week: 10 to 15
☐ Number of staffers needed for start-up (including founder): 1

Calling in an outsider for an objective opinion is a big business. Some experts estimate that over $4 billion in consulting fees are billed annually, with over 60,000 consultants working full-time and countless others making part-time incomes.

Getting paid for giving advice is lucrative, usually bringing in from $35 to $100 an hour. But moonlighting consultants will tell you that the biggest payoff is the satisfaction from finally having people listen to their advice. Here's how a Pennsylvania college administrator who moonlights describes his situation: "Around here [the college where he works full-time] I have to fight over every piddling decision, purchase, or change in policy. But when a small college in upstate New York asked me to evaluate their fundraising system, they rolled out the red carpet and hung on my every word."

For a moonlighter, consulting is a perfect option, according to Dr. William A. Cohen, professor of marketing at California State University at Los Angeles. "You can actually start in consulting part-time and ease your way in. Many successful people have started through part-time work after their full-time jobs, at nights and weekends."

WHAT DO YOU HAVE TO OFFER? _____

Sit down with a pencil and paper and list your areas of expertise and your professional accomplishments. Inventory any marketable skills. Perhaps you've developed a reputation in your present line of work—anything from running efficient food services on a tight budget to computer

87

programming expertise qualifies—and feel your experience could benefit others. Or maybe you possess a unique skill, such as operating a lie detector or having an expert touch with a video camera. Another possibility is that you have strong management skills and/or an impressive academic background in business. If so, you can market your advice to local firms in need of an established expert to recommend new procedures and operations. (Often, a consultant is brought aboard to prove a point, since outside expert opinion often carries more weight than in-house judgment.)

Successful consulting practices have been established in such diverse fields as

Office design	Labor relations
Security investigation	Telephone system installation
Insurance	Employee training
Computers	Investment

STARTING OUT

Professionals in certain fields may need some sort of license; for example, someone advertising his or her services as a "consulting psychologist" must first be able to legally use the title psychologist. Such professional licensing laws vary from state to state; check with the consumer affairs department near you.

Know in advance what sort of fee you want to collect and how the fee will be determined. Straight hourly or daily billing is a common practice, although some consultants work on a fixed rate or some sort of scale keyed to performance and results. However you figure the bill, don't sell yourself short. Because you are working for yourself, you must build in a cushion to absorb overhead and miscellaneous costs. This is a factor often overlooked in consulting because there's little visible "hardware." But a consultant does encounter considerable expense, such as travel costs and the time (time, of course, is money) spent in research. Also, it's common in the consulting business for clients not to hire low-priced consultants because they assume that they will get what they pay for.

The fee you charge is basically determined by what the market will bear and the particular demand for your specialty, but think in terms of getting at least $25 to $50 an hour.

FINDING CLIENTS

Many consultants have been successful with a direct mail approach. After all, you will have a pretty good idea of what types of firms need your services, and a well-written letter is an economical way to persuade an organization leader that he or she needs your help. You can often build your mailing list by a trip to the local public library. If, for example, you're trying to market your services to colleges, there are several reference books that list college addresses, phone numbers, and names of administrators. Libraries also typically have listings of area businesses and their executives. If you choose the direct mail route, try following up your letter with a phone call.

Sometimes firms in need of a consultant advertise directly in newspapers or trade journals, and a publication called *Commerce Business Daily* announces consulting contracts available from the U.S. Government. You can find this publication at Small Business Administration (SBA) field offices and in major libraries.

Send out press releases to local newspapers announcing the formation of your business. You can also publicize your consulting practice by speaking before professional business groups.

RESOURCES

The SBA offers many publications, some of them free, which can help a consultant, including *Profit Pricing and Costing for Services*. Two good books on consulting include *Cashing in on the Consulting Boom* by Gregory Kishel and Patricia G. Kishel (Wiley), and William A. Cohen's *How to Make It Big as a Consultant* (American Management Association). The American Association of Professional Consultants runs frequent seminars on how to establish a consulting practice and offers a wide range of support materials. Contact them at 9140 Ward Pkwy., Kansas City, MO 64114.

CRAFT COOPERATIVE ORGANIZER

☐ Start-up costs: Variable, depending on the type of cooperative you form. Generally not a major investment.
☐ Estimated hours per week: 5 to 15
☐ Number of staffers needed for start-up (including founder): 1 person can start the cooperative, but by its very nature you need a number of participants.

The value of cooperative marketing is apparent to many segments of industry. Agriculture has long used the co-op—pooled resources and expertise—to increase profits. You can use the same strategy to market your own crafts and those of your associates.

HOW A CO-OP WORKS

One highly successful craft cooperative in Manhattan pools the resources of members in order to rent an attractive loft space (very expensive throughout the borough) so that members can have a decent place to work and display their wares. In addition, members help each other with marketing by sharing their skills to develop a catalog and by contributing their individual mailing lists of clients to the co-op.

OPTIONS

You can follow this model or expand in almost any direction you'd like. The key is to pool resources and talent; using that tactic, almost anything's possible. For example, you and your associates could

- Publish a newsletter.
- Open a shop in a high-traffic business area which would be operated part-time by all members.
- Put together a mail-order house.
- Open a gallery. Co-op galleries often return an excellent profit to member artists because the gallery overhead is quite low.

Get the idea? Your personal profit could come from the increased amount of crafts you sell due to the cooperative effort, or it might also include fair compensation for services you offer the co-op (such as running the mail-order arm of the enterprise).

RESOURCES

There's economic power in numbers, and no one knows that better than the U.S. Government, which publishes a booklet called *The Cooperative Approach to Crafts*. You can obtain this or any other government document by writing the U.S. Government Printing Office, Washington, DC 20402. Better yet, ask your local library if they have a copy; many government publications are available on microfiche in many larger libraries.

Another excellent guide to the craft business in general and cooperatives in particular is Barbara Brabec's *Creative Cash: How to Sell Your Crafts, Needlework, Designs and Knowhow* (Aames-Allen).

CRAFTS: SELLING CRAFT WORKS

☐ Start-up costs: Quite variable, but usually under $200 for initial supplies.
☐ Estimated hours per week: 10 to 12
☐ Number of staffers needed for start-up (including founder): 1

Crafts are big business in the United States, and growing bigger. Psychologists theorize that we feel a need to do a job from start to finish, something rarely encountered in the modern workplace. Perhaps we are drawn to crafts just because they offer an outlet for creative skills. And most importantly—from the standpoint of a moonlighting entrepreneur—people buy completed craft works just because they like them.

WHAT YOU CAN SELL

The range of items you can sell is limited only by your talents and skills. Examples include

- Items made specifically for other crafters. An Albany, Georgia, firm has been racking up sales of over half a million dollars a year by marketing preprinted cloth for hobbyists who do cross-stitching. The kits are sold via mail order (see page 181).
- Crafts sold on commission. Getting an advance order for a project is a satisfying and secure way to practice your craft and make money, too. One example of this type of work is a handpainted tile business operated in Putney, Vermont, where the proprieter does such tasks as designing murals for kitchens and bathrooms.
- Crafts sold in flea markets. You may not make a great deal on each piece, but if you move several dozen potholders in one day the profits can certainly be worthwhile.

- Crafts sold to gift shops. Sometimes such sales are made on consignment, but more often items are purchased outright and marked up anywhere from 25 to 40 percent, although that figure can and does go higher. Gift shop owners are partial to local suppliers who have some flexibility in their schedules, meaning that they can supply larger amounts of the product when demand is high.
- Crafts sold to retail stores. Make an appointment to see the buyer of a local department store. (This is usually much easier than most people suspect.) Ask about their requirements and schedules for buying wholesale goods. A word to the wise: Be sure you have the capability to fill any order you take on.

RESOURCES

Many artisans report that a subscription to *Crafts Report* (700 Orange St., Box 1992, Wilmington, DE 19801) is useful for finding lists of shops and shows. Also, read Loretta Holz's *How to Sell Your Arts & Crafts* (Scribners) and *How to Sell Your Homemade Creation,* ed. by Allan H. Smith (Success Advertising & Publishing).

CRAFTS TEACHER

☐ Start-up costs: Minimal
☐ Estimated hours per week: 3 to 8
☐ Number of staffers needed for start-up (including founder): 1

There's a tremendous interest in crafts of all sorts; by some estimates, the collective category of arts and crafts is the nation's second largest hobby (next to gardening). But it is often difficult for people to get started in a craft. That's where you, the moonlighting crafts teacher, enter the picture.

ME? A TEACHER? _____

Crafts teachers are unanimous in their observation that skilled crafts-people have a great deal to offer others and that many prospective teachers simply don't recognize their own talents and abilities. If you've developed a reasonable proficiency in any craft, be it rug hooking, pottery making, or crocheting, you can profitably pass your skills along to others. Remember, people in your classes will generally be starting from ground zero. Even if you have only a moderate level of expertise, you'll be light-years ahead of your students.

STARTING A CLASS _____

Friends and acquaintances are good prospects for a first class. In fact, it's likely that several of them have already broached the idea of classes with you already. Take advantage of your talents and the demand for them; organize a class and hold it at your home.

THE PROFIT MOTIVE _____

You don't need to charge a fortune for your classes. A small fee can go a long way if you multiply it by five, ten, or however many people you can accommodate. A good way to start is to offer a series of four three-hour classes, once a week, for a total fee of perhaps $25 per student, with the students purchasing their own supplies. You can, if you choose, sell the supplies yourself and mark them up.

FINDING STUDENTS _____

Many crafts classes fill quickly by word of mouth. If you find, though, that you need to advertise, take out a small classified ad in the local weekly shopper. Crafts teachers report that those ads get surprisingly good results.

Another promotional tack is to offer classes and seminars in your local adult education program. While you won't make a lot of money teaching adult ed, you will produce many satisfied customers who will recommend you to their friends.

PROBLEMS AND PECULIARITIES _____

Crafts teaching is not without difficulties, and experienced teachers do have some words of caution. First, limit the size of the classes, at least at first. You'll probably be surprised at how difficult it is to teach a group of

15; crafts work is highly intensive in terms of student–teacher contact time.

Second, be sure to find out what your present insurance will and will not cover; if you're not covered for certain types of crafts-related accidents or liabilities, get the right type of coverage before you start teaching people at home. Crafts classes involve surprisingly frequent injuries, especially when you're dealing with heat-producing equipment such as kilns and wood-burning irons. Don't take chances with liability.

Finally, protect your home from damage. Fifteen people slinging oil paint can make a terrible mess of your carpet. Invest in drop cloths or whatever it takes to keep your furnishings from being spattered, burned, or gouged.

CUSTOM CURTAINS AND DRAPERIES _____

☐ Start-up costs: Under $1,000
☐ Estimated hours per week: 6 to 18
☐ Number of staffers needed for start-up (including founder): 1

If you can measure accurately and know basic sewing techniques, give some thought to starting a home-based custom curtain and drapery business. Chances are, millions of naked windows in your city need dressing, and each one could add up to a profit.

WHAT YOU DO _____

To start with, you measure—*accurately*. That's the key to success in this business; even a half-inch measuring error can seriously detract from the appearance of the curtains or drapes, so be scrupulous. After measuring, including allowances for hems, you cut the fabric to size and sew the hems.

Sizing involves some simple multiplication. Size a drape by measuring the length of the rod and the distance of the ends from the wall and add an allowance for where the drapes overlap a little in front; multiply that figure by 2¼ to determine the length of the drape. Curtain length is determined by multiplying the measurement by 2½.

Sound simple? Well, it is, with some experience. But remember that you're dealing with a lot of fabric and mistakes can be expensive. Also, you may have to deal with pattern problems; because you'll have to match up the pattern repeat exactly, some fabric may have to be thrown away if the end of one roll doesn't match exactly with the beginning of the next. This situation can play havoc with your fabric purchase estimates, so be aware of the pattern repeat dilemma.

BUSINESS ASPECTS

You can usually charge $10 an hour for residential work. This hourly fee includes the house call if you measure for your client (a good idea) and also should apply to your time spent shopping for fabric if your client requests that you pick it out.

Drapery businesses have a way of expanding on their own. One Wilmington, North Carolina, firm was born when the proprietor's guests (she sold antiques from her home) admired her flowing, handmade drapes. Word spread, and the curtain business soon occupied a garage, then a factory, and eventually ten stores, with an estimated yearly gross that exceeded $20 million.

So start small and rely on word of mouth. Small newspaper ads will help, but satisfied clients provide the best advertising for a custom drapery and curtain business.

RESOURCES

For further information, consult *The Curtain Maker's Handbook* by Frank A. Moreland (Dutton) and *Curtains, Draperies and Shades*, Sunset editors (Sunset Books).

DATING SERVICE ⸻

☐ Start-up costs: Plan on spending $4,000 to $5,000, much of it on advertising.
☐ Estimated hours per week: 10 to 20
☐ Number of staffers needed for start-up (including founder): 1

Meeting members of the opposite sex seems to be harder than ever for a significant portion of the population. The singles market is an enormous one, and offers some real opportunity for the energetic moonlighter who wants to start up a dating and introduction service.

THE MODERN MARKET ⸻

There are many large, well-established dating services, and the level of competition can be daunting to the newcomer who wants to market dating services to the general public. But the narrow, specialized market offers quite a bit of opportunity—and that's your angle. Small services have become successful by grabbing a specific segment of the singles market and running with it. For example, Health Conscious Connections in State College, Pennsylvania, specializes in making introductions for singles devoted to fitness. Other agencies specialize in matching people of Asian descent, or computer specialists, or disabled people, or singles with odd working hours.

Even if you don't have a particular, specialized market, you do need a unique approach. A Wayne, New Jersey, company called Compatibility Plus hires psychologists to interview clients and prepares a detailed profile for matching up those singles.

THE BUSINESS END ⸻

To start, you want to assess the local market and see if there's an angle you can use to establish a moonlighting dating service. Are there enough singles to support the service? You probably need to be in a reasonably large area in order for the service to succeed. Can you find the right angle? Perhaps there's a large Spanish-speaking community, and you feel you can meet their needs. Are there many high-tech types in your area? They might be the perfect clients for your dating service.

Many services use computers to match up potential clients; people looking for a date fill out a questionnaire and the computer matches up candidates. Some small dating services don't have a computer, though; they take their completed forms to a local data-processing service to do the matching.

Membership can work in a variety of ways. One California firm gives women a free membership and charges men $200 for five introductions. Other services charge in the $250 range for a yearly membership in which 10–20 introductions are made.

RESOURCES

A dating service, while potentially profitable, can be a relatively complex operation. Many options are available, including the aforementioned computer matching, as well as video matching. The American Entrepreneurs Association and its publication *Entrepreneur* magazine (2311 Pontius Ave., Dept. 500, Los Angeles, CA 90064) offer a start-up manual for a dating service.

DAY-CARE SERVICE

☐ Start-up costs: Extremely variable but not overwhelming, if you don't have to make modifications to your home.
☐ Estimated hours per week: 20 to 40
☐ Number of staffers needed for start-up (including founder): 1; veterans say 2 is a better number for preservation of sanity.

Recent surveys have shown that about 80 percent of children in day-care are in family day-care centers, meaning home-based day-care facilities. While the definition may differ among localities, family day-care usually applies to an organization in a private home which serves six or fewer children.

WHAT DAY-CARE INVOLVES

You'll be expected to do more than supervise and feed clients' children. A learning experience of some sort is essential; so are opportunities for play and interaction. Also, you must be prepared to deal with the ever-present problems relating to groups of children. What do you do about fighting? About questions dealing with religion? Sex? These are things you'll have to think about, because veterans of the day-care business have encountered all these problems—and more.

RULES AND REGULATIONS

It's not easy to get into the day-care business. There are many forms you'll have to fill out and more than enough hoops through which you may be compelled to jump. Licensing is usually done by the welfare department, but in some states, such as Maryland, permits are issued by the health department.

In addition, you and your associates will probably be required to take a physical to certify that you are free of communicable diseases.

For quite obvious reasons, your property must be up to snuff. Usually an inspection is done by the health department. In addition to any physical requirements, you must also make the whole house child-safe, and that means putting all poisons out of a child's reach.

Information on licensing can be obtained by contacting the National Association for the Education of Young Children (1834 Connecticut Ave., N.W., Washington, DC 20009).

BUSINESS PRACTICE: NUTS AND BOLTS

Contracts are important because they specify what you are and are not expected to do. Pay particular attention to working out details relating to

- Times parents will leave and pick up the children.
- What will happen on holidays. (Be specific: Will there be day-care on Thanksgiving? On Columbus Day?)
- Contingencies if children become ill during the day.

Regarding the last point: You'll need to get signed consent forms for medical treatment if a child is hospitalized in an emergency.

You'll need insurance coverage. The types of coverage available and the costs vary considerably; check with your insurance agent and be sure you specify that you're considering a *family* day-care center.

A fee of $30 to $90 a week per child is typical for home-based day-care.

RESOURCES

Betsy Squibb has written a comprehensive and useful book: *Family Day Care: How to Provide It in Your Home* (Harvard Common Press). You might also be interested in *Day Care for Other People's Children in Your Home,* a publication available from the U.S. Government Printing Office, Washington, DC 20402.

DELIVERY OF GOODS AND SERVICES

☐ Start-up costs: Highly variable, ranging from thousands for a specialized vehicle to extra gas for the family car.
☐ Estimated hours per week: 12 to 25
☐ Number of staffers needed for start-up (including founder): 1

Too little time and too much traffic are major turnoffs for many people; increasingly, busy people just go without rather than go to the place where traditional goods and services are provided. That's one reason why John Naisbitt, author of *Megatrends,* predicts that businesses that bring goods and services to the home will rise significantly.

WHAT KINDS OF BUSINESSES CAN DELIVER TO THE HOME?

You can bring many kinds of goods or services to your clients' homes. Examples include the following:

- A Wisconsin firm brings tires to the customer. That firm will install a new set of tires at the customer's home or place of work—anywhere as long as the client can leave the car sitting still for half an hour. Not only does the business attract clients because of the convenience, but the cost is actually less because overhead is lower than for a store.
- A Massachusetts audiologist (nonmedical hearing specialist) brings her services to the client. While working in a hospital-treated clinic, she discovered that traveling to the clinic was a real hardship for many of her patients. Some were elderly and could not drive; others experienced so much difficulty with traffic and hospital parking that they just ignored their hearing problems. Her mobile van is sound-treated and contains all the necessary equipment for basic testing. She pulls up to the client's home, and can do business literally anywhere as long as she's within 75 feet of an electrical outlet.
- A national firm says a $10,000 to $15,000 investment in a remote retail sales vehicle route brings in earnings of $24,000 to $75,000 annually. For instance the dealer-owned cooperative, J.T.'s General Store, brings a variety of merchandise to the customers' homes.

WHAT YOU'LL NEED

The requirements quite obviously vary with the job. A specialized vehicle can cost tens of thousands of dollars, but in many cases you'll be able to get by with a truck, station wagon, or the family car.

Give some thought to ways in which your particular skills or abilities could be marketed on a home-delivery basis. Nothing is too far out of the question nowadays. Home delivery services even include mobile dentists who will fill a tooth in your kitchen or living room. Consider home dog grooming, hair-styling, various shopping services, among others.

ANOTHER OPTION

If you have a dependable vehicle, you can use it to deliver someone else's goods or services. A good example—one which you might not have seriously considered—is newspaper delivery. This is an ideal moonlighting job for someone who works nine to five because morning papers will be delivered before work. Those with free afternoon hours can do some moonlighting delivering afternoon papers. Newspaper delivery is also an ideal part-time job for the person who likes to work a regular, defined chunk of time (and get a *regular*, dependable second paycheck!) —this may or may not be you.

Before you balk at visions of wearing short pants and shouting "Extra!," consider the fact that many newspaper publishers are tending to use adult motor routes today. Kids have just become too undependable in many circumstances, and newspaper delivery systems also must now depend on people with vehicles to ferry the papers around. (This could be a good job to take on with a partner—one person drives from point to point and the other jumps out and drops off the papers.) Sometimes the job won't even involve actual doorstep delivery of papers. Some adults on motor routes simply drop off the bundles of papers at distribution points. Rates vary for this type of job, but energetic adults can often earn $50 to $100 a week for only a few hours of work.

DESKTOP PUBLISHER

☐ Start-up costs: Possibly under $8,000; prices probably will continue to drop as technology advances.
☐ Estimated hours per week: 10 to 15. Heavy time investment initially to learn computer operations.
☐ Number of staffers needed for start-up (including founder): 1

There's a revolution going on, albeit a quiet one. Expensive typesetting machines and highly trained graphic artists are gradually being replaced by the magic of the microchip. Professional-quality publications are being designed, written, and edited by one person with a computerized desktop publishing system.

HOW IT WORKS

Modern computer technology allows graphics to be stored in computer memory. State-of-the-art software permits word-processed text to be "poured" into columns and headlines to be readjusted instantly to fit the copy. Special laser printers turn out a complete page at one time, producing densely painted copy that almost rivals professional typesetting.

Operators with an artistic flair can create original drawings or manipulate a variety of preprogrammed designs. If you're producing a restaurant menu, for example, a quick trip to the software store will turn up a package of preprogrammed line drawings of hamburgers, hotdogs, and sodas. Simply call up the picture on the computer screen and position it using an electronic wand.

WHAT YOU NEED

To start in desktop publishing, you need a computer capable of doing the work (not all can), appropriate software, and a printer, usually a laser printer, meaning that it uses laser technology to project and print an entire page at once.

The most popular systems used for desktop work are made by Apple, although IBM and many other firms have strong entries on the market. The Apple Macintosh Plus is one good choice for desktop publishing because it runs such excellent software as ImageWriter II, MacWrite and MacPaint.

WHAT YOU CAN DO WITH IT

The relatively low cost of the desktop option opens up a wide variety of possibilities for the moonlighter:

- Publishing books and newsletters. It's no longer necessary to find a publishing house to print and sell certain types of books. Armed with desktop publishing apparatus, you can give a typeset look to your work, lay out the pages and artwork, and print up a decent-looking book. Selling the book is another matter, but some books sell very well by mail order (see page 181). Cookbooks, how-to books, and tour guides are good bets.

    Newsletters (page 194) can be produced quite easily on a desktop system. A Tampa firm by the name of Newletters, Etc. currently publishes about 15 newsletters using a Macintosh computer and Pagemaker software. The fee charged by the company for producing newsletters for clients is usually between $25 to $50 a page; consulting fees run upwards of $50 an hour.

- Producing camera-ready work for clients. A computer consulting firm wanted to publish a series of 75-page manuals. But the firm president was horrified to find that the cost of typesetting and graphic art work would bring the cost of producing camera-ready copy to $36 a page—a total of about $2,700 per manual. A small Austin, Texas, company using desktop publishing was able to do the work for about $4 a page and still give the manual a high-quality appearance. If you know something about layout and design, you won't have much trouble convincing clients to forgo costly typesetting and purchase your desktop services.

GETTING STARTED

The impact of desktop publishing technology is just beginning to hit home. About $1 billion of desktop publishing gear will be sold this year, according to current industry estimates. How that equipment will be used in the next few years is anyone's guess. But right now desktop publishing is still an emerging business and there appears to be enormous opportunity for someone interested in setting up a part-time business as a pseudo-typesetter, or publisher, or both.

RESOURCES

If you're serious, read anything and everything you can find about desktop publishing. You won't have to look too hard, because a trip to the magazine rack of any major bookstore will turn up at least three publications dealing with the desktop revolution. Periodicals are your best bet for keeping up with the technology because things change very rapidly in the computer business. You'll need information that's as current as possible, particularly if you want to buy software or a printer. A number of books address the general topic, including Coleen Perri's *Publish It Yourself* (which, of course, she published herself), available from Possibilities Publishing (P.O. Box 520, Kenosha, WI 53141). Also check out Jacquelyn Peake's *Publish Your Own Book (and Pocket the Profits!)* (Columbine).

DIRECTORY PUBLISHER _____

- ☐ Start-up costs: A few hundred for a basic print job; high-volume printing will, of course, cost proportionally more.
- ☐ Estimated hours per week: 5 to 15
- ☐ Number of staffers needed for start-up (including founder): 1

A directory is a listing of where to find people, things, or services, and in some cases a directory passes along other specific information, such as prices of goods and services. One entrepreneur, for example, started a highly successful business by publishing a book that lists the prices of guns. More traditional directories have listed where to find services for the handicapped, or who produces a certain type of craft in an area. Publishing a directory can be a profitable enterprise and requires a low start-up investment.

FINDING CLIENTS _____

Identify a business or service that lacks a good directory and approach those involved in it, offering them the opportunity to be listed in your directory for a fee. When you make the initial sales pitch you'll have to be prepared to tell them how many copies will be printed and how they will be distributed. (Selling your directory at trade shows is a good idea.) You can also offer space for display advertising in the directory. There's a chance you can sell the directory, too, earning a profit at both ends.

So who would pay to be listed in a directory? There are no guarantees, but you might be successful in recruiting

- Local craftspeople. They could be grouped by specialty, and the directory could be distributed to department store buyers, specialty stores, and craft fair organizers.

- Moonlighters in a particular specialty. For example, freelance advertising copywriters and advertising artists might be willing to pay for inclusion in a directory to be distributed to ad agencies.
- Service providers. Think about compiling a directory of area service businesses (beauty parlors, for instance) that are accessible to the handicapped.

START-UP

You're limited only by your imagination. One note of caution: You *are* obligated to print the directory and distribute it according to the promises you made to people who bought the listings. Therefore, you could lose money on the deal, but printing a directory isn't all that expensive so it's not a huge risk.

Before starting, check out the entries in this book on *Desktop Publishing* (page 101) and *Book Publishing* (page 48); they may contain some helpful, relevant information.

DISC JOCKEY

☐ Start-up costs: Usually in the range of $2,000, although the figure can be lower if you buy used equipment and much higher if you buy new high-quality gear.
☐ Estimated hours per week: 5 to 12
☐ Number of staffers needed for start-up (including founder): 1

The rising cost of live rock bands has opened the door for the proliferation of disc jockeys who bring their records and amplification equipment with them to the site of a dance or event.

TOOLS OF THE TRADE

Disc jockeys use two turntables, high-quality record players, and a mixing console. The mixing console, as the name implies, mixes the signals from the two turntables and the microphone so that the records can be cross-faded and the disc jockey can speak over the music. Large speakers amplify the music. Some disc jockeys use strobe lights and other special effects to add impact to their presentations.

BUSINESS BASICS

Essentially, the jockey entertains the audience by playing records and keeping up an engaging patter during the affair. This can, under some circumstances, be far more complicated than you might assume. For one thing, it's essential to match the music and the delivery to the audience. You'll do your show quite differently for the Elks Club than you would for a junior high audience.

As a result, a disc jockey needs a wide knowledge of popular music and an extensive collection of records. Records you can buy; knowledge you have to pick up on your own.

GETTING STARTED

On the subject of buying records, you'll usually start out by picking them up the same way everyone else does—at the record store. As your business advances, you'll be approached by people in your area who will offer deals on regular purchases of new releases. Many disc jockeys find these services cost-effective, while others feel that there are too many dogs included among the new releases. Also, you may need a good collection of oldies; if that's the case, haunt used record shops.

Concerning the purchase of equipment: For a variety of reasons, people go in and out of the disc jockey business quite frequently. Watch for "for sale" classifieds in your local paper and you may pick up a good bargain. Many dj's buy their equipment from firms specializing in public address equipment (usually listed in the phone book under "Sound Systems and Equipment"). Many of these firms offer a service whereby they will provide you with loaner gear should yours suffer a breakdown. And break down it will—such equipment is touchy and, like any other electrical gear, it will have occasional problems. That's why a deal with a responsible firm and/or some personal repair talent is a good asset for a tyro in the disc jockey field.

MARKETING

Newspaper classifieds are quite effective, but good word of mouth is the best. Also, you can do a lot of productive spadework by printing up some brochures and dropping them by

College student affairs offices
Fraternity and sorority houses
Fraternal organizations
Bars and restaurants, especially those establishments featuring regular
events such as singles nights.

Weddings are the kind of work you're likely to get from your classified
ads. Nowadays, a wedding reception can fetch a dj $200 to $250 for an
afternoon's work. You usually won't be able to get that much for night
work in bars. The prime determinant of your rates is what other jocks
charge, which varies widely from city to city. People looking for a disc
jockey service do comparison shop, so price your service competitively.

PITFALLS

Before you invest, strongly consider the fact that you'll have to haul all
this gear around. You will need a truck, van, or a trailer. Bear in mind that
the stuff is heavy, and backing a trailer up to the rear door of a frat house
in the driving rain can be a hassle.

One other option to consider is buying the gear and hiring the disc
jockeys, usually from local radio stations. However, experienced pros do
caution that this business is most profitable if you do the work yourself.

DRAPERY AND BLIND INSTALLER

☐ Start-up costs: Only $100 or so for basic hand tools, but you will need an
enclosed van to transport the materials.
☐ Estimated hours per week: 6 to 16
☐ Number of staffers needed for start-up (including founder): 1

Sales of custom-ordered vertical blinds and custom draperies have soared in recent years, as upscale homeowners have come to appreciate the striking effects blinds and drapes can produce. But blinds and draperies can be very difficult to install, especially if you don't have the proper tools or aren't particularly handy. As a result, the moonlighting installer can make some significant part-time income.

WHAT INSTALLERS DO

Putting up vertical blind or drapery hardware involves more steps than you might imagine. You must:

- Measure the window precisely so that the proper size hardware can be ordered from the factory.
- Determine whether you'll top-mount the blind (on the molding above the window) or mount the blind inside the window frame for two distinctly different looks.
- Consider other aesthetic factors, such as what type of blind will permit the most light into a dark room, or which will best soften harsh light in a too-bright room, and help the client decide accordingly.
- Actually install the hardware, and in some cases do some minor surgery on the blinds themselves.

WHO HIRES INSTALLERS?

The best prospect for a moonlighting installer is to serve as an independent contractor for an existing retail drapery and blind company. You can locate them in the phone book under such headings as "Draperies and Curtains, Retail"; "Vertical Blinds"; and "Window Shades."

HOW TO START

Give retailers a call and let them know you're interested in acting as a freelance installer. Let them also know that you have a delivery vehicle and an insurance policy. (You'll need some insurance coverage because it's easy to accidentally break something; more than one priceless vase has met its end from a swinging drapery rod. The costs of basic insurance policies vary, but they usually are not very expensive.)

You might be better off by starting as a paid part-time employee on the retailer's crew, or the crew of an independent contractor hired by the retailer. Installation of blinds and draperies is very tricky work, and you almost have to learn it hands-on with someone showing you the way.

Working on a crew can bring you about $8 an hour; if you have your own vehicle and tools and take on the job as an independent contractor, you can earn well over $10 an hour.

ERRAND SERVICE_____

☐ Start-up costs: Minimal, although you do need a dependable vehicle.
☐ Estimated hours per week: 5 to 15
☐ Number of staffers needed for start-up (including founder): 1

It's no secret that many people are just too busy to get things done. And it's also true that many American professionals have a surplus of disposable income. Add these factors together and you come up with one of the prime growth categories of modern business: personal services.

Some new firms, such as the You Deserve It service in Auburn, Massachusetts, specialize in doing the unpleasant and time-consuming chores others don't have the time or the inclination to do themselves. One example is standing in line at the motor vehicle office; currently, one insurance agency pays You Deserve It to perform this chore for its employees.

WHAT YOU CAN DO _____

There are a variety of tasks an errand service can take on. Examples include

- Taking things places. Returning books to libraries and mailing or picking up parcels or dropping off and retrieving dry cleaning are jobs that are sometimes difficult for busy people to get to during a working day.
- Taking people places. One firm in the errand-related business picks up a businessman's guests at the airport and shows them around town when the businessman has other, unavoidable appointments.
- Buying things. When you limit your business to buying gifts, groceries, or other items, you've got a shopping service (page 255), which meshes perfectly with errand running.

PRICING

You'll want an hourly fee, probably in the neighborhood of $10 an hour, plus mileage, which nowadays is often billed at 22 cents a mile.

ATTRACTING CLIENTS

You may find, as other errand services have, that businesses are your best customers. As such, it's worthwhile to make cold calls at local businesses and drop off your flier. Insurance agencies and law offices are good bets.

Consider a direct mailing to likely clients. One idea is to target physicians; they're always busy, and like everyone else they have personal and possibly professional errands that need running. A direct mailing to physicians is easy. Just look them up in the phone book. You'll have to supply zip codes, but you'll be happy to note that physicians tend to cluster in certain parts of the city, often the same street, and many physicians maintain practices at a small number of hospitals.

ESCORT SERVICE

☐ Start-up costs: Minimal. Most of the initial investment is in time spent promoting your services.
☐ Estimated hours per week: 8 to 15
☐ Number of staffers needed for start-up (including founder): 1

Here's an idea that's limited only by your imagination and, to some extent, your personal inventory of skills. It's based on the premise that the business world involves increasing travel, and this travel produces many complications requiring the services of a professional escort.

WHAT ESCORTS DO

We're not talking about the sometimes semi-shady world of providing women to accompany businessmen; that's a whole other field in itself and not a particularly good opportunity for moonlighters. What we're dealing with is the ever-increasing need for people who know their territory and can iron out some of the problems faced by visiting VIPs. Examples include:

- A Houston woman makes $100 a day escorting visiting authors around town when they promote their books. She takes time off from her job at a mutual fund organization to do the escort work.
- A Massachusetts karate teacher and several other black belts escort visiting rock stars around town and lead them up the aisles before and after concerts.
- A Washington, DC, musician, who is fluent in English and Japanese, earned over $100 a day escorting visiting Japanese businessmen and diplomatic staff.

HOW TO START

There are many opportunities; all it takes is some creative thought and a little marketing. Contact firms in your area and explain your desire to escort visitors. Should you speak a foreign language, your services will probably be in demand (see also *Translator,* page 284). You can boost your chances of success by dealing with firms whose officers do a great deal of traveling and therefore are also likely to entertain many visitors. You can find out more about these likely targets by calling local travel agencies and asking which firms book a great deal of business flights.

Another winning strategy is to keep an ear to the ground concerning upcoming events. Is the local theater organization sponsoring a fundraising benefit featuring several out-of-town dignitaries? Chances are, somebody's got to show those people around—take them to meetings, local TV stations and newspapers—and that somebody could be you.

One caveat: Be careful about driving people around as part of your business because you could be putting yourself in the role of chauffeur and you may need a special local permit for that. There's nothing wrong with the chauffeur business, though, as long as you play by the rules (see *Limousine Service*, page 177); in fact, a limousine service makes an excellent complement to the work of an escort.

EXCHANGE SERVICE _____

☐ Start-up costs: Most services are computerized, so you'll need at least a bare-bones unit with some sort of database, usually costing more than $1,000.
☐ Estimated hours per week: 5 to 15
☐ Number of staffers needed for start-up (including founder): 1

Here's a business you can set up and run according to any parameters you'd care to draw. The idea is pretty basic; how you choose to work it is up to you.

WHAT'S AN EXCHANGE SERVICE? _____

Basically, it involves making a list of what people want to sell and matching the items to incoming inquiries. One example of how this technique is put into action is the Boston Computer Exchange, a thriving business which matches up people who want to sell used computers with people looking to buy them. The exchange service charges a 10 percent commission on sales that amount to several million dollars a year.

The secret of the exchange business, if there is one, is simply a matter of matching supply and demand. Computers are, and probably will continue to be, a good exchange product because the technology changes so frequently that the devices constantly become outdated. But what's out of date for one person might be a terrific bargain for another—and that's the business in a nutshell.

IDEAS _____

Matching up buyers and sellers for any product involves much more paperwork than you might imagine. That, of course, is why a computer comes in handy. If you have a database, you can match up inquiries quite simply. In fact, you might be able to get a very specific match if you've programmed the database in detail.

For example, if you're in the business of matching buyers and sellers for used office equipment, you might be able to enter

Desk
Wood
Under $250

and come up with an exact match. You might charge a commission on the sale, or you could assess a fee for listing the seller on your computer for a certain length of time.

MARKETING AN EXCHANGE SERVICE

Marketing an exchange service is largely a matter of reaching all the individuals who make up a group sharing some highly specific interest. One way to accomplish this is through direct-mail advertising. Purchase or rent a mailing list of persons likely to own or use the product or services you wish to exchange (look in the Yellow Pages under "Mailing List"). Another effective tactic is to advertise in specialized magazines, newspapers, or newsletters.

RUN WITH IT!

You can play commercial matchmaker for any product, but you'll probably have better luck if you stick to a product you know well. Computers could be a possibility; in fact, the Boston Computer Exchange (telephone 617-542-4414) has marketed a manual on how to start a similar operation in your area.

EXPORTER _____

- ☐ Start-up costs: Highly variable, mostly determined by the cost of your inventory.
- ☐ Estimated hours per week: 5 to 15
- ☐ Number of staffers needed for start-up (including founder): 1

Exporting is really nothing more than selling your product in a new market. While there are some problems you'll encounter in foreign markets that won't crop up in domestic sales, the business is really not as mysterious as you might assume.

BASICS _____

Many experts maintain that the most efficient use of exporting is to supplement the sales of a product you now market domestically. There must, of course, be a market for the product. Valerie Bohigian, author of *How to Make Your Home-Based Business Grow: Getting Bigger Profits from Your Products,* notes that medical and health care products, low- and high-tech consumer products, automotive equipment, and simple machinery are hot items in overseas markets. Also, any product that has a specific appeal because of the indigenous needs of that particular market (mosquito netting, for instance, in tropical areas) can prove a highly profitable export.

IS IT FOR YOU? _____

There was a time, not so long ago, when quick fortunes could be made in exporting, but the recent realignment of the world's economy has made immediate riches less likely. However, there is still a strong demand for many American goods overseas. If you have any doubt, just examine how many American firms operate multinationally.

It's also a little more complicated nowadays to cut the web of regulations—legal and economic—that surrounds exporting. Also, there are vast social differences in how business is done in various nations. In China, business transactions are elaborately formal. In Japan, a majority of business is conducted among personal contacts, making it a difficult world for the outsider. Be aware that to do business overseas you must also deal with banks and sometimes with foreign credit arrangements. But it can be done; after all, world trade is a trillion-dollar industry.

GETTING INTO THE MARKET

One way to break into exporting is to deal with a middleman. Export managers, representatives, and agents can grease the skids for a percentage of your profit. Generally, these firms buy your goods at deep discounts and take over the marketing details. Look under "Exporters" in the local phone book, or if you live in a small town with no listing for exporters, visit the library and check the phone directories for nearby large cities.

RESOURCES

You also can take advantage of the wealth of exporting information available to you. Exporting is a knowledge-intensive business, so learn all you can. *Building an Import–Export Business* by Kenneth Weiss (Wiley) provides the basics. The SBA offers various publications dealing with exporting, including *Is Exporting for You?* and *Market Overseas with U.S. Government Help*. The GPO also offers various works, including *Basic Guides to Exporting*.

These and other publications cover some of the ins and outs of the exporting business, including detailed summaries of special insurance options available to exporters and evaluations of other risks you may face.

EXTERIOR CLEANING SERVICE_____

☐ Start-up costs: Anywhere from a few hundred dollars to over $20,000, depending on your depth of involvement.
☐ Estimated hours per week: 5 to 30, possibly full-time or with a full-time partner.
☐ Number of staffers needed for start-up (including founder): 1

Buildings, trucks, airplanes, and other structures and vehicles can get very dirty. They have to be cleaned on occasion, and that's where an enterprising moonlighter can turn a profit. There are many levels at which you can approach exterior cleaning, but in any event your goal is to offer a service that's needed.

LOW LEVEL: MANUAL CLEANING _____

Buildings in most cities suffer from the blight of graffiti. Now, there are very few secrets to cleaning ink and paint from stone, cement, aluminum, and wood, other than very, very hard work. If you can secure some good cleaning chemicals (a janitorial supply house can fill you in on what works best for graffiti) and provide the elbow grease, you can generate some good, regular hourly income, often more than $12 an hour.

This is a fine opportunity if you're a hard worker and live in an urban area. Make up some business cards and drop them off to area merchants. They'll probably welcome your service, because graffiti can be a vexing problem.

116

HIGH LEVEL: HIGH-PRESSURE CLEANING

A variety of franchises will supply you with a cleaning unit and business support. As an example, a Houston firm called Ultra Wash (2335 Naomi St., Houston, TX 77054) will sell you washing equipment for about $25,000 and a van to cart it around in for $11,500. Ultra Wash asks a minimum franchise fee of $18,500. The Ultra Wash equipment can be used on just about anything, but is most commonly used to clean trucks. According to promotional literature supplied by the firm, you can clean eight tractors and eight flatbeds in two hours, for a fee of $136; "typical" days can bring in between $500 and $600.

Of course, that's if you operate full-time, which most owners of a major franchise will want to do (although there's no reason why you can't team up with a partner and keep your involvement part-time).

Incidentally, sometimes the pressure-washing principle is applied to interior jobs, too, such as range hoods in restaurants. A Vermont firm called Black Magic (1478 Mountain Rd., Stowe, VT 05672) offers equipment specially suited for this type of application.

FINDING YOUR NICHE

There's obviously a wide range of points at which to enter exterior cleaning, and you can find out more by scanning the ads of the companies that offer exterior cleaning equipment and franchises; magazines dealing with business start-up typically carry several such advertisements.

But regardless of the level at which you start, remember that there's quite a bit of opportunity; just about everything has to be cleaned eventually, and all you have to do is find the people who buy the cleaning services and offer them a better deal than your competitors.

FINANCIAL PLANNER

☐ Start-up costs: Minimal other than basic office expenses.
☐ Estimated hours per week: 10
☐ Number of staffers needed for start-up (including founder): 1

Financial planning is, without question, a growth market. Today, people of even modest means are looking for advice on how to invest in stocks, savings, and insurance. Should you have a handle on the ever-changing world of money, you can cash in on the demand for sound financial advice.

WHAT A FINANCIAL PLANNER DOES

In the most basic terms, a financial planner helps clients manage their investments, sometimes aids in tax preparation or at least in minimizing tax consequences of investments, and almost always sells clients recommended investment vehicles such as insurance policies.

This latter facet of the business puts the financial planner in something of an ethical dilemma, since selling policies to a client can be construed as a conflict of interest. And in a way, it is, but ethical planners do realize that it is pointless in the long run to sell clients what they don't need.

Some planners operate on a fee-only basis, meaning that they provide advice but don't sell anything. Most planners do some of both—selling and giving advice—and make a scrupulous effort to keep things fair and aboveboard.

QUALIFICATIONS

Because financial planning is a relatively new area, some of the regulations have not caught up to the realities of the marketplace. There is one major requirement of which you must be aware: the federal Securities and Exchange Commission requires anyone who dispenses financial advice for a fee to be registered as an investment advisor. You can find out about the application process by writing to the Chief Counsel's Office, Securities and Exchange Commission, 450 Fifth St., Washington, DC 20054.

You don't need a degree to be a financial planner, but with increasing competition for clients, a degree and specialized training certainly helps. The College for Financial Planning (9725 E. Hampden Ave., Denver, CO 80231) offers an independent study program which also leads to a certain type of certification. If you're interested in academic credentials, American College (270 Bryn Mawr Ave., Bryn Mawr, PA 19019) offers a master of science in financial service through a short residency and independent study. American also offers a plan of study leading to the title Chartered Financial Consultant (ChFC).

MARKETING

Making inroads into financial planning is not particularly easy, as advertising doesn't always produce the results one might expect. As a result, many successful planners advocate the contact/network system. You can develop contacts by joining every group that will have you (Rotary, Kiwanis, Elks, etc.) and speaking before any group that will listen. Seminars at adult education centers are also useful.

Here are some other options for finding a market:

- Hone in on a particular category of client you want to service, such as doctors, store owners, or dentists. If you can persuade a potential client that you have particular expertise in his or her profession, you may make some serious inroads into expanding your own business.
- Focus on a particular economic group. Most planners, of course, want high rollers, but some get their business off the ground by soliciting lower-middle-income clients. You won't make as much per person, but you can build a great volume this way.

FINAL THOUGHTS

A unanimous word of wisdom from the financial planning community: Never give advice in areas where you are not knowledgeable. Don't advise on real estate if you don't know the territory. Likewise, don't sell insurance unless you know what you're doing (and, in places where it's required, have the proper license to sell it).

RESOURCES

If you're interested in finding out more, investigate a very good book by Andrew M. Rich titled *How to Survive and Succeed in a Small Financial Planning Practice* (Reston).

FIREWOOD SERVICE

☐ Start-up costs: Between $600 and $1,000, depending on whether or not you buy a log splitter. You'll also need a truck.
☐ Estimated hours per week: 10 to 15
☐ Number of staffers needed for start-up (including founder): 1

Firewood is relatively profitable, but obviously the amount of profit varies according to location. In urban areas, a cord of firewood can sell for more than $150. In outlying rural areas, it might sell for under $80 a cord. If you can harvest the firewood in the country and truck it into the city, you have the opportunity to make good profits as a firewood service owner.

WHERE DO YOU GET THE WOOD?

You can't just walk onto someone's land and start cutting. In rural areas, people know the value of trees and keep pretty close track of the comings and goings of people with chain saws. A special term applies to cutting down a couple of trees that don't belong to you: grand larceny.

If you don't have your own forest, make arrangements with a rural landowner to harvest his wood. Sometimes he'll charge you a fee (which is highly negotiable) and sometimes you'll get permission to do it for free if he wants some land cleared. In fact, some proprietors of tree services (page 286) are paid for their land-clearing services *and* can keep and sell the firewood.

Publicly owned land can sometimes be harvested with the permission of the forester. You may also be able to work a deal with a logger who is harvesting building timber; he may not want the firewood-quality wood and might let you take it to save him the expense of hauling it out.

PREPARING THE WOOD

Once you have a good supply of wood, cut it into fireplace length (usually 16, 18, or 20 inches) and split it. Log splitting is very difficult to do the old-fashioned way (with a sledge and wedge); you'll have an easier time if you invest $600 to $4,000 in a hydraulic log splitter. Should your service really take off, you might consider investing in a wood processor, a machine that takes a 20-foot log and automatically cuts and splits it.

Bundle the cut wood in cords (128 cubic feet) and sell it. Keep some stored for a year to season the wood, and sell the rest unseasoned. (Be sure to specify whether the wood is seasoned or not, as many people will prefer one over the other.) You can find clients by placing ads in area newspapers and by leaving business cards in the doors of people in the neighborhood who burn wood. If you're unsure about who those people are, just look at the amount of smoke coming out of the chimneys on a cold day.

RESOURCES

Call your local representative of the state forestry service; he or she will be able to point you in the right direction.

FLEA MARKET ORGANIZER/ PROMOTER_____

☐ Start-up costs: About $800 and up as a rough estimate; costs vary signifi-
cantly by locale.
☐ Estimated hours per week: 10
☐ Number of staffers needed for start-up (including founder): 1

Flea markets have a new cachet—many are now trendy, chic, even
yuppified. People are no longer ashamed to admit they're bargain hunters.
As a result, an indeterminate number of flea markets (estimates range
from 2,000 to 50,000) thrive each week in the United States. Add up the
impossible-to-determine number of smaller scale garage sales, and you
can easily see that there's a thriving economy waiting to be tapped.

HOW YOU CAN CASH IN ON FLEA MARKETS _____

Basically, a flea market is just a large garage sale (or tag sale, yard
sale, or whatever terminology you use). The only difference is that in a
flea market one person usually sets up the affair and charges other participants rent (although that is sometimes done in larger garage sales, too). A
person who promotes a flea market generally does the following:

• Finds a good location and rents or buys a piece of land. Flea markets
can be held in the country, where rents are cheap, but population is low.
Conversely, you can hold a flea market in the middle of the city, but
you'll have to pay some stiff up-front rental costs.
• Promotes the event. Promotion is the key, both in getting dealers to rent
space and obtaining a large enough crowd to make the whole thing
profitable.

- Sells his or her own merchandise. There are some promoters who simply arrange events, but they are dealing with well-established, big-time operations. You'll want to have a generous amount of merchandise you can sell, even if only to other dealers the morning of the event. (This, by the way, can be quite profitable; you won't make a lot per piece, since dealers will probably want to mark the goods up by at least 50 percent, but you do stand a chance of moving a great deal of merchandise. Dealers are usually surprised to find how little they actually have when the goods are spread out the morning of the show, and they like some extras to fill in the gaps.)

PROBLEMS AND PITFALLS

As one veteran organizer and promoter points out, there are some big worries connected with the business. Foremost is insurance. The price of liability coverage for flea markets has risen precipitously, and in some areas you may have to fork over many hundreds of dollars for a small one-day event. Price of coverage, of course, will vary widely depending on your particular location.

Crowd control is another hassle. Should you attract a great deal of pedestrian and vehicular traffic, you'll probably need to employ off-duty police officers, and they don't come cheaply.

HOW TO GET STARTED

If you remain undaunted in your aspirations, the first thing you'll need to do is rent the site. Areas with some shelter (like a barn) are best, so the event can't be rained out. When you rent is just as important as where you rent, because during the summer there are many competing flea markets. You may be able to attract customers to two or more flea markets, but dealers won't want to pack up and move or split their inventory. You'll have to do quite a bit of checking and asking around, since comprehensive formal flea market schedules are usually not published.

A problem related to the scheduling difficulty is that you'll be competing against long-established markets—markets that may literally do no promotion because they're traditions. Steer clear of competing with them. In any event, you'll need to do some promotion to make your market attractive. Try advertising in the weekly shoppers in your area. They are very effective in reaching the crowd you want. One particularly cost-effective strategy is to take out classified ads which feature a boldface FLEA MARKET heading. Road signs ("Flea market ½ mile ahead") are useful, too.

BUSINESS BASICS

Decide how much you want to charge for exhibition space. Big flea markets charge about $100 a day, smaller affairs charge $5 or $10. It's likely that you'll be closer to the latter category when starting out, so be sure that you have a generous supply of goods you can sell to augment the rental income. Attend as many auctions as you can and load up on the bargains.

RESOURCES

You can pick up some valuable information about the way yard sales and flea markets work by reading such books as *The Flea Market Entrepreneur* by Charlotte Harmon (Pilot Books), and *How To Plan and Run a Rummage Sale* by Philip J. Dodge (How-to Books). Also, talk to promoters of other flea markets. They're generally quite willing to share their expertise.

FLEA MARKET SELLING

☐ Start-up costs: An inventory worth $200 (resale value) is a reasonable minimum.
☐ Estimated hours per week: 4 to 8
☐ Number of staffers needed for start-up (including founder): 1

Some aspects of flea markets are addressed in *Flea Market Organizer/Promoter* (page 122) and *Antiques Dealer* (page 30). In addition to the material in those entries, there are some basic principles which apply to all types of flea market sales.

HOW TO MAKE MONEY IN FLEA MARKETS

The basic principle is to buy low and sell high. In practice, that may not be quite so simple, but you can make a good profit if you do a lot of bargain hunting. One New York State woman who regularly earns $10,000 annually through flea market sales contends there is only one secret: "Go to auctions. Go to every auction you can visit. You've *got* to buy as many bargains as you can. Load up on stuff you know you can resell for a higher price."

With some experience, you'll have no trouble spotting bargains you can resell at a profit. Glassware, for example, often sells quite cheaply at auctions but commands a good price in flea markets. Also, remember that you'll be buying in volume so your purchase price will be lower due to economies of scale.

TIPS FOR EFFECTIVE SELLING

Rent a table in local flea markets. You'll have no trouble finding nearby markets, especially in the summer. Follow these suggestions:

- Mark prices for your goods. Some people don't mark prices, but those who do contend that it's the most efficient way to operate. For one thing, you'll keep a potential customer looking. That customer might otherwise tire of asking, "How much is this . . . and how much is this?" Mark on the high side so you can dicker down a little. Ideally, you want to double the price you paid for the item.
- Use every inch of space you can and *get as many goods on display as possible*. You can't sell it if it's in a box in the basement. Be sure to fill the spaces under the tables. In fact, that's where some flea market devotees prefer to shop, thinking they'll find better deals there.
- Don't be overly concerned with neatness. One flea market seller once made a diligent effort to organize and neatly display her inventory, only to find that sales dropped. She realized her customers wanted disarray —they felt that her lack of organization signified good bargains.

DETAILS

Learn as much about the business as you can. Talk to other dealers because they're usually generous with their information. Read up on the business. A good source is the *Flea Market Price Guide* by Robert W. Miller (Wallace-Homestead) and Robert G. Miner's *The Flea Market Handbook* (Old Main).

FLOWER ARRANGER ____

☐ Start-up costs: Materials—containers, vases, etc.
☐ Estimated hours per week: 5 to 12
☐ Number of staffers needed for start-up (including founder): 1

A skilled flower arranger can earn a very high hourly fee—in some cities as much as $20 an hour. But the work is not easy and getting assignments, as we'll see, involves a substantial amount of time marketing yourself.

BEGINNING ARRANGEMENTS ____

To get started, work for a florist shop. If your hours are flexible, you can work for several florists on an on-call basis. Finding work often will involve a screen test of sorts; you'll be given an assignment and asked to do an arrangement on the spot. A photo portfolio of arrangements you've done will be helpful, but you'll usually be given the on-site test. A good time to get started is during the holiday season when florists are especially busy.

Rates for flower arrangers range from $7 to $18 an hour. If you have lots of experience and a good reputation, you can charge much more.

QUALIFICATIONS ____

A flower arranger provides floral displays for funerals, weddings, bar mitzvahs, and similar occasions. The flowers can be arranged in a container, crafted in a number of creative ways, or bundled into a wreath.

Arranging is only part of the job. Cleaning and preparing the flowers is quite time-consuming.

RESOURCES

Some schools offer courses in flower arranging, but usually the skill is picked up on the job under the guidance of an experienced designer. In addition to knowing the technical aspects of floral design, you must have a thorough grounding in color and proportion. There are some very good books on the subject, including *Flower Arrangements: Month by Month, Step by Step* by Julia Clements (David & Charles) and *Flower Fingers: Step by Step Flower Arranging* by Bernadette Wright (Trans-Atl. Phila.)

FREELANCE MAGAZINE ARTICLE WRITER

☐ Start-up costs: Stationery, good-quality typewriter, and miscellaneous mailing and office supplies cost about $500. Add about $800 to the total if you want a word processor.
☐ Estimated hours per week: 5 to 25
☐ Number of staffers needed for start-up (including founder): 1

"It's not going to win the Pulitzer Prize, but it sells," commented a newspaper reporter who secretly writes (under a pseudonym) for a magazine specializing in recreational vehicles. While evaluating new tire designs or recommending campgrounds may not excite you, such specialized topics can provide up to $200 for a five- or six-page article.

Freelance magazine article writing is an ideal moonlighting job, and you don't have to be a Hemingway—or even a newspaper reporter—to generate sales. However, you do need some specialized knowledge or the ability to acquire that knowledge.

THE HUNGRY MAGAZINE MARKET _____

Fundamental changes have taken place in the world of magazines, and these changes work to the advantage of a moonlighter. Today, general-interest magazines are far outnumbered by highly specialized publications. General-interest magazines, such as *The New Yorker* or *The Saturday Evening Post*, are overloaded with material from recognized professional writers, but publications such as *Practical Woodworking* don't have that luxury. They need material and are willing to pay well for it. A recent writer's magazine article noted that the woodworking magazine pays $52 to $74 per published magazine page for how-to articles on such subjects as making cabinets, toys, and musical instruments.

If you don't know anything about woodworking, don't despair—you could sell articles on log homes, which might pay you $200 to $1,000 per article. An article for a magazine focusing on the real-life dramas of emergency rescue teams could earn you up to $400. And believe it or not, there's even a magazine devoted entirely to raising llamas; should you be an expert in that particular field, you can expect to earn up to $250 for an article.

The point is that if you can make yourself an expert in a field, and can write reasonably well, you can generate a substantial second income. Suppose, for example, you're a physical fitness buff. You can tap into a virtually unlimited market by writing articles about:

- The training regimen used by your local sports team.
- A type of diet a nutritionist you know recommends for building endurance.
- How a psychologist advises athletes to concentrate and focus their energies for maximum performance.

You can see how a working knowledge of almost any specialized area can be turned into profits.

CHECKING OUT THE TERRITORY _____

Get a copy of *Writer's Market* (Writer's Digest Books, published annually), which is available in almost any large bookstore or library. This book lists hundreds of specialized magazine markets and will help you identify customers for articles on virtually anything from aardvarks to xylophones.

Next, buy copies of the magazines you think you could write for. If you can't find copies on the stands, *Writer's Market* explains how to write away for samples. Closely examine the articles and learn to copy the magazines' styles. Also, read the listing for *How-to Writer* (page 157).

STARTING AND EXPANDING THE BUSINESS _____

Generally, you won't write a complete article and then try to sell it. Instead, you'll want to write a query letter to the editor and describe the article. The query should explain

- The general content of the article.
- The slant (the special angle which will make it of interest to the readers of the magazine).
- Why you are qualified to write the article.

Don't worry too much about the last point. You don't need a Ph.D. or a Pulitzer to write for magazines. A statement such as, "I have owned a personal computer for five years and have shopped for dozens of programs," might persuade an editor that you know enough to write "How to Pick the Right Spreadsheet."

The editor generally will offer to look at the complete article "on speculation"—meaning that he or she is interested but there are no guarantees. Established writers can often command a "kill fee," a specified payment in the event the article is not used.

You need a typewriter, some stationery, and a ream of good-quality 20-pound bond paper. Should you start racking up sales (an active moonlighter can make upwards of $5,000 a year), you might choose to invest in a word processor.

RESOURCES _____

As a beginning freelance magazine article writer, you'd be wise to invest in a library of reference works. In addition to the *Writer's Market*, consider such books as *Writing Nonfiction That Sells* by Samm Sinclair Baker (Writer's Digest Books) and Kirk Polling's *A Beginner's Guide to Getting Published* (Writer's Digest Books).

One other point: You can get some valuable insight and criticism by taking writing courses. Be sure, though, that the course you choose is geared specifically to article writing; a freshman comp course really won't be of much help. Check with the adult education department of your local public school system or with the extension department of an area college.

FREELANCE NEWSPAPER REPORTER _____

☐ Start-up costs: Negligible, except for occasional long-distance calls.
☐ Estimated hours per week: 3 to 8
☐ Number of staffers needed for start-up: 1 (including founder).

Believe it or not, your local newspaper needs *you*. Dissect an edition of a daily newpaper and you'll find that a fair percentage of the stories come not from full-time reporters but rather from moonlighters like yourself. And while the pay is not spectacular, you can find quite a bit of satisfaction as a freelance newspaper reporter.

WHAT A FREELANCE REPORTER DOES _____

A reporter writes in a different style from a magazine writer (see page 127). The newspaper reporter uses a lean, just-the-facts-ma'am approach to the news, focusing on the who, what, where, when, and why of the story. The facts are given in order of importance, so that if a story runs long, the editor can cut from the end to make the article fit the alloted space without affecting the gist of the story. This differs from the feature style used by the magazine writer, which involves a story with a beginning, middle, and end, and allows a more leisurely approach to the topic.

Most freelance reporters cover areas and events that are too marginal or too far away for the newspaper to cover; usually, this means that the news is not important enough to assign a staff reporter. And although reviewing is not, strictly speaking, reporting, many newspapers also hire freelancers to cover concerts and plays.

IDEAS YOU MIGHT EXPLORE

Here are some of the best possibilities for freelance newspaper reporting:

- Covering news of outlying towns. Metropolitan newspapers often can't send a reporter to cover town council meetings and the like. But that news is important, and the paper may want it badly. Town correspondents can earn upwards of $100 a month for covering weekly meetings and writing a couple of other short articles. If you live in a suburb, call the nearest metro daily and ask for the regional editor. See if the paper is interested in your services. (Note that many papers advertise for correspondents in their classified sections—there is a demand!) Incidentally, one advantage of going this route is that the regional editor will often take an interest in your training, assigning an experienced reporter to help you in your initial coverage.
- Reviewing events, especially those which occur at some distance from the newspaper offices. Consider the plight of the editor of the Sunday newspaper: He or she has eight concerts and plays on Saturday night and two available writers. There's only one way for all those events to receive coverage, and that's through freelancers. If you have some knowledge of music or drama, contact the entertainment editor of the local daily. You may be asked to attend an event and write a sample review. Pay is not extraordinarily high for this—$30 to $50 a night, perhaps—but you'll get to see a lot of free entertainment.
- Covering news for out-of-town papers. Suppose a U.S. Senator from Pennsylvania is visiting your hometown in New York and giving a speech. There's a good chance you could cover the event and sell the story to several Pennsylvania papers *if there is no other coverage*. Should the speech be covered by a wire service, or if the local newspaper has agreed to furnish the Pennsylvania papers with a story, you're out of luck. But very often there will be no other coverage sent back to the senator's state, and you can arrange for freelance assignments. Call likely prospects in advance (you can get the names of daily newspapers from the *Gale Directory of Publications,* available in libraries) and see if there's any interest. Ask for the city editor or city desk.

RESOURCES

A good newswriting textbook can get you started. An example of such a text designed for college courses, but which you can order through a local bookstore, is *Media Writing: News for the Mass Media* by Doug Newsom and James E. Wollert (Wadsworth Pub.). The same authors also wrote *Media Writing: Preparing Information for the Mass Media* (Wadsworth).

FURNITURE REFINISHER _____

☐ Start-up costs: Upwards of $1,500 for most basic hand-stripping operations, but less if you already have tools.
☐ Estimated hours per week: 12 to 20
☐ Number of staffers needed for start-up (including founder): 1

Quality furniture can last forever—if it can be patched up along the way by a competent furniture specialist who knows the right way to repair and refinish the piece. More and more Americans are finding that junky-looking chair stowed in the attic is, under the layers of paint and ripped upholstery, a fine and sturdy piece that just needs a little first aid. That, of course, is where you come in.

THE BUSINESS OF FURNITURE REPAIR _____

There are three basic stages in furniture fixup. Some furniture repair people do all three; some specialize in only one area.

- Stripping and refinishing. Here, the old finish is removed, usually by applying a chemical which loosens the old finish and scraping off the residue. Sometimes the whole piece is dipped in a vat of stripping chemical.
- Upholstery. A tricky and sometimes frustrating job, repairing upholstery or reupholstering requires a good touch with a needle and thread. It can pay very well, however.

Many older chairs have caned seats, and while recaning is extremely time consuming, there is an extensive market for the service.
* Fixing damage to the wood. Many pieces need to be redoweled, reglued, or sometimes even partially rebuilt. This is not extraordinarily complicated work, but it does take some know-how.

SETTING UP SHOP

You first must find out about factors such as zoning and insurance should you choose to actually open a shop. Be aware that there are certain hazards involved in furniture repair: some of the chemicals are corrosive and flammable. Certain operations, such as spray painting, can be very, very tricky.

Furniture repair can be a good income producer even from one piece a week, meaning that it's a reasonable corner-of-the-basement enterprise if you start and stay small. But you must avoid at all costs sanding and painting in the same area at the same time, because wood dust will instantly spoil a paint job. Some other caveats for a newcomer to furniture repair:

* Don't try to remove every imperfection. The small blemishes in old wood are what give the piece character. An excessively shiny new finish might make it look more like a piece of plastic-laminated motel furniture.
* You must know a great deal about existing finishes, because you can really ruin things by using the wrong remover for the existing surface. A furniture repair specialist has to know, for example, that a piece from the Queen Anne era is covered in spirit varnish, a substance best removed by alcohol and steel wool. But alcohol and steel wool would make a gummy mess of a colonial piece covered in layers of old-fashioned milk paint. You'll need ammonia for that job.
* You have to have the right tools. There's no improvising if you need a round-cornered putty knife or 2/0 steel wool. A square-cornered knife will gouge, and the wrong type of steel wool will mar the surface. Remember, though, we said the *right* tools, not the most expensive. Most of what you'll need comes relatively cheaply. A tourniquet for drawing legs of a chair together during gluing costs about a nickel for a few feet of cord and a scrap of wood to tighten the cord. It's cheap, but you must have it on hand in order to get the job done.

THE BUSINESS END

Word of mouth referrals through friends and acquaintances can often get you started. If you have an advertising budget, ads in the Yellow

Pages are reported to produce good results, as are small classifieds in shoppers and regional magazines.

How much you can charge depends to an extent on what the local market will bear, but keep in mind that people who take the time and effort to have furniture refinished want a good job and are more often than not willing to pay well for it. It's not unreasonable to expect to clear $20 an hour for your efforts. You'll charge more if you increase your overhead with such items as dipping tanks or spray booths.

RESOURCES

You can promote the business in many ways, but when it comes right down to it, you've got to be able to do the work and do it well. Three widely available books will provide you with a crash course in all aspects of furniture repair: *The Complete Book of Furniture Repair and Refinishing* by Ralph Parsons Kinney (Scribner's), *Furniture Doctor* by George Grotz (Doubleday), and *Restoring and Reupholstering Furniture: Learn How To Make Old Furniture New with Master Craftspeople*, by Kenneth Davis et al. (Beekman House).

GENERAL CONTRACTOR

☐ Start-up costs: Variable, from a few thousand dollars for up-front expenses to the full cost of a house you are building on speculation.
☐ Estimated hours per week: 20 to 30 during construction projects.
☐ Number of staffers needed for start-up (including founder): 2

Although home construction has its ups and downs, the business in general is on a steady upward climb, and has been for years. You can cash in on the building boom by going into business as a general contractor. You can do it part-time if you partner with an experienced builder.

TYPES OF CONTRACTING WORK

There are essentially two types of general contractors:

1. The contract builder, who builds a home according to a client's demands.
2. The speculative builder, who puts up a house and then looks for a buyer.

There are risks associated with each type of contracting job, and they should be mentioned up front. The contract builder generally sets a price and hires all the help; as general contractor, he must meet that price or eat the difference. Most general contractors working as contract builders add protective clauses into their contracts to isolate themselves from the risk, but too many clauses may turn off buyers.

The speculative builder faces the obvious risk of not being able to sell a house for a large enough profit. In some cases, he also risks not being able to finish the project because of weather or financial problems.

WHAT A CONTRACTOR DOES

The general contractor hires subcontractors—carpenters, heating and plumbing installers, roofers, etc. He or she coordinates the entire project and makes sure that it is finished on schedule and at the agreed-upon price.

If you take on a general contracting job on a moonlighting basis, it is essential that you have a relatively flexible schedule. You must be able to go to the construction site to handle an emergency or problem. At the very least, you must have a job that allows you to receive messages during working hours.

A GOOD COMPROMISE

You can see that acting as a general contractor is no small job. A Boston psychologist who moonlights as a general contractor suggests that if you're interested in pursuing the business you team up with someone who knows the building trade and can work on site. Perhaps you'll be able to complement that person's abilities; you may have great organizational abilities, for example, or an outstanding credit rating.

WHAT YOU CAN EARN

Contractors building on a speculative basis usually want to pocket about 20 percent of the final selling cost of the house. (No small profit—a $100,000 house can earn you $20,000.) Contract builders can take an even higher percentage since they are typically dealing with particular clients who have a lot of money to spend.

RESOURCES

McGraw-Hill publishes an excellent line of construction books, including *Management of Small Construction Projects* by Alfred P. McNulty, and *Building Design Construction Handbook* by Frederick S. Merritt. Also check out *Do-It-Yourself Homebuilding Step-by-Step* by Charles D. Neal (Stein & Day).

If you're really interested in learning the construction trade, invest some time in watching someone else do it. Take your vacation and work on a construction site; get a part-time job working for a general contractor; do anything you can to learn what often is a difficult and risky business.

GIFT BASKET DESIGN AND DELIVERY

☐ Start-up costs: About $2,000 for generous inventory and supplies.
☐ Estimated hours per week: 8 to 20
☐ Number of staffers needed for start-up (including founder): 1

What do you give to your boss? Your secretary? Your neighbor who's in the hospital? That's not such a simple question anymore; people eventually get tired of the same coffee mugs or floral arrangements. A new wrinkle in the gift business is the custom-made gift basket—an attractive option for a home-based moonlighter.

BUSINESS IN A BASKET

The essence of the business is to design a unique and appealing gift, whether it's food, perfume, or flowers, and market those gifts to potential clients. One Massachusetts firm, Sage Baskets and Moore, specializes in gourmet food gift baskets. A New York firm offers baskets filled with personal care items.

Who buys gift baskets? Examples include

- Real estate agents who send gift baskets to clients who have just purchased homes.
- Friends of hospital patients.
- Parents who have children graduating from high school or college.
- Bridal and baby shower guests.

WHAT YOU DO

You must come up with an idea that pleases the potential client and allows you to earn a reasonable profit. It you give some thought to the various categories of baskets, you'll have several good alternatives to suggest to potential clients.

Gift baskets usually range in price from $10 to $100. Some basket agencies make a practice of asking callers how much they want to spend, and then tailoring the basket to that price.

A QUALITY PRODUCT

Contents of the basket must be relatively unusual, attractively presented, and of high quality. In addition, you'll generate more repeat customers if you master the personal touch. Does your client's high-school-graduate daughter love cats? A gift basket including some stationery with cats emblazoned on it would be a welcome touch. Is the recipient of the basket entering the world of yuppiedom? A basket of brie and white wines might be right on target. Ask your client for some hints on the recipient's tastes.

You should buy wholesale as often as possible, and you'll really need to have a stockpile of items. (You can't run out to do some shopping every time you put together a basket.) Contact wholesale sources by writing to the manufacturers of distributors listed on the labels of the articles you buy.

By the way, you'll probably want to deliver the baskets. Some firms charge for mileage when delivering but often suspend that charge during the busy holiday season.

PROMOTION

Display ads in weekly papers are productive. You probably will need a display because the service is a bit too complicated to explain in a classified. Try mailings to realtors and other businesses that might want a basket to reward a client or promote goodwill.

GRANT WRITER

☐ Start-up costs: Minimal, unless you invest in a word processor—a helpful tool for this type of work.
☐ Estimated hours per week: 4 to 10, but highly variable depending upon demand.
☐ Number of staffers needed for start-up (including founder): 1

There are literally tens of thousands of different grants available today. Some are offered by the federal or state governments, others by private foundations. These grants are available to nonprofit institutions as well as to individual artists and writers. Just about every college receives some major funding from grants, and most social service agencies depend on the grant business for their very existence.

What does this mean for a moonlighter? Well, somebody has to write these grants—and that could be you, given the right set of circumstances.

THE BUSINESS OF WRITING GRANTS

Most freelance grant writers function as researchers for grants and as polishers of the final proposal. Many grant writers, of course, have a collection of duties.

Here are some examples of grant-writing assignments:

- A symphony orchestra is applying for a grant from a regional arts council. They need a writer who can assemble evidence that the orchestra serves the needs of the entire locality, offers a worthy product, and offers a cultural benefit that is not available elsewhere in the three-county area. The writer does local interviews with community leaders, scans files of newspapers for information, and organizes the documentation collected by the orchestra itself.
- A college is applying for a federal grant to train therapists. All the information is readily available in various forms, but someone has to pull it all together. The grant writer organizes the heaps of forms and documents and uses them to write the various entries. Those entries are in direct response to the questions in the grant application.
- A writer builds a grant from the ground up, for himself. He wants to write about the need for better East–West relations and finds an organization dedicated to just that goal. He writes away for application forms and composes a grant proposal based on those requirements.

QUALIFICATIONS

If you have good organizational skills and can express yourself in writing, you can write a grant. In fact, organization is the biggest part of the job, because an efficient grant writer has to juggle numerous facts and get information from hordes of people.

An important grant-writing skill is the ability to clarify highly technical material. Remember, most grants are written by specialists but read by bureaucrats, who typically will not understand technical jargon or relish wading through it. If you have the skill of translating technical jargon into plain English, be sure to stress it.

MARKETING YOURSELF

It helps if you've written a grant before. The question of experience will be the first issue raised by your prospective client (unless you're writing the grant for yourself, in which case you'll need a good project as well as the grant-writing ability). If not, you can sometimes talk your way into an assignment by citing the public relations, marketing, or promotional writing you've done. Be sure to bring samples.

If you have had no grant-writing experience, it might be a good idea to volunteer a small amount of research and writing for a grant-writing team at a local institution. Some colleges also offer night courses in grant writing.

You can find prospective clients easily enough. Any college or nonprofit organization (museums, social service agencies, etc.) will need someone with grant-writing skills. Some assign all grant writing to in-house personnel, but there is opportunity for freelance work. Call organizations such as the above and ask for the director of development. Have a resume on hand because development directors generally place great stock in resumes.

In some cases you may be able to establish connections and drum up business by offering your services for researching and applying for available grants. Hold off on this approach until you've had some legitimate experience.

BILLING AND PAYMENT

Some pros take a percentage of the money brought in by the grant, say 2 or 3 percent. But that's a risky approach for the newcomer because a failed grant means a lot of work for nothing. A fee arrangement is a better way to start off. Grant writers seem to favor daily fees and usually want upwards of $75 per diem. Should you become well established in your area, or if you can convince a client that you're an expert with indispensable knowledge, that daily fee can go much higher.

RESOURCES

Read up on the various books available detailing the grant-writing process. A good one to start with is *The Art of Winning Foundation Grants* by Howard Hillman and Karin Abarbanel (Vanguard). Various periodicals deal with available grants but are not always readily available. Ask your librarian which federal publications dealing with grants are subscribed to locally. Your U.S. representative's office can help you, too. Interested in writing a grant for your own work? Ask your local librarian for entry forms for regional arts grants, and check out Hal Borland's *How to Write & Sell Nonfiction* (Greenwood) as well as F. Fraser Bond's book by the same name (Arden Library).

GRAPHIC ARTIST

☐ Start-up costs: For the most basic setup, about $100.
☐ Estimated hours per week: 10 to 15
☐ Number of staffers needed for start-up (including founder): 1

"Anyone who's neat, precise, and who can work under deadline can start up a home business doing simple graphic arts," maintains a graphic artist who graduated to ownership of a successful Massachusetts advertising agency. "And you can usually get all the work you want from local ad agencies."

THE ART OF GRAPHIC ARTS

Graphic artists do work that, at the high end, is complex and requires years of training. But much of what graphic artists do is simple pasteup, meaning the process of taking typeset material and art renderings and laying them out on a board. The pasteup, also called a mechanical, is the camera-ready piece from which the ad, brochure, or article will be printed.

Pasteup is not complex—it usually involves rubber-cementing sections of type onto a special graph paper or cardboard—but it is time-consuming and demands a high degree of accuracy. That's why ad agencies don't like assigning their regular graphics people to the task, and that's also why the regular graphics people aren't crazy about doing it, either.

WHAT YOU'LL NEED

Buying a drafting table is the first order of business. You don't need an expensive drafting table; for starters, you can use the kind sold in department stores. In a pinch, even a card table will do, although being able to angle the table towards you makes things much easier. Some rubber ce-

141

ment or a wax gun (available in art supply stores) is essential. A ruler and a T-square are necessary, too. Add a set of business cards and you can get started—possibly for as little as $100.

GETTING DOWN TO BUSINESS

Call or stop in at local ad agencies; be sure you have something to leave behind, like a business card or brochure. Show a sample of something you've pasted up before, or dummy up a sample ad.

Remember, the work you'll be getting from an ad agency might not be all that creative or pleasant. You could, for example, wind up gluing 100 little words and letters to a paper, and you'll have to make sure that each is perfectly level and correctly spaced. For taking on such mundane tasks, you can usually make from $5 to $20 an hour, depending on your experience, the going rate where you live, and how badly the client needs the job done.

A word on the concept of supply and demand: You can make good money by taking on deadline work, but be sure you can handle the job. If you miss a deadline, you may very likely never get work from that agency again. So turn down work if you can't do it. No agency will hold it against you if you occasionally don't take a job because you're not able to meet the deadline. In fact, they'll probably respect your professionalism.

RESOURCES

There are a number of good books on graphics available in any library. One very good guide is *How to Do Your Own Pasteup for Printing* by Edmund C. Gross (Halls of Ivy Press). Another practical resource is *Pasteups and Mechanicals* by Jerry Demoney and Susan E. Meyer (Watson-Guptill).

GRAPHIC DESIGNER____

☐ Start-up costs: Usually $300 to $800 for basic art supplies, but in most cases nothing beyond that.
☐ Estimated hours per week: 5 to 15
☐ Number of staffers needed for start-up (including founder): 1

Graphic designers create visual images to communicate something, whether for a promotional brochure or for someone's self-published newsletter. For our purposes, a graphic designer is considered to be different from a graphic artist (see separate entry on page 141). We've defined a graphic artist as a person primarily involved in pasteup, while a graphic designer is an expert in creating overall design packages which may include illustrations. Note that there are no universal definitions of these terms, so don't automatically assume that someone calling himself or herself a graphic artist only does pasteup.

WHAT A DESIGNER DOES _____

In simple terms, a graphic designer puts together a whole visual package. This might involve a small job, such as selecting type, photos, and layout for a brochure, or it could extend to creation of an overall visual identity for an entire corporation.

Some possible jobs for a graphic designer:

- Designing logos. Those catchy designs just don't spring up full-bloom from the artist's pen. They must be drawn, redrawn, tested, and checked against other existing logos to be sure they don't infringe on a trademark. Logo design is a big and lucrative business.
- Designing corporate identity packages. A graphic designer will put together an entire package of material for a company wishing to put its

143

name before the public. For instance, a graphic designer might oversee the creation of point-of-purchase displays for a product, along with package design, visual components of the corporation's advertising, even the letterhead.

- Supervising production of collateral. Collateral design (page 21) is a major endeavor in today's corporate world. Remember that collateral is the term used in media enterprises to indicate any printed material used for promotional purposes. It includes brochures, illustrations, charts, and various other documents. Ad agencies don't usually relish this job (after all, they make most of their money placing ads) and are often willing to farm out collateral production. A graphic designer gets his or her slice of the collateral pie by specifying type style, planning layout, and making sure that the style of the piece coordinates well with other visual elements in the firm's image.

MARKETING AND PRICING

One graphic designer describes her marketing strategy as simply "handing out cards and knocking on doors." Some of those doors should belong to advertising agencies and some to major corporations. Your card should obviously be a graphic masterpiece.

What you charge depends on your experience and the local market conditions. Should you have a convincing background and a good portfolio, you can probably command upwards of $40 an hour.

RESOURCES

There's an endless supply of books on graphic design. One you might look at first is John Laing's *Do It Yourself Graphic Design* (Macmillan). Adult education courses and local art schools will also offer helpful courses. Some courses can be expensive, however, and cost upwards of $300.

GREASE COLLECTOR___

☐ Start-up costs: You'll need some sort of truck; other than that essential requirement, start-up costs can be anywhere from a few hundred dollars for pails and barrels to thousands for special vehicle tanks and attachments.
☐ Estimated hours per week: 10 to 15
☐ Number of staffers needed for start-up (including founder): 1

Now, here's one you'd probably never come up with on your own . . .

Restaurants are prohibited by law from throwing out the grease they use in deep frying. That grease, which today is typically a 50/50 mix of animal and vegetable oils, must be collected and disposed of in a sanitary fashion. An enterprising part-timer can take advantage of this regulation and earn some extra income through grease collection.

WHY GREASE COLLECTING? _____

Luckily for you, that grease (which can't be put into a dumpster because it causes sanitation problems) is actually in demand. Who wants old grease? Rendering companies—firms that distill fatty compounds. A rendering company will take the restaurant grease, purify it, distill it, and sell it to another company that can use it as a base for products as varied as soap and dog food.

THE OPPORTUNITY FOR INDEPENDENTS _____

Modernization has had a dual effect on the grease collection business. First, the demand for the stuff has made it something of a big business, and nowadays many grease collection routes are dominated by very large companies that field a fleet of trucks specially equipped to suck up the grease. But another aspect of modern life has created some opportunity for the small timer: In some major cities, streets have become so crowded that the big trucks can't find a place to park while they move in the mobile unit to suck up the residue of the deep fryer.

WHAT YOU DO

Basically, an independent grease collector has to devise a method for picking up the grease. The most basic tool of the trade is a five-gallon metal bucket, which you fill with grease (once the deep fryer has cooled down) and carry to your 55-gallon drum on the truck. This obviously will require a few trips, and the work is rather hot and messy. Sometimes, the restaurant will store the used grease for you in a shed outside the restaurant, and you can simply pick up the barrels—a heavy job which requires two people or a hydraulic lifting device.

You perform the service for free (until recently, grease collectors charged for their services, but no more) and sell the grease to a rendering company, which in today's market will probably pay about 2 cents per pound of grease. The grease, by the way, becomes solid once it cools off. Depending on the market and the fullness of the barrel, you may earn only about $9 a barrel, but remember that there's a lot of grease out there and restaurants produce it in large volume.

The frequency of collections and the amount of grease you'll pick up vary considerably according to the procedures of the restaurants on your route.

RESOURCES

See if there's a market for your services before making any investment. Call grease buyers, listed under "Rendering" in the Yellow Pages, and ask about local demand. They'll be able to fill you in on what kind of containers you need and where to get them. Should you perceive a demand for the recycled grease, find out whether there are local restaurants interested in your services. They probably have someone doing the job right now, but find out if there's some way you can improve on the present service: more frequent collection, possibly, or neater work. Contact restaurants that are opening or changing hands.

HANDYMAN_____

☐ Start-up costs: About $20 for fliers, more if you need to purchase additional tools.
☐ Estimated hours per week: 5 to 15
☐ Number of staffers needed for start-up (including founder): 1

Let's try a little amateur marketing analysis. If your ears have been operating properly for the past couple of years, you've heard homeowners make such complaints as the following:

"I can't find people to do small jobs. Carpenters, roofers, and repair people only want major contracts."

"It's impossible to get someone to come after work. If you want something fixed, you have to take time off from work to meet the repair person."

"These people never show up! If they're going to be late, can't they call?"

You know that homeowners have these feelings—and you've probably guessed by now that you can capitalize on them.

HOW TO BE A HANDYMAN_____

Frank was a schoolteacher who couldn't make ends meet on his salary of $19,500. However, he was also adept with a hammer and saw. As a result, he developed a sideline of fixing steps, floors, and small appliances for homeowners in his neighborhood. He does no advertising (in fact, he wants to keep his moonlighting job secret from the school administration and has so far been able to do so) and gets as much work as he can handle from referrals.

He started out by apprenticing himself to a handyman carpenter who advertised in the newspaper. When Frank started doing jobs on his own, he had a good base of knowledge from which to draw but scrupulously avoided taking jobs over his head. He knows—and you should, too— that certain involved jobs should be left to the experts.

TYPES OF JOBS

You don't have to be a master carpenter to help people with the kind of work they typically need. Fixing stairs and refinishing floors are good jobs to start with. Stripping woodwork is also a job in high demand. Replaning or refinishing doors is another highly desired service. Anything that you can do well can probably be marketed.

HOW TO FIND CLIENTS

Moonlighting handymen (and handywomen) seem to agree that advertising in the newspaper is not the right approach, at least not initially. There are two reasons:

- You'll waste time with people who are just shopping.
- You'll probably get jobs farther from your home than you'd like.

Here's a better idea: Make up a flier and distribute it to people in your neighborhood. Make it simple, but be sure to note that you

- Can handle a variety of repairs
- Are available nights and weekends
- Are reliable—you keep your appointments
- Are insured

On that final point, check with your insurance agent to find out what type of coverage you need for a handyman service, both in terms of liability and personal accident insurance. Insurance is an added cost—and quite candidly many handymen do without it—but more and more homeowners are insisting on some sort of proof of coverage before they engage a workman. You can also save yourself from personal financial disaster by having the right coverage.

RESOURCES

There are many books on home repair available in libraries and bookstores. Time-Life publishes a particularly helpful series on *Home Repair and Improvement*, which gives details of the exact types of jobs you'll probably encounter. Also check out *The House Doctor's Guide to Simple Home Repair* by Herb Baum (Pinnacle).

HOME CLEANING SERVICE

- ☐ Start-up costs: **$200** to **$300** minimum, more if you want an advertising budget.
- ☐ Estimated hours per week: 5 to 10
- ☐ Number of staffers needed for start-up (including founder): 2 or more

People are busy these days, and there's sometimes just no time left over for cleaning the house. Of course, some people just hate to clean, period. If you don't mind hard work done on a tight schedule, you might look into the possibility of moonlighting with your own home cleaning service. If you live in or near an area that's reasonably affluent with a high percentage of two career households, there's a market waiting for you.

HOW THE BUSINESS WORKS

Although sometimes described as a "maid service," the idea of home cleaning really does differ from the maid concept. Home cleaning, in order to be efficient, is usually a *team* effort. It's very difficult to make a decent income from a one-person cleaning job. It's not easy to make money from multiple-person cleaning, either, but you do stand a better chance of regularly working on a reasonable profit margin.

The secret to keeping the profit rolling in, according to experienced home cleaners, is organization. Three people working in tandem can clean a house in a fifth of the time it takes one person. Aside from the fact that a team can more efficiently do things like move furniture, there also is additional motivation due to on-site supervision and teamwork.

THE PROFIT MARGIN

Efficiency is important because home owners don't like paying much more than $40 or $50 for a thorough housecleaning. If the job is going to be done once a week on a regular contract basis, you'll have trouble extracting much more than $20 or $30.

But the essential problem is estimating the job. You'll have an hourly minimum you need to bring in to cover salaries and provide a reasonable profit; let's say $26 for three people on-site. You then need to accurately estimate how long the job is going to take. Estimate too many hours and you probably won't get the job. Estimate too few and you take a bath. That's why it might be a good idea to work for someone else's home cleaning service first before establishing your own. That way, you can learn something about the time requirements.

GETTING STARTED

Ads in weekly papers are reported to be very effective in getting initial clients. Also, don't overlook friends and aquaintances who might want your services.

Getting help can be a problem. One obvious solution is to pay very well ($7 an hour and up); you will have a smaller profit margin but more willing workers. At first, it's advisable to stick with people you know; a house cleaning service is a good business to start with a group of friends. For one thing, you won't have initial recruitment problems. Also, you won't have to deal with the touchy business of employee honesty. For some people, the home cleaning business is dangerous because the temptation to steal is just too great. In fact, you might find it necessary to have your employees bonded.

MAKING THE BUSINESS GROW

Do good work and you'll have many calls coming in. Make sure you have business cards to give to clients and give some thought to developing a memorable name for your service. Once the business is off the ground, it probably will be worthwhile to spring for a business listing in the Yellow Pages so that interested potential clients can locate you.

Veterans of the business note that what at first seems impossible—making a decent profit from home cleaning—gets much easier as you learn shortcuts and efficient practices. Also, you're going to be ahead of the game if you turn down difficult and time-consuming jobs like windows and ovens.

HOME INSPECTOR_____

☐ Start-up costs: Probably close to $30,000 if you purchase needed equipment and do necessary advertising; an advertising budget may be considerably smaller in less competitive parts of the country.
☐ Estimated hours per week: 16 to 20
☐ Number of staffers needed for start-up (including founder): 1

Home inspection is a rapidly growing business. Just a few years ago, most people buying a home didn't know what a home inspector was or where to find one. But today a home inspection is often mandatory to secure a mortgage. In many areas of the country, home inspectors are in short supply.

START-UP BASICS _____

You can make a substantial part-time income from home inspection if you've got the knowledge and the tools, but it is definitely not a business for rank amateurs. You've *got* to have a comprehensive store of knowledge about buildings and building practices, which you may have learned as a contractor or builder yourself. In addition, you must be prepared to do a thorough and painstaking job on each home you inspect because careless oversights and omissions can result in legal action against you.

You'll need such specific equipment as an electrical tracer, circuit tester, and gas detector, and such basic tools as screwdrivers, flashlights, and a ladder. If you live on the East Coast, you'll have to do some extensive Yellow Page advertising because there is much competition. Insurance will vary from location to location, but you can bet it's going to be expensive. In our increasingly litigious society, home inspectors are attractive targets, and the cost of liability insurance reflects that fact. While certification for this type of work is not universally required, there may be a variety of licenses and permits you'll need in your area. Check with your town or city clerk or secretary of state.

LEARNING THE INS AND OUTS

Assuming you have a good general knowledge of buildings, it's a good idea to do some inspections for another firm before starting out on your own. Without exception, experienced home inspectors recommend this practice. One of the major inspection associations, the American Society of Home Inspectors (1010 Wisconsin Ave., N.W., Suite 630, Washington, DC 20007), requires just such an apprenticeship for certification. Incidentally, you'll find society membership helpful not only because the membership is a good marketing tool, but also because you'll avail yourself of numerous contacts and knowledge at association conventions. In any event, you certainly will want a good deal of experience doing inspections under someone else's aegis before you even think about starting on your own. Send resumes to home inspectors in your area. You can find them in the phone book or write to the American Society of Home Inspectors and ask for a roster.

Once you've gotten your feet wet (perhaps in a client's leaky basement), you are ready to start on your own. The work can be quite enjoyable. "You're on center stage for three hours," says one inspector, "and there's no question that during the inspection you're the star of the show."

By the way, the perks also make it incumbent upon the inspector to develop good people skills and verbal abilities. You'll be doing an enormous amount of face-to-face work with clients, and your reports—which are vitally important documents to those affected—must be legible, expressive, and accurate.

THE BUSINESS AND ITS FUTURE

Because home inspection provides a good second income, many inspectors never open up their own business. Instead, they're perfectly happy to let someone else pay the expenses of the business.

WHAT TO CHARGE

A home inspection costs about $300 in most parts of the country and takes about three hours. Never try to shave that time period, because you'll be looking for trouble as well as for termites. The fees for home inspection will probably increase in the next few years as more banks require inspections and the service becomes more of a necessity. You'll have to set your fees to be in line with those charged by other home inspectors. Customers do shop around before contracting an inspector.

The East Coast has a glut of home inspectors (but it also has a lot of homes), while there is a shortage out west. As more banks and realtors demand inspection, the business of inspecting homes grows healthier. It's a promising field if you like the spotlight and can handle the pressure.

HOUSE AND PET SITTING

☐ Start-up costs: Nothing if you do the work yourself; a few hundred dollars if you set up an agency.

☐ Estimated hours per week: If you live in the house, you'll be there full-time. But actual chores—maintaining the home and/or feeding the pets—take no longer than normal housework. Agency work can be 10 to 20 hours a week.

☐ Number of staffers needed for start-up (including founder): 1

America is an increasingly mobile society. We travel more than ever, and our houses sit vacant while we're gone. Unfortunately, ours is also an increasingly crime-ridden society, and those people who leave their homes for extended periods need some protection for their house and their belongings. That's where you come in.

WHAT A HOME SITTER DOES

Essentially, you move into the house, feed the pets, water the plants, clean, take care of minor maintenance problems, and give the house that lived-in look. Looking lived-in is critically important from a house's point of view, because vacant homes attract vandals and burglars. It's also prohibitively expensive to insure an unoccupied home.

THE MONEY ANGLE

There are several ways the money can change hands. In some cases, the homeowner simply lets the sitter live for free; in other cases, there's a small fee paid to the sitter. Sitting agencies charge a fee for setting up clients and sitters; usually that fee is charged to the client, although some agencies, such as a large Washington State firm, charge the occupants of the home $100 to $150 a month. Another agency charges $24 a night for a sitter, and splits that fee evenly with the sitter.

What you charge—and how you charge it—depends entirely on local supply and demand.

SETTING UP AN AGENCY

Can you operate a successful home sitting agency part-time out of your home? "You sure can," says Jane Poston, head of Housesitter Security Service in Tucson, Arizona. "I've run it part-time for ten years. You can do as much or as little as you want."

The work isn't particularly hard, but it does require conscientious screening of your sitters. There are several principles that apply to selecting sitters for your service:

- Associate with them as independent contractors. Clearly lay out in writing that they do not work for you in a formal employer–employee relationship.
- Screen them carefully. Look for reliable people, not itinerants. Some home sitters feel that recent college graduates are often good bets. Jane Poston maintains that older sitters are best. Should you look for young sitters, you can advertise for sitters on college bulletin boards or in local newspapers; for older sitters, try putting up notices on church bulletin boards. Regardless of the age of your sitters, be selective about whom you take on. Check references.
- Have your sitters read and agree to a list of restrictions and regulations. Be very careful about letting your sitters entertain visitors while in a client's home.

RESOURCES

The concept of a house and pet sitting business is quite simple, but the arrangements can be complex. Jane Poston offers a manual for starting a home sitting service; it includes price breakdowns and contracts which you can reproduce. The manual costs $36, postpaid. Write to Ms. Poston at 1708 E. 9th St., Tucson, AZ 85719.

HOUSE PAINTER

☐ Start-up costs: $1,000 minimum.
☐ Estimated hours per week: 15 to 20 during painting season, full-time during summer if you're on an academic schedule.
☐ Number of staffers needed for start-up (including founder): 1, but 2 or more is more practical.

"The first time you do it, you'll be up on a ladder, your knees will be shaking, and you'll wonder how you got yourself into this," says one successful moonlighting house painter who makes an excellent income to supplement his salary. "But after you get used to it, and after the first few paychecks, you start to enjoy painting."

House painting is an ideal moonlighting job, especially for teachers or students who can work in the late afternoon during the school year and full-time during summers.

WHAT YOU NEED

The most essential piece of equipment needed by a house painter is a good extension ladder, which isn't cheap. A 40-foot aluminum ladder can cost $250 to $300, and if you have a crew of painters you'll need a couple of ladders. In addition, you need smaller ladders, brushes, buckets, scrapers, liability insurance, and in, many communities, a rigger's license. A rigger's license is usually granted after you pass a short written exam in which you demonstrate that you know the concepts of erecting and securing ladders and rigging. More elaborate jobs require additional equipment, such as scaffolding.

HOW TO START

Many house painters get all the business they want without any ongoing advertising. Some have never advertised, relying simply on word of mouth. If you're starting up, try the word-of-mouth strategy and supplement it with some fliers left in the doors of houses in your neighborhood. You'll know which houses are the likely prospects; just look for the structures most in need of painting. Also, leave your fliers at the very neatly kept homes (the ones with the trimmed lawns and hedges) because meticulous owners have frequent paint jobs.

In the beginning, stick to your neighborhood. There are two advantages to this:

1. People like dealing with someone in the neighborhood because they feel that person will have a vested interest in doing a good job; the painter doesn't want an unhappy neighbor and certainly doesn't want an ugly-looking house down the block.
2. A good share of your time will be spent in transporting ladders and supplies. You can cut travel time by working close to home; also, if you find yourself missing a certain brush, you can go home and get it.

WHAT TO CHARGE

You'll have to make an estimate that brings in a certain hourly or daily rate. Estimating the time needed for a paint job is something that comes with experience, but it comes quickly. One novice painter noted that he can now estimate the time required for the job within two to three hours. A rate of $100 per full working day is common.

PITFALLS

Be aware that painting can be a difficult and physically tiring job, especially in the summer. Also, painting is not the ideal job for someone who has a fear of heights.

Experienced painters recommend that you get some experience working for someone else before you start lining up and estimating jobs. For one thing, some of the work is tricky and you'll need a guiding hand to demonstrate. Also, estimating time and cost is difficult at first. It's pretty easy to estimate how long it will take to paint the broad surfaces, but windows are trickier. It may take an inordinate amount of time to remove, paint, putty, and replace certain windows. You'll have to learn to spot potential problems before doing an accurate work–time estimate.

HOW-TO WRITER_____

☐ Start-up costs: Negligible, except for basic writing equipment and postage costs. Investment in a camera can be helpful.
☐ Estimated hours per week: 5 to 15
☐ Number of staffers needed for start-up (including founder): 1

What writing field offers the most opportunities? Novels? Hardly: only a few are published each year, and many are by established novelists. Biographies? Check the bio shelf in a bookstore, and you'll see that there are only a handful of biographies for sale at any given time.

Take a close look at the shelves in your local bookstore and you'll see that the overwhelming majority of titles are of the how-to variety. And don't forget magazines. They're usually bursting with articles on how to do something and how to do it better than anyone else.

If you're a reasonably skillful writer and have some expertise you'd like to share, the burgeoning field of how-to writing may be for you.

THE MARKET _____

There is a vast and unquenchable demand for how-to-do-it materials. Examples include

How to refinish furniture
How to fix your car's engine
How to be healthier
How to be happier
How to be more organized
How to help your child do better in school

If you can think of other examples, you're already started on your second career.

HOW TO DO HOW-TOs

A how-to author has a distinct advantage over many other types of writers because he or she only needs to write part of the book in order to sell the work. In most cases, book publishers will issue a contract on the basis of one or two complete sample chapters and a detailed outline of the work. Magazine editors often assign how-to articles based on a query letter (see *Freelance Magazine Article Writer*, page 127).

When preparing your sample and outline, you must show the editor that you can impart information in a simple, easy-to-follow style. A good how-to writer never assumes too much knowledge on the part of the reader. In addition, you'll want to express the information in a reasonably engaging way.

FINDING A TOPIC

Anything you can do well and explain clearly probably has potential. Wallpapering, repairing old cars, using a computer—all are activities in which other people have an interest. You don't need extensive formal qualifications to be a how-to writer (although formal qualifications do help), but you must know the subject and be able to communicate the information authoritatively.

Once you've come up with an idea, the next step is to scope out the competition. Should you visit the bookstore and find that the shelves are overloaded with high-quality works on radio repair, for example, you might want to pursue another topic. Should there be nothing on your subject, that may indicate that there's either a great deal of opportunity or no interest. The best scenario is when there are only a limited number of books available on your chosen topic and those books have what you feel are obvious flaws.

RESOURCES

For such a wide-open field, there was, until recently, a dearth of books on how to write how-to books. Duane Shinn's *How to Write "How-To" Books and Articles for Publication* (Duane Shinn) is a good one. Writer's Digest also publishes *Writer's Market*, an indispensable guide to finding publishers intersted in your category of writing.

IMPORTER_____

☐ Start-up costs: Variable, but remember you'll need to invest in inventory first, then sell it later.
☐ Estimated hours per week: 5 to 10, more if you travel to foreign destinations.
☐ Number of staffers needed for start-up (including founder): 1

Importing is a difficult business to enter, usually much more so than exporting. (See exporting business entry on p. 114.) For one thing, you won't get as much help from the U.S. Government when importing as you would when exporting (for the quite obvious reason that the government wants to encourage sales of U.S. goods to foreign markets but not the reverse). Additionally, you take some greater risks because *you* place the order—meaning you shell out the up-front money.

BASICS OF IMPORTING _____

In essence, you want to buy a product that is cheap and common in an overseas market, but that will be unusual and expensive in the U.S. To do this, you'll have to sort through some complex and rapidly changing regulations. Also, it's imperative that you be able to relate to foreign marketers and understand their currency and ways of doing business.

Many importers ease the way by having a contact overseas. For example, a Maryland couple began a highly profitable importing business after a friend married a Japanese woman and moved to Tokyo. The Japanese woman had introduced the Maryland couple to kimonos, and, to everyone's surprise, there was a brisk U.S. demand for the beautiful ceremonial garments. This home-based business sold to friends and retailers, and eventually became a full-time retail firm itself—grossing more than $200,000 a year.

159

GETTING STARTED

Give it some thought: Do you have a contact overseas? A relative? A neighbor who works as an overseas tour guide? Any contact can be helpful. You can also try to generate some contacts by getting in touch with embassies of foreign governments: U.S.-based foreign embassies often make referrals to people interested in starting import businesss.

After making initial contacts, you must

- Identify a product that is marketable here. You'll need to rely on instinct as much as anything else. Trends come and go, and it's important that you be able to spot a trend early, like the Maryland couple who caught on to the growing American interest in the Orient.
- Find a market for the product. To importers, this usually means a *definite* market. You probably will need to buy in bulk to make a decent profit, so you must have an outlet for those crates of goods. It's essential to line up as many local commitments as possible before putting a lot of your cash on the line.

Incidentally, don't forget that importing can turn your vacation travel into a profitable sideline. Many home-based importers use their travels to line up deals and sometimes to purchase the goods.

RESOURCES

Consult Kenneth Weiss's *Building an Import–Export Business* (Wiley). Also, consider dealing with an importing firm now in business; you can contract for the firm to do the importing for you, then you'll take over the marketing. The profit will be smaller, but so will the risk and complexity. Importers are listed in the Yellow Pages.

Being an importer involves being able to spot trends in order to capitalize on them. A valuable guide to developing this ability is *Supermanaging* by Arnold Brown and Edith Weiner (McGraw-Hill). The authors contend that you can predict trends by scanning a core of publications, which include the *New York Times, American Demographics*, and the *Wall Street Journal*. In addition to identifying many other useful trend-spotting publications, the authors give hints on how to scan them and what to look for.

INDEXER _____

☐ Start-up costs: None, other than mailings to clients.
☐ Estimated hours per week: 5 to 10
☐ Number of staffers needed for start-up (including founder): 1

Should you have an orderly mind and a love of words, indexing books may be a good way for you to generate some extra income in your spare time. Generally, publishing houses hire indexers on a freelance basis, although some publishers assign the task in-house and occasionally the author indexes his or her own book. While publishers are always in need of indexing services, they are wary of newcomers, and any experience you can garner will work to your advantage.

TOUGH DUTY _____

Lest you think that indexing is a simple clerical task, be forewarned that a good index requires great creativity. You have to be able to approach the subject from a reader's point of view. As an example of the difficulties involved, consider the author of a child-care book who wanted to do the index himself because he felt that no indexer could better anticipate the headings under which a mother would search for information. But even he couldn't cover all the bases; a reader of his book wrote a letter to a library science magazine complaining that she could find no entry for "swallowed objects." There was an entry under "O" for "objects, in nose and ears" but nothing for "objects, swallowed." And while the child wasn't choking, she assumed that a doctor might list it there, and eventually found what she wanted in a paragraph subhead titled "swallowed objects and choking."

Though this is just one example of an incomplete index cited by master indexer G. Norman Knight, it does demonstrate that an index is a critical portion of a book—not an afterthought—and can be a critical factor in its success or failure.

HOW IT'S DONE

Many indexers use index cards for making initial notes on entries. They read through the proofs (copies of typeset pages), jot down the appropriate reference and page number, and file the card alphabetically. (These days, most professional indexers use a computer.) Now, the indexers must develop cross-references and include as many variations as can be reasonably anticipated. For example, under the heading "software" would be listed related subcategories ("word processing," "spreadsheet," etc.). These subcategories would in turn be listed individually, with a cross-reference to the general heading "software." For instance: "Spreadsheet, 122, 177; see also *software*."

SETTING UP THE AGREEMENT

First, find out how detailed the index must be. Next, clarify deadlines. You will probably agree on a certain pay figure or a range of figures based on anticipated number of hours or lines in the index. Hourly pay for indexing is not especially high at first—$7 to $8 an hour might be a reasonable minimum—but as your reputation grows, the hourly price grows, too.

GETTING INTO BUSINESS

Write letters to nearby publishers and explain your experience, if any, and your desire to undertake part-time indexing work. It helps if you're located near publishers, because certain transactions are best handled in person.

RESOURCES

Literary Market Place runs listings of qualified indexers; you can find out about getting a listing in this popular sourcebook by contacting the publisher, R.R. Bowker (245 W. 17th St., New York, NY 10011). The book *Jobs for Writers* (Writer's Digest Books) addresses indexing as well as a number of related part-time jobs for moonlighters with good language skills. And for a complete guide to the process of indexing, check out the surprisingly readable *Indexing Your Book: A Practical Guide for Authors* by Sina K. Spiker (Univ. of Wisc. Press). There are also indexing associations, including the American Society of Indexers (1700 18th St., N.W., Washington, DC 20009).

INFORMATION BROKER _____

☐ Start-up costs: Usually in the range of $1,500 for computer gear, plus $500 for online database services.
☐ Estimated hours per week: 5 to 15
☐ Number of staffers needed for start-up (including founder): 1

Consider the following situations:

- A drug company researcher wants a listing of all press articles published during the previous month that dealt with product tampering.
- A public relations executive wants to read anything and everything about a new, important client.
- The manager of an import–export firm needs weekly updates on worldwide commerce in gold bullion.

Where do these firms turn for such information? Possibly to their in-house research department, if they happen to have one. If not, they just might turn to you, should you establish yourself as an information broker.

JUST THE FACTS _____

Buying and selling of information is, by some estimates, a $13 billion business. You can have a chunk of that business if you have (a) a personal computer with a modem and (b) the kind of mind that lends itself to database research.

Before specifying the talents you need, let's talk about the basics. What, exactly, is a database? It's a computerized bank of information that can be scanned by telephone via computer. To access the database and initiate the computer searches, you need a modem, a device for encoding and decoding the computer code used to transmit over the phone. Special software is usually needed to communicate via modem, although some computers have communications software built in. A printer is a necessity, too.

There are literally hundreds of databases into which you can tap. Some specialize in financial news and information; others contain abstracts of research findings in various fields. There are also super-specialized databases in such topics as packaging technology and food science.

PROFITING FROM RESEARCH

Basically, as an information broker, you have to find someone interested in certain knowledge who is willing to pay for it. That may present some difficulties because the whole business of computer-based research is new. However, you can do some helpful spadework by determining the kind of information certain firms will need and offering them your services. Write to or call the firms and see if there's any interest. Consider taking out small classified ads in trade journals. If you have expertise in a certain professional area (finance and banking, for example) you'll probably know what kind of information is in demand and who needs it.

THE BASICS OF THE BUSINESS

Why would firms pay for an outsider to use a service which they could just as easily tap into themselves? For one thing, accessing a computer database and finding the desired information is far more complicated than flipping through an encyclopedia. Database research requires determining the correct source to search (so you'll have to know what's available) and then using the appropriate keywords to start the information-gathering. In addition, each database system has its own codes for responding and prompting (known as control vocabulary), which you will have to learn. It takes a resourceful, experienced, and creative researcher to do quick and accurate work on a database.

That's why a competent researcher can earn upwards of $20 an hour in profit, although profit and the method of determining that profit varies. Computer expert Dana K. Cassell writes that one way to determine your bill is to mark up the cost of online time by approximately 20 percent and add on a flat $35 fee to cover the cost of planning the search.

With that strategy you could stand to make some serious money, since some of the online services are expensive. Should you access LABOR-LAW (Bureau of National Affairs) through Dialog Information Services, the bill for an hour's searching will come to $120, plus miscellaneous costs for such items as printing out a record. Remember that you'll be paying the bill initially (usually through a charge card), so be sure you have a concrete pay and reimbursement agreement with your client before running up too many charges.

RESOURCES

It takes some effort to learn about databases. An easy and fun way to begin is to subscribe to CompuServe, a consumer-oriented service with relatively easy-to-use information banks. CompuServe even publishes a magazine, *Online Today*, for its members. For information, write to CompuServe, 5000 Arlington Center, Columbus, OH 43220. More research-oriented databases include Dialog Information Services (3460 Hillview Ave., Palo Alto, CA 94304) and Newsnet (945 Haverford Rd., Bryn Mawr, PA 19010), an online service compiling 300 business newsletters.

INSURANCE SALES

☐ Start-up costs: None
☐ Estimated hours per week: 8 to 16
☐ Number of staffers needed for start-up (including founder): 1

Direct sales offer you an excellent moonlighting opportunity—an opportunity limited only by your own ambition and perseverance. There are many kinds of products and services you can sell, but insurance is particularly attractive because most companies offer training programs, even to part-timers. In addition, insurance selling is regarded as a profession, so there's some status attached to the field.

WHAT YOU'LL DO

You can sell many types of insurance. Life insurance is one of the easiest for the moonlighter because the demand for this type of insurance is high. Disability and auto insurance are also relatively easy to sell. The job can be done after typical working hours and on weekends. In fact, those hours are often the best times to reach potential buyers.

FIRST CONTACT

You can find out about local opportunities by contacting a general agent in your area. A general agent has overall charge of a particular geographic area for an insurance firm. In most cases, the general agent will either enroll you in a company training program or at least give you some personal coaching on sales techniques and practices. You'll also need a license before you hit the streets; the license is granted after an exam given by the state government at various locations within the state. (If you live near a state border and want to work both sides, you'll need to take exams in two states, as the licenses typically are not reciprocal.)

SELLING THE GOODS

Many people have a very unflattering view of insurance sales—the image usually involves a hardnosed salesman browbeating a prospect. As successful salespeople point out, it's really not like that. Insurance sales can be quite pleasant, and often involve dealing with people who really want the product and need advice as to the best plan.

Your goal is to circulate, meet as many people as you can, and follow up on likely prospects. Sometimes, you'll limit yourself to a certain group—businesspeople, perhaps—and use your network of contacts to generate sales. In that regard, insurance sales can be a good complement to your regular job, especially if you deal with a large number of people during the day.

PROFIT POTENTIAL

Payback works differently with each company, but you'll usually get a large percentage of the first year's premium payment and a smaller percentage after that. For example, if you sold a policy with a $100 premium, you might get 50 percent—$50—the first year, and 5 percent each year after that until the policy was fully paid. Larger policies can produce attractive commissions, and if you sell many policies the yearly income can be substantial.

STARTING UP

Call local insurance companies and ask to speak to the general agent. Inquire about opportunities for part-timers and the training that is available.

Remember that even though you'll be selling for a company, you'll be working for yourself. In fact, that's usually part of the deal: you're an independent contractor and can work at your own pace in your own territory.

INTERIOR DECORATOR

☐ Start-up costs: About $400 and up.
☐ Estimated hours per week: 4 to 15
☐ Number of staffers needed for start-up (including founder): 1

If you have a flair for color, an eye for balance, and an appreciation of the classical principles of design, interior decorating might be the field for you. It can be done part-time, and the rewards—financial and creative—are sometimes exceptional.

STARTING IN THE BUSINESS

There are several options for the novice. One decorator, for example, started with a $400 investment, which allowed her access to a company's samples and catalog. She now specializes in draperies and upholstery, and reports that the business is showing great promise.

Another very successful decorator started in her home and announced the start-up of her business by having her children put fliers on the windshields of cars in the parking lots of upscale furniture stores. To this day she does very little advertising but does a whopping business—all from an enterprise she started from scratch.

Basically, you can start at almost any level, from a no-investment operation based in your garage to a full-fledged franchise. But remember, you have to be able to do the work and you must interact well with people.

QUALIFICATIONS

Anyone can call himself or herself a decorator, but not everyone can actually put together a coherent decorating scheme. To do this, you need

- A certain amount of training, whether formal or informal, in the rules of design.
- A good sense of color and color mix.
- A knowledge of the products and workings of the home decoration field. You need to understand such things as the structure of furniture and the composition of wallpaper.

The American Society of Interior Designers (1430 Broadway, New York, NY 10018) offers certification following a series of exams. In addition to the prestige of belonging to the association, you can take advantage of special reports and programs dealing with professional practices.

HOW TO START

One good option is to start doing jobs for friends and relatives. Also, speak before groups, especially women's groups, and give some courses in interior decoration at the local adult education center. Once you're established, you might take out a Yellow Page listing. Some decorators contend that for their field, a small ad in the Yellow Pages works just as well as a large one.

THE BUSINESS OF BEAUTY

A decorator often generates income by marking up a customer's purchases, charging 20 percent of whatever amount the customer spends on furniture, draperies, and floor coverings. If you take a job on an hourly rate, that rate generally will be between $35 and $50 an hour.

RESOURCES

You can learn a great deal about decorating trends and about advertised franchise opportunities by reading *Interior Design* magazine (475 Park Ave. S., New York, NY 10016). Good reference books include *The Home Book* by Terence Conran (Little, Brown) and *The Complete Book of Home Design* by Mary Gilliatt (Little, Brown).

INVENTOR

☐ Start-up costs: Highly variable, but in most cases you'll need several thousand dollars for models and marketing studies, and if you elect to seek a patent, several thousand more could be required. But some inventions have been made on minimal budgets.

☐ Estimated hours per week: 5 to 15, but this is obviously quite variable.

☐ Number of staffers needed for start-up (including founder): 1

You don't have to be a scientist to be an inventor, and you don't have to have a totally original brainstorm. In fact, most inventions are simply improvements on existing ideas. Thomas Edison, for example, did not really invent the electric lamp, but he did improve existing models and make them workable and marketable.

IDEAS INTO CASH

Regular people across the nation have come up with ideas that proved profitable:

- A California couple, irritated that portable cassette players with earphones prevented them from hearing street sounds when jogging, invented a set of speakers that clip on to a collar or cap. At last count, the units were expected to bring in $100,000 annual revenue.
- An Italian immigrant from San Rafael, California, became outraged that corkscrews would deposit cork debris in bottles of fine wines. As a result, he invented a grabbing device to remove cork fragments from the bottle. The company reported close to a million dollars in sales in one year.

None of these people were scientists, mad or otherwise, or had extensive laboratory facilities. They were typical people who *had a better idea*.

HOW INVENTING WORKS ─────────────────────

That, of course, is the heart of the inventing business. Most often, someone has a pet peeve and comes up with a working model that does something better, more efficiently, or more cheaply. In this regard, people who are mechanically inclined do have an advantage.

But as long as you can illustrate the idea somehow and document that it is yours (documentation, step by step, is a very important part of the business), you might be able to sell your concept.

THE BUSINESS END ─────────────────────────

You can sell an idea in a number of ways, but these are the three basic processes:

- Selling an unpatented idea. Many firms will agree to discuss your idea if you sign a disclosure form up front, pledging that you will not sue them should a similar product turn out to be profitable for them. Firms do have a realistic fear in this regard, since they may have already conducted substantial research into the same area you're investigating. If you sell the idea outright, you may receive a few thousand dollars. While you won't get rich doing this, you also won't have to go through complex model building and patenting procedures, and you'll also generate some valuable contacts within the company.
- Selling a patented and/or well-developed idea for a down payment and future sales royalties. If you have a really good idea, and have protected and documented your interests, a company may be willing to buy it for up-front cash and a royalty, usually 2 to 7 percent of the selling price. You can get rich on a widely marketed product.
- Selling the product yourself. You'll have to make a huge investment in development and marketing, but the profits can be staggering.

RESOURCES ─────────────────────────────

Invention is a complex area, so you'll need to do a great deal of homework before setting out. Read *The Inventor's Guidebook: A Step by Step Guide to Success* by Melvin L. Fuller (Geothermal Press) and *The Art and Science of Inventing* by Gilbert Kivenson (Van Nostrand Reinhold). Also look at *The Inventor's Handbook: How to Develop, Protect and Market Your Invention* by Robert Park (Betterway Publications). Should you be interested in scoping out the market first, visit the library and consult directories of manufacturers, most notably *Thomas's Register* and *MacRae's Bluebook*.

INVESTOR _____

☐ Start-up costs: Highly variable, depending on how much financial cushion you have beyond your needs and obligations. Whatever your level of speculative investment, it must not be done with money you cannot afford to lose.
☐ Estimated hours per week: 10 to 15
☐ Number of staffers needed for start-up (including founder): 1

While he cautions against any get-rich-quick schemes, California mathematician Charles Huff, a successful part-time speculator, notes that by speculating in investments, "you can quite possibly add appreciably to your annual income with little or no physical effort on your part."

Huff, the author of a book on commodity speculation, is one of the growing number of experts who feel that average people who are willing to devote a great deal of attention to the subject can make a part-time income from investments.

THE NATURE OF INVESTMENT _____

We're basically talking about speculative investments, that is, investments in which there's a potentially high return but an accompanying level of risk. Safer investments are a worthwhile and practical idea, but probably won't qualify as a part-time moonlighting income because returns are so low. But the moonlighting factor enters into speculative investments because, in addition to the gambling aspect, these investments require work—hard work—to keep up with the various markets and to amass the knowledge necessary to compete in the high-pressure world of professional money-makers.

KINDS OF INVESTMENTS _____

You're probably most familiar with typical investments in banks and securities. (Real estate investment is an area unto itself, and is covered on page 231.) While many securities are quite safe, some are speculative, as are investments in commodities.

Here are some basic kinds of investments in which you can make money if you're willing to put in long hours of study and stake a good chunk of your own cash:

- Common stocks. There are no guarantees in common stocks, and some are quite risky. The speculative investor typically looks for "bargain" stocks, which sell for an artificially low price, or "cinderella" stocks, which offer the possibility of quick turnaround.
- Bonds. High-rated municipal bonds can be a very safe investment, but the speculative investor stands to reap higher profits (or losses) from riskier, lower-rated bonds. In addition, many speculative investors buy "zero-coupon bonds," investments which return no cash at all until the day they are due. The risk, of course, is that the issuer of the bond will default and the bondholder will be stuck with no profit. (Normally, bonds pay periodic dividends.) A zero-coupon bond can be worth the risk, though, since some have been known to pay 20 times their purchase price on maturity.
- Commodities. Raw commodities, such as grains and livestock, are bought and sold by people who might not recognize a cow if it sat down at the computer terminal. It's all a game of speculation on the future supply and demand of commodities. It's a risky business, but payoffs can be extraordinary.
- Precious and strategic metals. Any substance can be valued as money as long as its supply is limited; many metals, such as gold and silver, fit that category. Other metals are valuable because of their use in technological operations. Investors frequently flock to metals during times they feel are economically perilous.

RESOURCES

The first thing you'll want to do is learn about the investment business. For an overview of stocks, try reading *Street Smart Investing* by George B. Clairmont and Kiril Sokoloff (Random House); for metals, check into *New Profits in Gold, Silver, and Strategic Metals* by Peter C. Cavelti (McGraw-Hill); for stock investors looking to catch the next Xerox train, check out Roger W. Birdwell's *High-Tech Investing* (Times Books); the world of bonds is covered very well in Robert Lamb's *How to Invest in Municipal Bonds* (Franklin Watts); and for commodities, try *Commodity Speculation for Beginners: A Guide to the Futures Market* by Charles Huff and Barbara Marinacci (McGraw-Hill).

JUNK REMOVER _____

☐ Start-up costs: Assuming you have a truck of some kind, the only additional costs are minimal advertising and promotional fees, plus occasional landfill fees.
☐ Estimated hours per week: 6 to 12
☐ Number of staffers needed for start-up (including founder): 1 or 2

Modern American society turns out a disproportionate share of junk. There's junk everywhere, but especially in attics and basements. Should you subscribe to the theory that a strong back is a terrible thing to waste, you can turn other people's junk into profits.

BUSINESS IS—AHEM—PICKING UP _____

The problems most people face when confronted with a junk-filled attic or basement are

How to take it somewhere.
How to find a place to take it.
How to work up the energy to pick it up in the first place.

Point #1 is easily solved by you if you have a truck or at least a trailer of some sort. Point #2 can be simple if it's only a matter of knowing where the nearest landfill is (many homeowners don't). However, note that in some localities you will be expected to pay dumping permits as a commercial hauler. The situation varies in every community, so find out what's expected of you. Also, learn something about disposal regulations at the landfill; you might not be allowed to dispose of certain kinds of trash or other substances.

Point #3 is what makes you marketable. Cleaning trash out of base-

173

ments and attics is hard work, and busy (or lazy) people are always willing to pay for someone else to do the dirty work.

WHAT'S INVOLVED

Essentially, you'll be doing a lot of lifting and hauling. In many cases, the stuff you'll be lifting and hauling is what the commercial trash hauler won't take or will charge extra to deal with, such as couches, stoves, and old refrigerators. (Again, check local laws, because there are sometimes specific regulations pertaining to disposal of particular items.)

You can do the work alone, but since some things are very difficult for one person to carry, two people are better than one.

MARKETING

Some attic cleaners advertise in weekly community newspapers and report good results. Excellent results have been reported from fliers handed out door to door. This is a good neighborhood-oriented moonlighting job, by the way. It's wise not to book jobs too far away because you'll spend too much time traveling to and from the sites.

Word of mouth will work for you, too.

JUNK AND MONEY

You're not going to make a fortune in attic and basement cleaning, although you can often turn your part-time job into a steady source of income. Try for $8 or $9 an hour, including driving time to the dump. Don't bill by the hour; bill for the whole job, and quote the price up front on your best estimate of how much time the job will take. You'll have to do estimates—accurate ones, at that—but if you stick to your neighborhood, doing the estimates won't be terribly time-consuming.

TIPS FROM PEOPLE WHO'VE LEARNED THE HARD WAY

Be *very clear* with your client about what you will do and exactly what you will and won't throw away. Don't leave any expectations unfulfilled and don't take on jobs you can't handle. Also, be sure you can throw away what you take. In many landfills, for example, you can't throw away old tires; they have to be shredded first at a special facility. Old tires simply will not stay put in a landfill; they rise to the surface with distressing regularity. Should you agree to take a load of tires from a customer's basement, you may wind up with a bunch of bulky souvenirs.

LAWN SERVICE _____

☐ Start-up costs: About $300 for basic equipment and promotion, more if you need to buy a lawn mower.
☐ Estimated hours per week: 5 to 10
☐ Number of staffers needed for start-up (including founder): 1

People who earn second incomes taking care of lawns know two ways *not* to do the work:

- Don't compete with the kids who do quick-and-dirty lawn mowing.
- Don't compete with the high-priced, well-equipped professional lawn services.

What you will do is offer a level of reliable service in-between these two extremes: a careful and thorough lawn job, including trimming, along with occasional seeding or fertilizing.

WHAT HOMEOWNERS WANT _____

Busy people typically want to pawn off the most time-consuming and disagreeable tasks, and those tasks include weeding, trimming lawn borders, and trimming around trees. If you can provide this type of service, you may be able to establish a regular clientele. You'll do more than the casual lawn-mowing 12-year-old, and you'll do it more thoroughly. (Also, remember that it really doesn't take much time just to mow the lawn. Even the busiest executive can usually find time to do that. It's trimming, weeding, and other details that eat up the hours.) At the same time, you'll do less than the lawn services which spray mysterious mixtures of chemicals and charge hefty fees. Sure, you might lay down a bag of fertilizer here and there, but you won't have a tanker truck.

175

WHAT YOU'LL NEED

A decent power mower is essential, of course. You'll also want your own rakes and a reliable power trimmer. Note that when it comes to trimmers, it usually pays to shell out a little more in the beginning for the heavy-duty models. An inexpensive spreader is handy. Most other equipment you can rent. If, for example, a client wants you to aerate the lawn, you can rent the aeration roller (basically a device to poke holes in the ground) usually for less than $20 a day. By lining up several aeration jobs for the same day, you can more than recoup the rental fee.

A pickup truck is handy, but most of the gear you would ever use on a lawn will fit into a station wagon and even, with some maneuvering, into the trunk of a large sedan.

WHAT YOU'LL DO

Provide the services people need: the aforementioned mowing, trimming, and occasional fertilizing and seeding. Try to get the mowing and trimming scheduled on a regular basis—once a week or once every ten days, whatever—with the special services like fertilizing done and billed separately.

Think in terms of earning $10 to $12 an hour. That certainly is a reasonable price, considering the equipment you'll be using and wearing out. To make your hourly fee, you'll have to do some reasonably accurate estimation. However, your experience in doing this type of work on your own lawn will serve as a guide. For example, you know that a medium-size suburban lawn (half acre) takes about half an hour to cut. If the front lawn has a split-rail fence, that'll take about 20 minutes for a thorough trimming. Getting the weeds out from between the flagstones and giving the hedges a quick trim takes another 15 minutes. Sum total: an hour and five minutes, which will probably amount to an hour and 15 minutes including arrival and setup times. If you bill $10 an hour, the total fee is $12.50. Charge your hourly fee plus the cost of fertilizer or seed when doing special jobs.

HOW YOU'LL FIND CLIENTS

The circular-left-in-the-door approach works well. So does word of mouth. Remember, you want to stay close to home to minimize travel time, so limiting your services to the immediate neighborhood has definite benefits. It's just not worth it to drive across town to cut a lawn.

RESOURCES

You don't have to present yourself as an expert gardener, and you don't want to mislead people into thinking that you are. But it is a good idea to pick up some basic knowledge concerning lawns and their care. There are a variety of books available in any store or library, but it's probably more productive to check with your local extension agency to see what publications are available. Booklets from the extension agency will specifically address local vegetation and growing conditions, which are very important factors. A lawn in Florida is quite different in composition and care requirements from a lawn in Michigan.

LIMOUSINE SERVICE___

☐ Start-up costs: $10,000 or more, depending on how much financing you get for the vehicle(s).
☐ Estimated hours per week: 10 to 30
☐ Number of staffers needed for start-up (including founder): 1 or 2

The type of service commonly associated with limousines is the stretch limo which ferries executives from meeting to meeting or takes well-to-do suburbanite teens to the prom and back. While that can be a profitable business, it's a hard one to manage part-time. After all, what do you say when a client wants to be picked up during your full-time job's hours? But there is a type of limo service that can be manageable for one—preferably two—part-timers. For lack of a more precise term, it's often called a fixed-point shuttle.

HOW IT WORKS

One successful service has two Dodge vans that shuttle passengers back and forth to a major airport at specified times during the day. The ride costs $25, and four or five people are often accommodated at once. You can see the advantage of such a service for part-timers:

- You know when the runs are, so you can plan the rest of your life around them.
- You know almost to the minute (barring unusual traffic problems) how long each run will take.
- There's no problem with drivers not knowing city streets because they travel the same route each time.

The shuttle leaves from a specified location (such as a parking lot), which is much easier than picking up passengers at their doorstep: drivers for other limo services report consistent problems with late customers. Also, drivers don't have to hunt down obscure street addresses.

CAN IT WORK FOR YOU? _____

If there's a need for a fixed-point limo and you can build the service around your working hours, it could provide a profitable return. You can assess need by informally checking on how many people want a service such as the one you propose. Is there a big demand for airport service? How about trips to a certain shopping mall? Do existing services meet those needs well? Can you take away some of their business?

In addition, check the type of people who live in your area. Are there many businesspeople who travel a great deal? You can check into people's occupations by scanning the town or city directory, which will be available at your library.

The formula is simply this: find a demand and fill it. That's exactly what the Los Angeles-based Super Shuttle did, starting with ten vans and expanding rabbit-fashion to more than 250 vans.

START-UP _____

If there's a demand and you feel able to meet it, check into the permits you'll need. In many states you don't need a special driving license, but check with your state's Department of Motor Vehicles to be sure. Make sure you're properly insured. Also, check to see if you have to pay a fee to the airport or other destination where you unload.

To be sure you know what you're getting into, start with a part-time job driving someone else's limo, preferably a fixed-point shuttle. You'll learn the ropes, and find out whether you like the business and what your competitors are up to. You'll probably have no trouble finding such a job, since demand is high.

LIVESTOCK RAISER

☐ Start-up costs: $200 to $300 for several small animals, more for larger animals.
☐ Estimated hours per week: 10 to 30 if animals are hand-fed, less if pastured.
☐ Number of staffers needed for start-up (including founder): 1

The modern emphasis on self-sufficiency has generated new interest in the methods of raising livestock. People with a little land and a lot of ambition have found that their food costs can be greatly reduced by raising their own beef and pork, and a decent sideline income can be earned from the sale of animals not kept for consumption.

A MATTER OF ECONOMICS

Livestock raising combines elements of the predictable and the unexpected. As an example of the former, note that it is relatively easy to calculate the profit from raising a calf. You can buy and sell a calf for approximately 70 cents per pound. The reason you profit, of course, is that the calf you buy at 70 pounds will tip the scales at almost 600 pounds when you sell it.

But the unexpected plays a role, too. Prices for all agricultural commodities are subject to wide fluctuation, and it's conceivable to lose money on livestock, too. You can protect yourself against such market vagaries by keeping a percentage of your animals for individual consumption. For instance, you might buy three pigs, raise them, and sell two; have the third slaughtered and keep the meat frozen. You'll make a slight profit on the resale of the adult pigs, but you will get a major profit from the difference between buying your pork and bacon at the store and raising your own. The "buy-three-sell-two" formula can be applied year to year and, of course, can proportionally be applied to any number of animals up to the limits of your personal consumption needs.

BREEDING AND BUYING

The small-scale livestock raiser often buys young animals, raises them, and then sells them to another person who will raise them to full adulthood. Cattle, for example, are usually purchased by the small-scale raiser when they are practically newborns and then sold as "feeder calves" when they gain 500 pounds or so. Feeder calves are bought by the proprietors of feed lots. Those buyers are equipped to transport and then feed the calves until the animals are *really* large—almost double their weight when bought. You can expect about a 25 percent profit per calf from this strategy.

Sometimes, a small-scale raiser will breed animals from scratch—that is, purchase a cow and produce calves through artificial insemination or, more rarely, natural insemination. While this sounds cost-efficient, be aware that there's a great deal of overhead involved in housing, breeding, and feeding a cow, and that's why many small operators prefer buying young calves. On the other hand, livestock raisers without a great deal of time to feed and care for young animals elect to travel the mother–cow route, because the mother will take care of much of the cattleman's duties.

LEARNING ABOUT THE BUSINESS

Be careful about rushing headlong into animal raising, because there are some difficulties. First of all, animals must be fed and cared for and always deserve humane treatment. And no matter how diligently you tend your flock, you must be prepared for some attrition. One veteran cattleman estimates that 10 percent of his calves die due to illness before they can be sold.

You also need to know something about supply and demand. Buying low and selling high is the name of the game, and as you get more involved in the business you'll find that some specialized knowledge helps the business quite a bit. For example, you can frequently pick up a real bargain when the market is low for certain breeds, but you've got to know where to find those breeds and how much to bid for them.

That's why involvement with local and national organizations is important. On the local level, cooperative groups often pool their herds and flocks (especially lambs) to get a better price at the market.

RESOURCES

National organizations provide helpful information on prices and breeding. There are many such organizations; two you might investigate are the National Cattleman's Association (P.O Box 3469, Englewood, CO 80155) and the Livestock Marketing Association (P.O. Box 901402, 7509 Tiffany Springs Pkwy., Kansas City, MO 64110).

MAIL ORDER _____

☐ Start-up costs: Varies, but at minimum you should allow about $500 for initial advertising costs.
☐ Estimated hours per week: 3 to 10, but higher during start-up.
☐ Number of staffers needed for start-up (including founder): 1

Pulling checks out of the mailbox is an intriguing notion. The fact that many people really do make a sizable part-time income from their mail-order businesses makes that picture all the more attractive. It *can* be done, if you know how.

The technique of mail order is rather complex, so it's wise to invest some time in learning the ropes. After all, you have to make yourself something of an expert in marketing, advertising, and product design.

THE BASICS _____

Essentially, mail order involves placing advertisements, usually classified ads, in various publications. Less often, direct mail advertising is used. Direct mail is expensive when you consider you have to buy a list of, say, 1,000 names, and you can't expect your response rate to be much more than 2 percent. You pitch a product—a product that customers cannot obtain easily in a local store (why else would they shop by mail?) and/or a product that offers great value because of the low overhead involved in mail order.

All sorts of products have been sold by mail. Scanning the advertisements in various publications will turn up pitches for

Books	Appliances	Toys	Artwork
Makeup	Assembly kits	Foods	Recipes
Novelties	Instruction	Job information	

HOW IT'S DONE

An ideal product for mail order should be easily described in small ads and, of course, easily distributed by mail. You'll need a wholesale supply source for your product (unless you've invented your own) and a sound marketing strategy. Where can you advertise to reach an interested buying audience? Many selections are obvious: you can get a pretty fair idea of where to advertise your miracle fishing lure, for example, by scanning the outdoor magazines available at your local newsstand.

Advertising must then be designed and paid for. Because you pay by the word for classified ads, every word counts. Be sure to include explicit ordering directions, including how you will ship the product and payment methods you'll accept. Eventually, you'll probably want to move into larger display ads, and the services of an artist or ad agency will then be helpful.

The ongoing business of mail order depends on your ability to gauge response from ads and realign your strategies with an eye toward the most productive return. People who do this intelligently and diligently can make a great deal of money. One present-day millionaire made his fortune entirely by selling all sorts of strange and unusual gadgets through the mail. Other successes have hinged on medallions, books, and self-improvement courses. Want more proof? Scan the magazines you read regularly. Note that many of the mail-order ads appear month after month, year after year. Those ads wouldn't keep running if they didn't produce.

RESOURCES

Three widely available books give very clear and detailed instructions on the entire gamut of mail-order opportunities. Be sure to read J. Frank Brumbaugh's *Mail Order Made Easy* (Whilshire) and *How Mail Order Fortunes Are Made* by Alfred Stern (Arco) as well as Cecil Hoge's *Mail Order Moonlighting* (Ten Speed Press). In addition, invest a small amount of time and money in reading and answering other people's mail-order ads; you'll find out quite a bit about how the field works.

MANUFACTURER'S REPRESENTATIVE_____

☐ Start-up costs: Allow several thousand dollars for initial travel and telephone costs. Other than that, you won't incur costs other than standard business expenses.
☐ Estimated hours per week: 10 to 20
☐ Number of staffers needed for start-up (including founder): 1

Being a freelance manufacturer's representative is a wonderfully flexible business because you can represent a variety of products and, in some cases, sell goods you manufacture yourself. The latter option can be highly profitable.

WHAT'S A MANUFACTURER'S REP? _____

Essentially, he or she is the link between the manufacturer and the wholesaler or retailer. The rep takes a sample of the product to the wholesaler or retailer, or in some cases a manufacturer who uses the product in a manufacturing process, and sells it.

Many firms have armies of full-time reps, but there are freelancers out there and many of them are quite successful. If you have the flexibility to do a little traveling and make some telephone calls during business hours, this might be a good moonlighting option.

WHAT YOU'LL DO _____

Simply find a product you like and contact the manufacturer. Ask if you can represent the line in your area. If you work on straight commission, no one has anything to lose and you might find such deals surprisingly easy to consummate. All the manufacturer has to risk is a set of samples.

The commission rates will vary, but you'll probably want to receive somewhere in the neighborhood of 20 percent on the first order filled, and 10 percent on repeat orders.

Of course, if you're representing a product you manufacture yourself (see *Manufacturing and Merchandising*, below), you're much farther ahead in the game since all the profit is yours.

RESOURCES

A couple with the unlikely names of Leigh and Sureleigh Silliphant have written a very detailed and well-organized book titled *Making $70,000 a Year as a Self-Employed Manufacturer's Representative* (Prentice-Hall).

MANUFACTURING AND MERCHANDISING

☐ Start-up costs: Depends on what you manufacture or merchandise
☐ Estimated hours per week: 10 to 20
☐ Number of staffers needed for start-up (including founder): 1

Many of the businesses profiled in this book could come under the heading of home manufacturing, including some of the entries related to crafts and woodworking. You can make a profitable business from items made at home, if, of course, you have the capability to manufacture them in your home. In addition, it's possible to sell what you make (or to sell anything else, for that matter) through your own home-based merchandising business.

BASICS

Many home manufacturing businesses have prospered, even grown to full-time. A man who started making antique chair reproductions in his kitchen now has, according to *Forbes* magazine, a multimillion-dollar business.

The choice of what to manufacture is yours. You probably have a good idea of your particular skills and may have gotten some inspirations from this book. Your method of marketing can vary. For example:

- You might sell your product in a "mobile showroom," which can be nothing more than the family car driven from place to place to display the merchandise. You can combine this method of home merchandising with home manufacture or you can supplement your stock with other items you've bought wholesale.
- You can sell mail order. The thriving chair business described above is conducted by catalog. Another highly successful business—which literally started in a bathtub—markets a cleaning fluid through the mail, as well as to retailers.
- You can set yourself up as your own manufacturer's representative and sell the product to industrial consumers. (For details, see page 183.)

RESOURCES

You can get details on the particulars of manufacturing an item from a variety of resources, many of which are cited in the relevant entries in this book. For some good advice on merchandising, read Barry Z. Masser's *$36,000 a Year in Your Own Home Merchandising Business* (Prentice-Hall).

MODEL _____

☐ Start-up costs: $100 or so for a basic set of photos
☐ Estimated hours per week: 3 to 10
☐ Number of staffers needed for start-up (including founder): 1

You may not look like a high-fashion model, but keep in mind that all models are not of the high-fashion caliber. If you have any doubt, pick up the Sunday advertising sections of your local paper and notice the variety of models' sizes, shapes, and appearances. This is not to say that you don't have to be good-looking to be a model; in most cases you do, but there is some latitude in the kinds of faces and body shapes that appear on the modern printed page.

THE MODEL MARKET _____

There are several different types of modeling jobs available:

- Print fashion modeling. Here, you'll pose for the camera wearing a designer's or store's latest fashions. This type of work is quite difficult to come by, since you generally need to be a certain age (usually 18 to 35) and between 5'8" and 5'11". Should you qualify for fashion, though, the jobs are lucrative.
- Wholesale modeling. This involves wearing a designer's clothes during trade shows. Often, this is done at luncheons and dinners.
- Specialty modeling. This includes hands, hair, and teeth.

While most modeling jobs are for women, there is also plenty of opportunity for men, although the requirements are a bit tighter.

REQUIREMENTS

All models do not need to be stunningly beautiful, but general attractiveness is requisite. Large-size models, for example, are needed to show larger women how fashions will look on them.

For wholesale modeling, you'll need to be the right dress size for that particular designer. Different sizes are used, so you'll need to check with the designer or your agency (more on agencies in a moment).

Men face more stringent requirements than do women. While female models can come in a variety of sizes and shapes, male models usually must be 6′ to 6′1″ and wear a 40 regular jacket.

MARKETING FACTORS

Almost all models work through an agency. Modeling agencies take a cut of the model's income—sometimes 15 to 20 percent—in return for finding jobs. You are expected to work exclusively with one agency; if you wish to change agencies, it's considered proper etiquette to quit one before joining another. Modeling agencies are listed in the Yellow Pages.

Sometimes you can make arrangements for wholesale modeling directly through a dress shop, but that can be difficult. Also keep in mind newspaper advertising supplements for local department stores, fashion shows at local stores and malls, and mail order catalogs.

You can make quite a bit of money as a model. High-fashion models in major cities routinely make $75 to $150 an hour, and $25 to $75 an hour elsewhere. Wholesale and department store showings usually pay less, often $5 to $15 an hour.

RESOURCES

There are many techniques models need to know. You can learn about the field in a local modeling school, but be careful when you sign up. Watch out for long-term contracts or unrealistic promises. Be wary of any newspaper ads for models that involve your spending money.

Two books are especially helpful for people intersted in breaking into modeling. For women: *The New Complete Book of Fashion Modeling* by Bernie Lenz (Crown). For men: *Male Model* by Charles Hix with Michael Taylor (St. Martin's).

MONOGRAMMING _____

☐ Start-up costs: Anywhere from $50 to $20,000, depending on the equipment you buy and the level of service you intend to offer.
☐ Estimated hours per week: 10 to 25
☐ Number of staffers needed for start-up (including founder): 1

In the beginning, there was silk-screening, an incredibly messy process in which you would rub ink across a layer of silk, which in turn covered a stencil; the ink would soak through the open areas of the stencil and leave a design on your intended item or article of clothing . . . not to mention the clothes you were wearing at the time, and your kitchen floor. Silk-screening became quite refined, though, and today with the right preparation, you can do this type of work in your home without destroying your immediate environment. In addition, thermal transfer devices and computer-aided sewing machines have made the whole business of putting a design on fabric relatively simple.

You can sell monogrammed items in a variety of ways, and you can start a part-time home-based business at virtually any level.

THE MOST BASIC SETUP _____

Starting at the bottom of the scale, you can buy a Speedball fabric screening kit for about $50 at a large art supply store. This kit gives you the basic materials and explicit instructions to put a design on cloth—say, for instance, a T-shirt. If you want to move up in price and sophistication, check out the professional-quality kits, one of which is offered by a firm called Ulano.

No matter how you start, though, the object is to put a design on cloth. This can develop into a very creative and complex enterprise. For example, one woman, using lithographic film (available in any camera store), produces negatives which she then projects in her home darkroom (see *Photographer,* page 207) onto a special silk-screen stencil material called Hi-Fi Green (available in art supply stores). The stenciling material produces a pattern that can be used to silk-screen a T-shirt, in this case, it carried the likeness of a person she photographed. You can easily get from $12 to $25 for a custom-printed T-shirt, not a bad profit when you buy the shirts wholesale, possibly for as little as $2 each. You can sell shirts at an indoor or outdoor booth, or you can do custom work for retailers or even ad agencies.

THE HIGH END

Now, consider the type of business done by the proud possessors of Meistergram machines. These devices are basically computer-driven monogramming and embroidery machines that can place an emblem on shirts, sweats, towels, and many other materials.

A spokeswoman for the company says that many Meistergrammers (the company was started more than 50 years ago by two brothers named Meister) start at home, and a good percentage of them are homemakers. Many of the Meistergrammed articles are sold to schools (such as sweatshirts emblazoned with the school emblem) or to small retail shops. One South Carolina woman makes her living primarily by emblazoning fabrics with corporate logos.

A Meistergram machine and the related accessories can cost from $16,000 to $20,000, but you'll benefit from having a company representative come to you and help you set up. The firm also provides ongoing telephone support and a newsletter.

RESOURCES

You can write for more information on the Meistergram machine to P.O. Box 1378, Greensboro, NC 27402. There are, of course, many other types of monogramming processes and machines; you can find out about them by reading the ads in various business and trade publications, including *Impressions* magazine (15400 Knoll Trail Dr., Suite 112, Dallas, TX 75248).

Take full advantage of the expertise of the clerks and owners of your local art supply shops. They're usually experienced in many facets of art, and they can be quite helpful if you're considering starting this type of business.

MULTILEVEL SALES _____

☐ Start-up costs: Variable but usually minimal.
☐ Estimated hours per week: 8 to 20
☐ Number of staffers needed for start-up (including founder): 1

Multilevel selling means marketing a product by recruiting salespeople and taking a commission from their sales. Those salespeople are also expected to recruit other "levels"—hence the term. Most multilevel sales organizations are based on selling home products, a subject examined on page 247.

THE BASICS OF MULTILEVEL SELLING _____

What happens is this: You answer an ad or are recruited personally, and attend a meeting with other hopefuls. You then either start selling the product or devote all your energies to organizing your own sales force. The former is probably the best bet for a novice. A more experienced person might do the latter. If you develop your own sales force, you'll want to motivate those people to form *their* own sales forces, since you receive a commission from each tier of the sales effort.

PLUSES OF THE BUSINESS _____

You really can make money in multilevel sales. You earn a generous commission on the goods you sell yourself, sometimes up to 50 percent of the retail price. If you're selling a product such as cosmetics, the Christmas rush can earn you about $15 an hour.

Some people do scale the multilevel mountain and eventually earn substantial incomes solely from the sales of others they've recruited. One Maryland couple used an Amway dealership to finance extensive world travel. A Los Angeles Shaklee distributor maintains that her sales work allowed her to take an early retirement. She also asserts that a part-time salesperson can bring home $5,000 a year, more if he or she recruits new salespeople.

MINUSES

There are some drawbacks. First of all, as in most sales jobs, you'll have to deal with skeptical people. Recruiting is not always the most pleasant of tasks. You'll occasionally encounter people who become quite upset that you've invited them to your house only to participate in a multilevel marketing business. (Some recruiters don't give guests the full story when the invitation is given, saying only that they'd like to talk about a "business opportunity.")

Also, you must invest quite a bit of energy in the work. Your income is directly tied to the amount of time and effort you invest. That's good if you're highly motivated and persuasive. That's not so good if you're laid back, chronically tired, or reticent when it comes to calling on strangers.

RESOURCES

How to Make Your Home-Based Business Grow: Turning Products into Profits by Valerie Bohigian (New American Library) contains a detailed section on sales and multilevel marketing. *Pay Yourself What You're Worth: How to Make Terrific Money in Direct Sales* by Shirley Hutton and Constance Deswaan (Bantam) is a good general guide to the topic. For a guide to sales techniques, check out Carole Hyatt's *The Woman's Selling Game* (Evans).

MUSIC TEACHER

- [ ] Start-up costs: About $200 for advertising, sample lesson books, etc.
- [ ] Estimated hours per week: Anywhere from 3 to 15 hours, depending on the number of students you have.
- [ ] Number of staffers needed for start-up (including founder): 1

It's not often that a person gets a chance to spread a little culture and make a steady income. But if you play an instrument or sing well, you can share your love of your art and make a profit, too. A perfect home-based operation, giving music lessons won't make you a member of Fortune 500, but you can earn a steady $15 to $30 an hour. And in many cases the business can be expanded to fill virtually as many hours as you have available.

WHO CAN TEACH MUSIC?

Those who teach music in public schools need a music degree and certification. Private schools also usually ask for formal credentials of some sort. However, a talented and respected musician probably can teach in private institutions with no degree. And until there are more academic programs in rock music, musicians of that genre usually will find employment with less formal training.

As a home-based instructor, you won't need degrees or certification, although such credentials are useful for establishing your reputation through school-based teaching and impressing potential clients. However, you do need a measure of self-marketing skills, a willingness to get involved in local music organizations, and an infinite amount of patience when it comes to working with students.

NETWORKING

Making acquaintances in the local music community is an important first step because private lessons are frequently arranged on a referral basis. Make a point, too, of contacting the director of the civic band and the directors of church choirs.

Classified ads in newspapers are another useful marketing tool, although their effectiveness varies according to the local market. Private teachers generally agree that the key to attracting students is a steady ad, run at regular intervals throughout the year. Weekly newspapers are good bets as the daily classified sections are often crowded with ads. Many teachers report excellent results from the so-called "alternative papers," the ubiquitous tabloid weeklies aimed at younger readers.

Direct contact with public school teachers can do nothing but benefit your business. Send letters and business cards to teachers in the school music departments. Be sure to mention your playing background as well as your training, including any "big names" with whom you've studied. A follow-up call usually will be welcomed.

With budget cutbacks and the general trend toward so-called relevant education, music programs have been trimmed significantly in many public schools. There may be no instrument or voice instruction offered in some curriculums, or such lessons may be given in groups. A conscientious music teacher, therefore, will often refer a talented student to a private teacher.

Finally, learn to promote yourself. Put up circulars in supermarkets, and leave your business cards in local music stores and in other locations where musicians gather. Or try posting a sign at the community theater. The more visible you are, the more students you're likely to attract.

DEALING WITH STUDENTS

Any experienced private instructor will tell you that keeping students is a bigger battle than getting them in the first place. The attrition rate is quite high, often because the student and/or the teacher is frustrated or because the student is working at too high or too low a level.

That's why a good teacher starts with an exploratory lesson, usually given for free. Listen to the student play or sing; get a firm idea of the student's goals and current level of playing. Respect those goals: if the student wants to play jazz, don't push classical pieces just because that's your great love. Never give unrealistic assignments, because frustration kills a student's ambition as well as your teaching business. Make sure you've picked out a good lesson book relevant to the student's needs and interests. (Don't insist on the book that was right for you.) Visit a large music store and peruse the selection.

If you and the student feel comfortable after the exploratory lesson, you can set up a schedule. Half-hour lessons are usually best for young children, while adults and more advanced youngsters usually need one hour a week. Many experienced teachers recommend that you schedule students one after the other during a certain time period. For example, you might schedule four hour-long lessons for Sunday afternoon from one to four. Students have a tendency to arrive late and linger after their lessons, so you'll avoid wasting time if you have another person waiting in the wings. This encourages on-time conclusion of the lesson and—because it will be apparent that others will be inconvenienced by tardiness—timely arrival.

The rate for beginner's lessons is about $10 per half-hour class, $15 for hour-long classes. If you live in a large city the price might be higher, while small-town teachers may have to shave the price a bit to meet supply and demand. A noted musician can charge from $35 to $60 an hour, but be aware that you can't bluff your way into this level of teaching. Your students will be advanced (often emerging professionals) and will be able to gauge your musical skills quite accurately.

NEWSLETTER PUBLISHER_____

☐ Start-up costs: Between $500 and $1,000 to cover initial printing and mailing costs if you publish the newsletter, under $500 if you edit and design for someone else.
☐ Estimated hours per week: 10
☐ Number of staffers needed for start-up (including founder): 1

No one really knows just how many newsletters are in circulation today. They are seemingly everywhere and deal with every imaginable subject: petroleum prices, stock trading tips, personal health, and so on. Basically, there are two reasons for the newsletter boom:

• Growing demand for specialized information.
• Greater availability of inexpensive layout and duplication machinery.

You can profit from newsletters in many ways, and your business may overlap into several other categories discussed in this book. For additional information, see *Desktop Publisher* (page 101) and *Public Relations Counselor* (page 225).

WHAT IS A NEWSLETTER? _____

Good question. New publishing technology blurs the distinction between a newsletter and a full-blown magazine or newspaper publication. Most people consider a newsletter to be relatively short (one to eight pages, perhaps) and to require less elaborate layout than a newspaper or magazine. Also, a newsletter typically differs from a newspaper in that it contains highly specific information, rather than material intended for the general public. In addition, a newsletter is usually sold by subscription, rather than on newsstands.

Most major firms have newsletters of some description, and these publications are frequently quite a bit more sophisticated than the old-style house organs, which usually focused on such items as company bowling teams and babies born to employees. Today, the in-house newsletter is a tool for motivating production, instilling company pride, and, not infrequently, addressing personnel problems.

NEWSLETTER PROFITS

There are two ways to generate income from the newsletter trend: moonlight as an editor for someone else's newsletter or publish and sell your own. The first option is a good way to start and involves no financial risk on your part. Assuming you're comfortable with words and can learn how to lay out a page, here's what to do:

- Contact the people in charge of publishing newsletters for firms in your area. Almost every large firm will have such a department—ask for corporate communications.
- Offer your services: writing stories, laying out pages, and if you know how, taking photos.

You can easily charge upwards of $15 an hour for newsletter work. If your duties involve farming work out to printers, you may be able to mark up the printing services (adding, say, 10 pecent of the cost to your bill as compensation for soliciting bids, dealing with printers, etc.).

Publishing and editing your own newsletter is a gamble, but the initial investment can be kept quite low, so you stand to lose more of your time than your money. The only prerequisite: you must have information desirable enough to a particular audience that they are willing to pay well for it. For instance, a pair of entrepreneurs created a virtual publishing empire by circulating a free restaurant-review newsletter. Today, the *Zagat Restaurant Survey* is a highly profitable publishing venture with yearly editions for major cities such as New York, Los Angeles, and Chicago.

Ideas may come easily, but finding the market is not so simple. Experts recommend that you do some digging first; identify a suitable market and compose a forceful direct-mail letter to sell your newsletter. You can target likely prospects by obtaining mailing lists. Examine the Standard Rate and Data Services' *Mail List Directory* available at many libraries. You can rent or purchase mailing lists from companies that specialize in the direct-mail business (check the Yellow Pages under "Mailing Lists"), or you can borrow, rent, or buy lists from specialized organizations. An organization of importers and exporters, for example, would be a perfect audience for your newsletter on international trade issues.

Once you've identified the audience, send a sales letter extolling the benefits of your newsletter. Be sure to provide complete, specific information on what the newsletter costs, how to order it, and how many issues will be sent on what schedule. Consider sending a sample copy of your newsletter to prospective customers.

How much to charge? That's a decision that depends on what the market will bear, but err on the high side. Remember, the whole idea of a newsletter is to provide specialized information that people can't get elsewhere. Your target group should be willing to pay well for your inside information, so upwards of $5 to $10 per issue is not out of line for a six-page newsletter. While the initial costs for getting your newsletter off the ground can be quite high, you won't need to spend much on the second and even less on the third issue. Because you're selling your product by subscription, you can use those initial dollars to pay for printing costs and the mailing list.

OFFICE CLEANING SERVICE_____

☐ Start-up costs: About $600 for basic supplies, up to $5,000 for purchase of a specialized machine, plus the price of a vehicle if you need to purchase one.
☐ Estimated hours per week: 12 to 18
☐ Number of staffers needed for start-up (including founder): 1, but usually 1 or 2 helpers are soon needed.

A former museum administrator who ran a moonlight office cleaning service offered this explanation of why he eventually left his day job: The money, he said, was just too hard to resist. Surprised that a white-collar executive could make janitorial work a profitable moonlighting job and eventually a full-time business? Well, the misconception that janitorial work is dirty and demeaning is precisely the reason it's so profitable.

AN IDEAL JOB

According to several cleaning service owners, the business is just about the best moonlighting opportunity available. For a small investment you can run your own business without interfering with your current job because all of your work can be contracted for evening and weekends when offices are empty. And if you don't mind cleaning up your own surroundings, why should you mind cleaning up someone else's?

One successful business owner started his service with an investment of $5,000, which today he feels was a little too much because he purchased expensive rotary floor scrubbers and special carpet soil extraction machinery. You can start a business with considerably less: two good upright vacuum cleaners; a portable canister vacuum; and a generous supply of mops, buckets, and cleaning solutions are all the supplies you'll need. You will, of course, need a dependable vehicle, but the family car will suffice for starters.

GETTING STARTED

If you want to know more about the business, particularly the methods of estimating how much time a particular job will take, start out by working part-time for someone else's janitorial firm. Because of the high turnover in the field, you'll have no trouble getting work. Next, visit a janitorial supply house and talk with a sales representative. These people are experts in cleaning products and practices, and have a vested interest in helping your business succeed. Purchase the supplies and equipment you think you'll need, but don't overbuy.

One problem you'll face is the need for repairs on equipment. Vacuum cleaners in particular suffer frequent breakdowns, so mechanical aptitude on your part is a plus. Buy your equipment with an eye toward ease of maintenance and repair.

PRICING

A small janitorial firm can charge upwards of $20 an hour for cleaning work. Ironically, a large firm won't charge nearly that much because it will deal exclusively in big contacts and volume business. For you, huge volume isn't the key to steady profits. You want good, regular accounts, the accounts a large firm won't want to bother with—but jobs that will supplement your income nicely. Cleaning a small office, for example, might involve two hours a week, with a major scrubdown every month. If you charge $20 an hour, that can add up to over $3,000 over a year.

THE BIGGEST MISTAKE IN THE BUSINESS

Getting too big too fast can kill a janitorial business with frightening speed. One service owner, for example, went from prosperity to bankruptcy when he spread his staff too thinly—neglecting his small accounts —in order to service a major industrial firm. But when the bid for the major firm came up in a year, he lost the contact. Major firms solicit bids for services every year, and price is often the only factor. Smaller firms often don't solicit bids as long as they're satisfied with your service, and they usually are not so concerned with seeking the absolute, rock-bottom bid; quality of the job is important to them. The moral: In the janitorial service business, bigger is not necessarily better *or more profitable*.

FINDING CLIENTS

How do you get your business? Word of mouth is surprisingly efficient. Check first with friends who own businesses that need cleaning; they in turn may have friends who own businesses that need cleaning, and so on. Spread the word. In addition, make some phone calls to local small businesses and ask for the procedure for submitting bids. You might also consider placing an ad in a local business-oriented magazine. While cleaning for businesses probably will be more profitable for you, don't exclude yourself from the domestic market. (See the listing for *Home Cleaning Service*, page 149.) You can find those residential jobs by placing an ad in the local newspaper or in the Yellow Pages.

A final note: You'll probably want to hire help somewhere down the line, and that's often when problems arise. It's hard to convince young men and women to do this kind of work, but remember that money talks. Small janitorial firms are advised to pay their help well—seven or eight dollars an hour, if possible. The payoff for your investment is a reliable staff of dedicated workers.

PARTY ENTERTAINER___

☐ Start-up costs: A few hundred dollars for supplies and business cards if you start out as a one-person operation, several thousand should you start an agency.
☐ Estimated hours per week: 5 to 15
☐ Number of staffers needed for start-up (including founder): 1

Parties are no longer the simple affairs they used to be. Nowadays, a good soiree requires the services of at least one entertainer. And for children's parties, the entertainer is almost a necessity for keeping order. If you have some marketable talents, you can fill this increasingly profitable void. Even if you don't have any talent, you can cash in by starting an agency.

KINDS OF ENTERTAINMENT OPPORTUNITIES ___

Musicians are finding a great deal of work in the party entertainment business. Pianists, in particular, are in high demand. Small combos also do the party circuit; duos, such as flute and guitar, are becoming quite popular.

Clowns do a good business at children's parties. This is difficult work, but people who enjoy children and clowning around in general find it satisfying as well as profitable. Mimes, jugglers, and magicians also can get party bookings.

HOW TO MARKET YOURSELF ___

Newspaper advertising works well for some people, but word of mouth and direct contact seem to be the most effective strategies. Call or send a card to people you see in the society pages of your local paper; those

199

people have a lot of money and are in the habit of entertaining. Also, leave a supply of your business cards at local party supply stores and rental centers.

HOW TO MARKET OTHERS

Should your business take off, you might want to involve some other entertainers. Or you could start an agency, making bookings for a cut (it varies—10 to 20 percent is common) of the fee. Be aware from the start that this involves receiving many phone calls at your home; also, you'll be the one apologizing if a performer doesn't show up. You'll also have to bear the costs of advertising, since an entertainment agency does require a good amount of promotion.

But should your business take off, you could really strike the big time. Some firms, such as New York's Completely Entertained by Colucci, stage elaborate shows using several entertainers and are able to earn hundreds of thousands of dollars a year.

RESOURCES

There are some good resources for anyone thinking about this line of work. Some skill-specific books are *Professional Magic for Amateurs* by James R. Gibson (Dover) and Walter Gibson's *Fell's Beginner's Guide to Magic* (Fell). To learn about the agency business, read *Clowns, Clients, and Chaos: Starting a Hometown Talent Agency for Fun and Profit* by Tom Elliot (TEP Publishing).

PARTY PLANNER

- ☐ Start-up costs: Only a few hundred dollars for advertising.
- ☐ Estimated hours per week: 5 to 15
- ☐ Number of staffers needed for start-up (including founder): 1

Harried hosts simply don't make very good hosts. It's hard to relax and enjoy your guests after being worked into a state of nervous and physical exhaustion during the planning stages of the big bash. That's why professional party planners—often moonlighters with a good sense of organization—are profiting from the boom in entertainment.

WHY A PARTY PLANNER?

A complex party can overwhelm the host or hostess. When many guests are invited or when the arrangements involve hiring an orchestra or a caterer or a florist (or all three), there are just too many loose ends for one person to tie up. Party planners take care of the details and offer their creative touches. In addition, they use their network of contacts to get top-quality help and entertainment for a client's function.

WHAT YOU'LL BE DOING

Essentially, you will

- Coordinate the idea or central theme of the party. Should the client throw a costume party? Is it possible to throw a party with a South Seas theme? You'll have to have the answers (and in some cases, the ideas), but with a little planning and forethought you'll certainly be able to guide your client.
- Manage the details. For starters, you'll line up all the vendors: caterers, musicians, florists, furniture and tent rental agencies, and clean-up services. In addition, you'll be responsible for picking the vendors who provide the best service at the best price or the ones most suitable to this particular occasion.
- Control disasters. Things do go wrong in the business of party entertainment, and that's why you'll usually want to be on hand during the event. You'll make sure that there's enough liquor available, or you'll get on the phone to track down a missing member of the orchestra.

HOW TO CHARGE

There's no set method of determining charges for party planning. Some common methods are the following:

- Flat fee. This has some advantages, because after a few parties you'll be able to gauge what's involved and know how much you want to make.
- Commissions. You take a commission from every vendor you hire. This requires some advance planning, of course, since the vendors will have

to agree in advance to work on a commission basis. You can also turn the equation around and add a markup to the services.
- Per-guest charge. This is usually done when the party planner is supplying an extensive meal. Also, the per-guest option is a good way to price an affair during the preliminary stages when the client isn't sure of the final attendance figures.

You can, of course, modify the above methods of pricing and use combinations of the three. How much to charge depends on how much you want to make and how much you realistically think you can get. Because of the nature of the business and the elasticity of the kinds of affairs to be planned, party planners are usually pretty vague about a "typical fee." (One New York planner puts it at "between $100 and $25,000.") But a realistic bottom fee seems to be about $250; some planners say they average about a $1,000 per party when staging really big shindigs. A Virginia firm which charges by the guest will plan a 20-person holiday dinner party for about $10 to $12 per peson, including food but not including rentals or vendors' fees.

PROMOTION

Yellow Page ads are useful, and newspaper ads in the entertainment section have paid off well for some planners. Send a mailing to the movers and shakers in your area, describing your service. Hints: Mail to people you see listed in the society pages of your newspaper; if you do a mass-mailing, target a zip code in the most prestigious area of town; leave promotional material with satisfied clients and ask them to spread the word.

Also, be sure to leave some literature with vendors, such as florists and orchestras. It will be in their best interests to promote you if you in turn scratch their collective back.

RESOURCES

Party planning requires some basic organizational skills, and you probably either have those skills or you don't. But in addition you need to develop a creative grasp of the concept of entertaining. *Party Planner: For Planning Weddings, Conventions, Business Meetings, Seminars, Parties* by Milly Singletary (Sunset-Phoenix) will give you a great deal of inspiration. Also see Patricia Mahany's *Party Ideas* (Standard Publishing).

PERSONAL DEVELOPMENT ADVISOR

☐ Start-up costs: Minimal in most cases. Advertising and marketing will be the biggest costs. Brochures will cost upwards of $250.
☐ Estimated hours per week: 5 to 15
☐ Number of staffers needed for start-up (including founder): 1

Personal development is probably one of the fastest growing businesses in the country. Everyone, it seems, wants to know how to make a better impression, or how to be a more effective communicator, or how to overcome the psychological stumbling blocks that prevent them from advancing in their careers.

Should you be a patient individual and a good people-person, you can market your skills to folks who are willing and able to pay well for your advice.

SELLING PERSONAL GROWTH

For example, one Boston woman makes hundreds of dollars for relatively brief sessions in which she teaches businesspersons how to communicate more effectively in meetings. She herself is an expert communicator, but bolsters her marketability considerably by offering her advice in an understanding and nonthreatening way.

Should you possess practical knowledge and the essential people skills, you can start your advising business in almost any area. Examples include

- Teaching corporate executives how to talk to the press. If you've had experience as a reporter, you can market this service to press-phobic corporate leaders.

- Helping salespeople present themselves and their product or service more favorably. You can serve as advisor, observer, and practice target for salespeople in any business.
- Assisting people in dressing better for the business world. (See *Wardrobe Consultant*, page 297.)
- Coaching for job interviews. Interviewing consultants mock up employment interviews to provide their clients with practice, feedback and specific interview techniques.

The list is virtually endless and can extend into the areas of public speaking, health, appearance, and management, just to name a few.

MARKETING

Brochures are essential for a personal development advisor, regardless of the particular field. Spend some money and have a quality brochure prepared. Be sure to list any special qualifications, degrees, or experience you possess.

Likely businesses are usually the largest firms in town; they have discretionary monies for training and development. If you can crack a large industrial firm, remember that there are many different departments within a typical firm, and you may generate a lot of repeat business.

The basic problem is making sure that your brochure and other promotional material get to the right person. If you're a specialist in business communications, for example, the initial query might go to the director of training. Should you be an advisor on dealing with the press, direct your inquiry first to the firm's CEO.

BUSINESS MATTERS

Charge whatever the market will bear, but be aware that when people purchase advice they often equate the worth of that advice with what they paid for it. As a result, don't be afraid to ask for a healthy fee; $25 an hour is certainly not out of line for most consulting, and you can charge considerably higher.

RESOURCES

For information on how to set up a practice dispensing advice, see Robert Kellye's *Consulting: The Complete Guide to a Profitable Career* (Scribner's).

PET BREEDER

☐ Start-up costs: Basically, the cost of the animal, which in the case of a breedable pet is usually upwards of $400.
☐ Estimated hours per week: 2 to 5 if you own a breedable male.
☐ Number of staffers needed for start-up (including founder): 1

It's a scene played out in backyards and living rooms across the nation. A human and a pet come to visit; the humans have coffee, while the pets have a...romantic interlude, shall we say. But it's all in the name of profit, as pets can occasionally bring their owners a second income if they—the pets—have the necessary credentials.

WHAT KIND OF PET TURNS A PROFIT?

In most cases, a breedable pet is registered and pedigreed through a breeding organization, such as the American Kennel Club (AKC). But it's more than simply having papers. Today, there are hundreds of dog and cat shows, and the animals that have the winning characteristics are the ones in demand for breeding purposes. Perhaps a certain breed of dog might be prized for its broad chest, and you happen to have a strain with a very broad chest; if so, you're in business. (You could breed horses, too, if you have substantial capital, but we recommend sticking to dogs and/or cats.)

The owner of a male animal of good breeding stock collects a stud fee once it is clear that the female has conceived. The fee might range from less than $100 to more than $1,000 if the animal is a national champion. Sometimes the owner of the male will negotiate for pick of the litter, as well (although this is not so commonly done with cats since litters are smaller). If you own a female, you breed her and sell the offspring.

PITFALLS

It sounds so easy and so natural—and, in some cases, it is—but don't count on your pets to reliably support you through your retirement. Things can and do go wrong. Sometimes newborn animals get sick and die, and it's not uncommon for some of the litter to be too small for show (and therefore for sale) or to have other unwanted characteristics. Some of the desired characteristics won't be shared by the whole litter, either. For example, a breed of cat called Scottish Fold has ears that fold over, but only half the litter will have that salable characteristic. Also, don't forget that even the most self-reliant of animals can't take care of themselves; it's quite a bit of work to take care of a litter of puppies.

LEARNING THE ROPES

You'll have to go to a lot of shows to make contact with other breeders and those who will buy your services. You also will have to learn about the many specialty publications for owners of certain breeds of pets. Another way to make connections is to place ads on the bulletin board in your vet's office.

RESOURCES

Before you start buying animals, learn all you can about dogs and/or cats. Consider the memberships and publications offered by the American Kennel Club (51 Madison Ave., New York, NY 10010) and the Cat Fanciers' Association (1309 Allaire Ave., Ocean, NJ 07712).

PHOTOGRAPHER

☐ Start-up costs: Under $1,000 for a reasonably good-quality SLR 35mm camera, wide-angle and telephoto lenses, flash attachment, camera bag, and other accessories.
☐ Estimated hours per week: 5 to 15
☐ Number of staffers needed for start-up (including founder): 1

It's very difficult to directly compete with professionals at their own game. You wouldn't box with Marvin Hagler, would you? Not for long, you wouldn't. Well, an amateur has something of the same disadvantage when it comes to complex full-color tasks like weddings or industrial photography. The pros have the equipment, the know-how, and, in most cases, the in-house color-processing gear. An amateur can't match the quality and, because he or she will need to pay for color processing and other out-of-house needs, can't undercut the pro's price by very much.

But you *can* make money with your camera by tapping into the exploding in-house publication market. Most major businesses and almost all colleges today have house organs (in-house publications), along with other publications such as annual reports and promotional brochures. The editors of these publications need photos, and they're usually willing to pay quite well for them. How does $200 for one afternoon's work sound? A freelance writer who has only a passing acquaintance with a camera recently added that to his bank account because an editor friend desperately needed a picture of a certain alumnus for a college brochure—and he needed it in a hurry.

GEAR YOU'LL NEED

A 35mm SLR camera (35mm refers to the width of the film) is the workhouse of the industry. SLR stands for *single lens reflex*, meaning that you focus and take pictures through the same lens, with the special reflex system allowing you to look in the viewfinder and see directly through the lens you're going to use to take the photo. This is an important feature, because you'll need to see the different fields of view created by different lenses, such as close-up (telephoto) lenses and wide-angle lenses. Instead of buying two lenses, you may elect to buy a zoom lens, which gives you some (but not all) of the advantages of a separate zoom and wide-angle. You'll also need a flash attachment, and maybe a tripod.

Equipment for developing film and photos may or may not be practical for you. For the type of photo assignments outlined in this section, you can still turn a profit by having your photos printed up at a local custom lab. A lab will usually charge about $10 to print up a black-and-white 5 x 7 or 8 x 10 print; you can easily sell that print for $25 or more. Call around and check on developing prices, but don't bother with those little yellow buildings in parking lots because they specialize in arranging for processing of snapshots.

Most of the photos you'll take for publication will be black and white. The most versatile black-and-white film is Eastman Kodak Tri-X.

PHOTOS YOU CAN SELL

Start by contacting area public relations or marketing people. You can often arrange assignments such as the following:

- Taking photos at a weekend sports event. College public relations offices need photos for publication and for their PR files. You may find yourself welcomed with open arms because the PR director, who might be the one taking the photos now, is probably not crazy about working weekends for free.
- Accompanying a writer and illustrating his or her story. Many writers either can't take photos or simply don't want to be bothered with the chore. You can work with staff or freelance writers for company newsletters or with freelancers writing for newspapers and magazines.
- Photographing company executives. Most PR offices have extensive files on their prime movers, but they may need current portraits to provide to the press.
- Photographing local attractions for the chamber of commerce. Chambers usually provide stock photos for travel writers and for production of brochures. This is a perfect weekend assignment, and a lot of fun, too.

SETTING PRICES

You'll want to make a good average hourly wage, $35 to $40 an hour, perhaps, to start. You'll find that taking and developing photos (or having them developed) is quite time-consuming, and you'll need to charge enough to cover all your time and materials. So a portrait, which takes you three hours to arrange, shoot, and develop, would cost the client at least $115. When the exact amount of photos you'll take isn't specified in advance, you may want to charge a per-diem rate, perhaps $150 for an all-day shoot.

MAKING YOUR CLIENT LIST GROW

Call local firms, colleges, and hospitals and ask for the public relations department. Ask the PR director if he or she uses freelance photographers. If so, ask for an appointment to show some of your samples. You'll make a good impression if you walk into the office with about a dozen good prints mounted in a folding portfolio case.

Phone the editors of house organs and ask if they need a photographer to accompany article writers. Also, contact freelancers whose writing appears in the local paper. Freelancers are usually identified as such in bylines and almost always have listed phone numbers.

If you're skilled with a camera, send resumes to local professional photographers. They frequently hire part-time moonlighters, but be aware that they'll want high-quality work.

RESOURCES

For advice on how to become a better photographer, check out the dozens of how-to books available in camera stores and pick the one right for you. Most are quite good. To find additional markets for your photos, examine a copy of *Photographer's Market* (Writer's Digest Books), available in most libraries and bookstores. More ideas for selling your photos and some practical business guidance can be found in Ted Schwarz's *Starting Your Own Photography Business* (Focal Press) and *Sell Your Photographs: The Complete Marketing Strategy for the Freelancer* by Natalie Canavor (New American Library).

PLANT SPECIALIST _____

☐ Start-up costs: Variable, but usually quite low.
☐ Estimated hours per week: 5 to 10
☐ Number of staffers needed for start-up (including founder): 1

Plants are big business in the United States, and there's a host of ideas you can use to put yourself in business if you're an expert on the subject.

WHAT YOU CAN DO _____

There are a number of possible avenues. Consider setting yourself up in business as one of the following:

- Plant doctor. Some people love their plants but are killing them because of inexpert attention. You'll be one of the few doctors who make house calls, and you can probably save a high percentage of your patients.
- Plant rental service. If you have the space and can cultivate and store plants, you may be able to rent them to area businesses. Here, you'll combine plant rental with plant doctoring, because it only makes sense that you will do the caring and watering of the plants.
- Plant advisor. Consider writing a column for your local paper or doing a telephone call-in program for a radio station. Don't ignore the opportunities afforded by adult education, either; give some seminars at your local community college.

It's difficult to estimate incomes for any of the above businesses, but you'll be able to gauge the going rate once you determine what other plant experts make for their services. Join your local horticultural society or botanical garden, if you're not already a member. You will make connections by going to events they sponsor.

RESOURCES

Assuming you're already knowledgeable about plants, you probably need a reference book for a quick brush-up. You might try David Black and Anthony Huxley's *Plants* (Facts on File). *Entrepreneur* magazine (2311 Pontius Ave., Los Angeles, CA 90064) offers start-up manual for a plant rental service. Check the magazine for an order form.

PLAYWRIGHT

☐ Start-up costs: None except for postage.
☐ Estimated hours per week: 10 to 15
☐ Number of staffers needed for start-up (including founder): 1

A second job is always more satisfying if it fulfills some of your creative urges — giving you a break from the routine of everyday life. Attorney and part-time playwright Ken Ludwig, in an interview in *Money* magazine, noted, "As a purely financial venture, playwriting is no bonanza, especially if you consider what I might earn if all those hours were spent on legal work. But it enriches my life enormously."

Writing for the theater is one of the most rewarding of all the literary crafts because you *see* your work come alive. And you can earn some money at the same time, if you know how to market your work.

THE BASICS OF PLAYWRITING

It's important to start small. Doing plays for local school or church groups will give you an idea of how your words sound when coming out of the mouths of actors. But before you can begin — even at the lowest level — you must know something about dramatic structure and characterization. It's essential to master the techniques used to create suspense, or to place characters in conflict, and to resolve that conflict.

WHAT MAKES A PLAY MARKETABLE? _____

Essentially, a producer buys a play because he or she believes people will want to see it. This might seem simplistic, but the principle of audience supply and demand requires that you keep up on theater trends; know what's playing, and you'll have some idea of what's selling.

Comedies, for example, are currently very hot, especially in dinner theaters. Murder mysteries are also popular.

The ideal play length varies. A few years ago, there was a tendency to shorten plays because audiences were believed to lack the patience to sit through a major work. But today, producers feel that too-short a play makes theatergoers feel cheated. So while there's no set formula, you'll probably want to make your full-length play about 2½ hours long; a one act usually runs 30 to 35 minutes. One act plays are currently enjoying a small resurgence in popularity.

MARKETING _____

You can find a list of play producers and publishers in the *Writer's Market* (Writer's Digest Books), which is available in most libraries. The book also gives explicit directions on how to send in your plays.

RESOURCES _____

Raymond Hull has written two useful books which address both the writing and marketing of plays: *Profitable Playwriting (Funk)* and *How to Write a Play* (Writer's Digest Books).

PRINTING: PRINT BROKER_____

- [ ] Start-up costs: Other than standard costs for business cards and stationery, next to nothing.
- [ ] Estimated hours per week: 5 to 10
- [ ] Number of staffers needed for start-up (including founder): 1; additional people can easily be added on a commission basis.

Print brokers are largely unfamiliar to anyone other than printers and the broker's customers. However, they have a hand in many transactions, and some manage to garner quite respectable part-time incomes.

WHAT'S A PRINT BROKER AND WHO NEEDS ONE? _____

A print broker is an independent liaison between customer and printer. A broker typically does all the legwork for the customer, helps the customer with choices relating to design and typeface, and solicits bids from several printers on the client's job.

Most customers do go directly to a printer, but some simply don't have the time, inclination, or expertise to do so. They hire a broker to handle the details—details that can be intimidating to someone without a knowledge of the business. To familiarize yourself with the business, take a tour or two of a printing plant and ask a lot of questions. *Pocket Pal,* published by the International Paper Company (to order write to Box 100, Church St. Station, New York, NY 10046), is a good introduction to the printing process. Bear in mind, however, that each printer prepares estimates differently, so you'll have to learn each printer's system. You won't be able to build a client list unless you make yourself an expert on printing and, to some extent, graphic design.

LOCATING CLIENTS

Print brokers often take out a Yellow Pages ad under "printers." If you do this, you'll field the same calls that would ordinarily go directly to the printer; it is certainly proper form, by the way, to let the inquiring client know that you're a print broker, not a print shop.

In addition, call on local businesses and offer your services. Restaurants and convention centers, for example, use a great deal of printing services and might welcome your help.

Remember, you're selling a service, so lean heavily on that point in your sales pitch. Let the client know that you can

- Get the best for the job by fielding bids from printers.
- Make sure that the client only buys what is needed and is not oversold by a printer.
- Advise the client on money- and labor-saving tricks of the trade; also, assist the client in eye-catching layout.

THE PROFIT MOTIVE

A print broker makes money in two ways: by marking up the price of the printing job or by securing a discount from printers for having brought them the business; the printers charge the client the normal fee and the print broker earns the amount of the discount. Sometimes the fee will result from a combination of the two methods. There is no universal figure for how much a printer will discount for a broker, and there's no guarantee that the printer will give any discount whatsoever. And, of course, there's no way of knowing for sure just how much a client will pay for convenience. You'll have to decide how much you want to make and strike whatever deal you can to bring in that figure.

INCREASING THE PRINT RUN

Most brokers use a simple trick to keep the money flowing: make the customer reorder through you and not through the printer. Simply include a convenient reorder slip with the first order. To ensure that the customer does not circumvent you, remove any identification of the printer from the work.

RESOURCES

A part-time job in a printing plant will teach you a great deal of what you need to know. Those jobs are easy to get in many parts of the country and are often at night.

Printing is a pretty sophisticated business, so the more you learn, the better. Consider taking some classes in printing and graphics. Also, read *Do-It-Yourself Graphic Design*, edited by John Laing (Macmillan), an excellent guide to the basics of graphics and printing. *Pocket Pal: A Graphic Arts Production Handbook* is useful, as is *The Print Production Handbook* by David Bann (Writer's Digest Books).

PRINTING: SMALL-JOB PRINTER___

- [ ] Start-up costs: a minimum of $7,000, although people handy at repairing old equipment can get by for less.
- [ ] Estimated hours per week: 2 to 10
- [ ] Number of staffers needed for start-up (including founder): 1

Printing is an equipment-intensive business, and as such it is not an easy market to crack if you plan to do it only part-time. The previous entry on print brokering (page 213) described a virtual no-cost way to get a piece of the business. Now, we'll look at a way to get a bigger slice of the printing pie—but first, a word of warning.

Be very careful about investing money in printing equipment unless you already know quite a bit about the field. Most small-job printers who operate out of their homes have had at least some experience in the field, and many work as printers during the day. You can spend a lot of money in a hurry when you buy printing gear, so it's essential that you know enough not to get stuck with a poor piece of equipment or a setup that just isn't right for the job.

PRINTING YOU CAN DO AT HOME ___

Some people, however, do make steady and reasonably attractive part-time income from a home print shop. If you're interested in such a setup, you'll need two basic pieces of equipment:

- A platemaker. This is the photographic device that produces the plate from which the printing is done. A new 11 × 17 platemaker can cost more than $10,000. Used platemakers are considerably cheaper, perhaps $5,000 and up.
- An offset press. An offset press uses the image from the photographic plate to impress a sheet of paper. This process achieves high-quality, sharp detail. A new offset press can easily cost $15,000; used models can be found for under $5,000, but you'll have to be pretty handy to keep them operating perfectly.

In addition, you will need some way of having type set. Much of what you'll print will be "camera ready"—that is, all set to reproduce by the time it reaches you. But clients will certainly want some original typesetting done, too. Unless you're prepared to make a really major investment, typesetting is best farmed out to regular print shops. Modern typesetting equipment is extraordinarily expensive. However, some basement-and-garage printers still set type by hand, which is a craft in itself. Prices for old-fashioned type and frames vary widely. You can also produce near-typeset-quality work by computer (see *Desktop Publisher,* page 101).

Don't forget you'll also require a supply of papers, inks, and miscellaneous equipment.

JOBS YOU CAN DO

The basic equipment described above can only be used for what printers call "one-color" jobs. You can, of course, use any color for which you can buy ink; should you want a piece using two or more colors, you can change plates and inks and run the whole job through the press again, this time imprinting the separate characters or drawings in the other color. But you can't do "process" color work, in which primary colors are actually mixed; this is the method used in making a photo. When printers talk of a "four-color" job, they mean process work in which four primary colors are shot on plates known as separations and laid over one another to reproduce the full range of colors.

This limitation means that you'll only be able to do simple work like business cards, stationery, and some business forms. But there's profit in those products—quite a bit if the work is steady. Experienced printers advise that you can squeeze $30 an hour profit out of most home-based printing jobs through good planning and quick setup.

FINDING CUSTOMERS

You can advertise in the Yellow Pages and in local newspapers, but you'll probably have to refuse most of the inquiries because you won't have the tools for more complicated jobs. Most of your jobs will come from word-of-mouth referrals. Try spreading the word in your neighborhood; many merchants will opt for the convenience of dealing with a nearby printer, even if the work is done in the basement. Also, think about combining home printing with a printing brokerage business; you can always use your gear for the smaller jobs that won't be handled efficiently by the big firms.

RESOURCES

Check out *Do-It-Yourself Graphic Design*, edited by John Laing (Macmillan) and *The Print Production Handbook* by David Bann (Writer's Digest Books). You can also learn about printing by taking classes. If there's a printer's club or association in your area, be sure to join.

PRODUCE GROWER

- [ ] Start-up costs: Variable. You need land, of course, which can be rented if you don't own any; seeds are minimal in cost. Fertilizers and other chemicals can be expensive, but the biggest investment is labor.
- [ ] Estimated hours per week: 12 to 20 during growing and harvesting seasons.
- [ ] Number of staffers needed for start-up (including founder): The more, the better. Good opportunity for large families.

Growing things is not as difficult as the uninitiated might be led to believe. It's largely a matter of being willing to invest the time and labor. Knowledge, while important, is easily obtainable, so don't be intimidated if you don't know a cucumber from a cantaloupe.

THE OPPORTUNITY

If you own or have access to one, two, or three acres of land, you may be able to raise a reasonably profitable cash crop. In addition—and this is a big factor—you can grow a great deal of your own food. So when you add up potential profits, remember to factor in the expenses you won't have at the grocery store.

What to grow? Given the right local conditions, you can grow just about anything, but take an informal survey of local stores and produce stands to see if there are any crops that are in short supply. Flowers, while profitable, often require intensive care and specialized growing conditions. Grains are a large-scale crop, requiring large amounts of land and harvesting equipment.

But small-scale produce raising is a good option for the moonlighter. In most cases, the best bets include crops such as peppers, tomatoes, green beans, and cucumbers. You can harvest a substantial crop of these from a small patch of land. Herbs might also be in demand—deliver them fresh to area restaurants.

THE LAND

What about the land? How much should you cultivate? Five acres is about the most a part-time grower can handle. And in some states, you don't want to go above five acres of cultivated land because it will change the way the land is assessed and taxed.

HOW IT WORKS

Three acres of peppers might be a good option. With some intensive cultivation and really hard work, you could produce about 2,000 bushels of peppers during the growing season. Those peppers can sell for anywhere between $5 and $9 per bushel. Under ideal market conditions, the price can go even higher. (Although it can go lower, too.)

You have a number of options for selling your peppers. Farmers' markets are a good start. Contact your local office of the Department of Agriculture to find out where and when these markets are held. Usually there's only a small rental fee for joining a farmer's market, and all you have to do is set up your produce, agree to clean up before you leave, and play by whatever rules are in force locally. (For example, most farmers' markets insist that you sell only what you personally have grown. There are also some health laws regarding the display of produce; usually, these laws relate only to displaying your goods—produce has to be displayed on a table or some other elevated platform.)

In the case of peppers, you might also sell directly to pizza parlors. Some of these establishments will buy a huge load of peppers in the fall and freeze them for year-round use. Should you have a large crop, you may be able to sell it wholesale to local stores and produce markets. Make some calls on local produce merchants; bring a sample of the crop and tell them how much and when you'll be able to deliver.

RESOURCES

All levels of government in the United States have a firm commitment to agriculture. While you may not realize it, there are many representatives of extension agencies, the U.S. Department of Agriculture, and other services waiting to help you. Expert, *free* advice is as close as your telephone. Start by calling your local extension agent (usually a county agency) and the local office of the Department of Agriculture (start by looking under U.S. Government listings in the white pages). The people you contact will be able to recommend relevant reading matter.

PROMOTER: EVENTS

☐ Start-up costs: Variable, but you'll need enough to cover the up-front costs of paying everyone associated with the event, and that can run from several hundred to several thousand dollars.
☐ Estimated hours per week: 5 to 15
☐ Number of staffers needed for start-up (including founder): 1

Promoting an event is really a simple matter of arithmetic: you have to take in more than you put out. If you can add up two columns of figures *and* come up with an idea that will attract paying customers, promoting events might be a worthwhile gamble.

THE ROLL OF THE DICE

And gamble you will, because the world of promotion is always a toss of the dice. Take, for example, the experience of a Connecticut woman who promoted a Dixieland concert. "We barely broke even," she says. "And the reason apparently was that we booked a high school auditorium;

everyone associated 'high school' with 'amateur' and didn't feel that the ticket price was worth it."

Those are the vagaries of promotion—and good reasons why successful promotion is about 90 percent audience research.

While procedures vary, an entertainment promoter will usually follow these steps:

1. Come up with a concept. Perhaps a rock concert will sell well in your community. Possibly a chamber music event will pull a sizable audience willing to pay well for tickets. Can you book a noted speaker? Maybe he or she would pull a good audience in your community. Again, it's a matter of careful audience research.

2. Scout out the available entertainers. If you're thinking of booking a band, listen to as many as you can, even if it involves traveling to distant cities. You'll not only learn about the bands, but you'll be able to gauge the type of audience they attract.

3. Make the bookings. Here's where you need to get out the calculator. Make sure that expected profits minus anticipated costs will turn a profit.

   Your income is based on the number of tickets sold. Many promoters work on the premise of filling 80 percent of the house for concerts and other entertainment events. People who promote meeting-type events often work with direct mail; since direct mail has about a one percent return rate in this type of marketing strategy, you can anticipate mailing 10,000 pieces to attract 100 audience members. Should you have a very specific mailing list, a list full of good prospects, the return rate can be substantially higher.

   Your expenses include more than the cost of renting the hall and paying the entertainment; you also must cover advertising, printing of tickets, and cost of security for the event. (Many towns and cities have very strict rules relating to the need for police security both at the event and for directing traffic outside; call your local police department and ask for the "off-duty assignments" departments for more information.)

4. Promote the event. Paid advertising is expensive but makes the point directly. Public relations—getting the press to write articles about the event and giving it free mentions in calendar sections—is cheap but sometimes unreliable.

5. Plan auxiliary services. Are you planning to sell food and drinks at the event? Then you'll probably need several permits from the health department. If you plan to sell alcohol, you'll need another permit and some liability insurance.

START-UP

You can profitably invest some time in conversations with officials of the chambers of commerce for the localities in which you plan to promote the event. They're experts on this type of business, and can offer you some valuable help. Another worthwhile way to spend your time is by researching the economics of the community; this has a direct bearing on setting your ticket price. If the surrounding area is poor, for example, a high ticket price will be a turnoff. By the same token, a rich community is often turned off by a low ticket price, because they feel the event won't be worthwhile if they don't have to pay heavily for it.

RESOURCES

There are many books about arts marketing. One which might be of particular use is *Marketing the Arts* by Michael Mokwa and William Dawson (Praeger). You can also benefit from an out-of-date but still pertinent book titled *How to Plan, Produce and Publicize Special Events* by Hal Golden and Kitty Hanson (Oceana).

PROMOTER: PEOPLE___

☐ Start-up costs: None, except for basic promotional pieces such as business cards and brochures.
☐ Estimated hours per week: 5 to 15
☐ Number of staffers needed for start-up (including founder): 1

Promoting individuals is a specialized branch of public relations (page 225). If you can master some of the basics of people promotion, you can test the waters in your locality at little financial risk, and you'll find that the work can be interesting and relatively lucrative.

WHO NEEDS A PROMOTER? ───────────────────────

People promoters find their biggest market in politics. Elections are a very good field in which to specialize because they occur with regularity and often involve generous budgets.

You might be surprised to learn that there's not an awful lot of good, professional help available to the aspiring politician, or even the established politician. This is particularly true in small cities and towns. The mayor of one upstate New York city, with a population of over 30,000 people, has hired college students to work as press secretaries. He simply couldn't find other qualified, even marginally qualified, help.

In addition to politicians, you may also find a demand for personal promotion among local executives. Many CEOs need personal promotion services, which may involve writing speeches or articles under their name, or working mentions of them into press coverage.

HOW TO FIND CLIENTS AND HOW TO SERVE THEM ────────

Politicians are all too easy to locate. They're everywhere. Just give them a call (people running for public office are almost always listed in the phone book) and make your pitch. If you want to mine the corporate world, write directly to CEOs.

You'll probably have the best success with political candidates. If you do get on a politician's payroll, you'll probably be turning out press releases, distributing photos, coordinating the production of advertising and purchase of advertising time, and writing speeches. Promoting personal appearances (and taking care of all the related details) is also a big part of personal promoting.

There's no set fee, nor is there a standard set of duties in personal publicity. But you probably shouldn't take less than $10 an hour, unless you're taking on jobs primarily for the experience, which is an excellent idea if you don't really know the PR business.

RESOURCES ────────────────────────────────

You can see that the duties you'll perform take some specialized skills. There's no substitute for experience, so sell yourself cheaply at first if you have to, particularly if you don't have any background in PR and promotion. If necessary, volunteer to help with the public relations and promotions for a political candidate.

There are many good guidebooks to public relations and promoting people. You can pick up some valuable insights from Herb Schmertz and William Novak's *Goodbye to the Low Profile: The Art of Creative Con-*

frontation (Little, Brown). The *Professional's Guide to Publicity* by Richard Weiner (Public Relations Publishing) is widely available in public libraries and offers an excellent introduction to promotion.

PROOFREADER, COPY EDITOR_____

☐ Start-up costs: $30 to $50 for mailing of resumes, plus incidental business expenses; $50 for resource materials, about $250 if you take a class to learn the basics.
☐ Estimated hours per week: 10 to 25
☐ Number of staffers needed for start-up (including founder): 1

Are you a stickler for details? Do your friends chide you for constantly correcting their grammar and syntax? If so, you can turn your predilection for accuracy into a profitable sideline as a proofreader or copy editor.

MINDING THE STORE _____

A proofreader checks for typographical errors. In the case of publishers, you'll be reading already typeset material which is destined for the printer. In addition to the many book and magazine publishers that employ freelance proofreaders, law firms and other businesses that require accurate documents also hire proofreaders. Also, printing houses hire proofreaders to scan items such as menus and brochures before they are run off in large quantities. It is more difficult to obtain at-home work from printing houses than it is from publishers because they generally want people in-plant to proof many quick jobs. Printers do have some freelance work, though, so don't write them off.

Copy editing involves additional responsibilities. Besides correcting grammatical and spelling errors, a copy editor also checks for consistency in usage, logic of arguments, and accuracy of content. Publishers are usually grateful to find a copy editor who has knowledge in a certain field (e.g., medicine or law).

Some types of copy editing require extensive knowledge of typefaces and design. A word of advice learned the hard way: don't even think about trying to fake your way through this type of work. If you really want to be good at it, take a look at *The Chicago Manual of Style* and take a class in copy editing.

FINDING CLIENTS

Send copies of your resume to publishing houses, magazines, and printers in your area. To construct your mailing list, ask a librarian for the *Gale Directory of Publications,* which lists periodicals, and the *Literary Market Place,* which includes book publishers. With publishers you can often work at quite a distance, although it is handy to be in geographic proximity. Printing work is almost always local.

Your resume should stress any proofreading experience you've had, or at the very least point out your penchant for accuracy and familiarity with the language. Needless to say, any typos in your resume or cover letter automatically disqualify you.

BUSINESS ASPECTS

How much can you charge? If you're just starting out, not much. Think in terms of $8 or $9 an hour initially. As you gain experience and build a reputation, you can charge more; one Boston-area proofreader charges as much as $15.50 an hour for her top-quality skills.

Remember that you've got to do a careful, high-quality job *every time*. One error can embarrass a publishing house or result in a total recall of a large printing order. Some errors, such as in medical texts, could have potentially disastrous results. Even popular books must be scrupulously checked. (Did you hear about the sex guide that omitted the word *not* when discussing safe times for sexual encounters under the rhythm method?)

Copy editors can generally build a fine business if they possess specialized knowledge. Be sure to mention any unusual qualifications you may have (for instance, a master's degree in biology) when submitting your resume to publishing houses. Much special interest work could be sent your way if your skills match up with the house's needs.

RESOURCES

You'll need a good dictionary, of course. And good, to a proofreader, usually means unabridged. You'll have to check highly unusual words and will need a source to verify how words are pluralized or spelled in different tenses.

The Chicago Manual of Style is an essential tool for checking usage and other details. For more specific information pertaining to the printing and publishing process, read *Words Into Type,* by M. Skillin and R. Gay (Prentice-Hall).

PUBLIC RELATIONS COUNSELOR

☐ Start-up costs: None above the standard office equipment.
☐ Estimated hours per week: 5 to 15
☐ Number of staffers needed for start-up (including founder): 1

The field of public relations has undergone something of an identity crisis recently. Because PR can be taken to mean anything from being a corporate vice president of a New York City PR firm to handing out sausage samples in a supermarket, the people who view themselves as professionals in the field have tried to impose some strict definitions on what, exactly, PR is.

Although no one as yet has really succeeded in clearly defining the field, it's generally accepted that a professional PR person usually will perform one or more of these duties:

• Interact with the media, answering press queries and presenting an organization in a positive light.
• Promote the organization, usually by getting free media publicity.
• Prepare written materials, such as press releases, newsletters, brochures, and in some cases advertising copy.
• Work to increase public awareness of the organization, attempt to gauge public opinion of the organization and maintain good relations with the public.

If you can handle these tasks, it's likely that you can succeed as a public relations counselor.

WHAT SERVICES TO SELL

Many organizations need good public relations counseling, whether they realize it or not. (Which is something of a catch-22, because the reason they don't realize their need is usually because of a poor PR effort.)

Unfortunately, the term *public relations* is an immediate turnoff to many organization leaders because they don't know what it means. They may have vague notions of a cigar-chomping press agent parading the company president down the street on an elephant, or worse—from a businessperson's standpoint—they simply feel that the PR results will be too nebulous to measure in dollars and cents.

That's why you should *never* try to sell public relations in your first contact with firms and organizations. Sell specific skills; better yet, sell specific *solutions* to an organization's problems. For example, a freelance public relations counselor offers

- A method to control damage after negative publicity about a chemical company's waste disposal practices.
- Ways to get better play for a company's press releases.
- Brochures that will boost lagging attendance at a museum by exciting tourists' curiosity about a specific exhibit.

HOW TO SELL YOUR SERVICES

Develop your moonlighting PR practice by grabbing a little corner of the market and working your way into more general duties. Writing press release and brochure copy is a good way to start, since many firms need that kind of help. Send a letter to some firms and organizations in your area. For small businesses, direct the letter to the president; small museums and colleges are best approached through the director of development; reach large organizations through the public affairs or corporate communications department.

Even if the organizations you approach have existing PR departments, there's always extra work that needs to be done or a task that the in-house PR person can't handle. Take care when you approach large corporations, however, as you don't want to unwittingly threaten the person in charge of PR. For example, instead of pointing out the department's failures, offer to add something to their already spectacular efforts. Note that PR people are not always journalistic professionals. Sometimes PR duties are assigned to the already overworked director of personnel or marketing, who would probably welcome a freelance PR expert.

Be sure to contact advertising agencies, who are frequently asked to perform PR duties. Smaller agencies sometimes don't have the expertise to do the entire job in-house.

Use your first contact to develop more contacts. The best way to make a PR business grow is through word of mouth via satisfied clients, supplemented by your diligent cold-calling over the phone or through the mail. It's probably not a good idea to circulate a brochure about yourself, because part of a PR person's duties is brochure preparation; so unless you have the skills and money to design and prepare a real blockbluster, you'll be undermining your own marketing efforts by sending a second-rate flier. Listings in the Yellow Pages, in the experience of this author and other PR practitioners, have proven to be largely ineffective for PR counselors.

RESOURCES

Since PR is a broad area, you'll probably need to brush up on skills you now have and acquire new talents and abilities. *Do Your Own Public Relations* by Philip Benoit and Carl Hausman (TAB Books) explains the field from the ground up. *Getting Publicity* by David M. Rees (David and Charles) is a good choice for a PR person interested in generating product publicity. *Fundamentals of Public Relations,* edited by Lawrence W. Nolte and Dennis L. Wilcox (Pergamon), is one of the best textbooks on the topic.

READING SERVICE SPECIALIST _____

☐ Start-up costs: Minimal
☐ Estimated hours per week: 10 to 15. Note that this business is easily combined with a clipping service, and many of the time-consuming tasks involved
with each overlap.
☐ Number of staffers needed for start-up (including founder): 1

There is just too much published material for anyone to keep track of.
Anyone, that is, except for the reading service specialist. If you're a good
reader with an agile and retentive mind, you can cash in on the information overload by doing other people's reading for them.

BASICS _____

You can tailor your reading service any way you like. All you need is a
good library and some basic research skills. Basically, you will read and
digest stories that have a direct bearing on clients. Then you'll prepare a
summary, hitting the high points of the story, and crediting the source.
(Essentially, you're preparing a detailed index, letting the reader know
where to find the whole story.) You'll have no trouble getting material: In
any large or medium-size city there are dozens of daily and weekly general interest, business, and specialty publications which have stories of
vital interest to local business executives.

What might an executive want to see? Examples include:

• Summaries of stories that directly mention the firm or the executive.
• Digests of general-interest news items with a particular bearing on local
  firms. A multinational corporation wants to know about political unrest

in host countries. Companies dependent on particular supplies, such as gold and silver, want to know about anything affecting those markets.

• Summaries and references to stories in specialized publications. A chief executive officer or other high-ranking official in a manufacturing business probably needs to know about developments in literally dozens of related fields. But most executives simply don't have time to read the reams of newsletters and trade journals which have a bearing on their business. A keyed index of story summaries would, in many cases, be a highly valued commodity.

OTHER OPTIONS

Should you be an early bird, you can offer firms in your area an executive summary and index of local and related national news first thing in the morning. If you live near an all-night store, you can generally get local and national papers by 4 or 5 a.m. Should you be a computer whiz, consider delivering your summary to the firm via computer.

PROBLEMS

Some publications won't be available at your local library, and you may find yourself making frequent trips to the offices of clients to scan their trade journals. It probably would not be cost-effective to subscribe to a plethora of journals yourself, but in some cases the company may be willing to buy you a subscription or wheedle a free subscription for you.

Be certain not to appropriate material wholesale from publications. Always give credit to the source and stop far short from reproducing any of the article verbatim. Otherwise, you may be in violation of copyright laws.

PRICING AND MARKETING

The price you can command will vary with location, but you can probably get at least $10 an hour for your services. How many hours will you need to do a particular project? Since you can do the job at many levels of complexity, that answer will primarily depend on how much work you want to put into the project. But here's a valuable hint: Construct a dummy digest for a local company. Make your best estimation of what sort of news they'd want to know about; you'll probably be pretty close. So for your time investment, you now have a marketing tool and a good idea of how long it takes to produce. Show the digest to your prospective customers. They certainly will want modifications on the final product, but you'll have a concrete example of your service to help sell it, and a good idea of the pricing structure.

RESOURCES

Ask your reference or periodical librarian for a basic lesson on using periodical indexes. Computer databases may also be available to you. If you can use an index—and you'd be amazed at how many people never bother to learn the fine points—you'll be able to do the work at an amazing speed. Check out Alden Todd's *Finding Facts Fast* (Ten Speed Press) for information on how to use indexes.

REAL ESTATE APPRAISER

☐ Start-up costs: Basically nothing more than standard office equipment and initial advertising. You'll almost always want to start by working freelance for someone else, and that entails virtually no expense.

☐ Estimated hours per week: 5 to 15

☐ Number of staffers needed for start-up (including founder): 1

First, the good news: Appraisers have a lot of work. There's an enormous amount of property that must be evaluated and valued daily. For example, when a divorce case comes up for trial, an appraiser is often hired to determine the fair market value of the home in question in the case. The same process happens in bankruptcies, seizures of dwelling by eminent domain (for example, when the city wants to build a highway and needs to tear down houses to do it), inheritance cases, and granting of mortgages.

Now, the not-so-great news: It's often difficult to break into the appraisal field. The people at the banks or law offices have usually gotten into the habit of working with a particular appraiser. But veterans of the business do note that there's room for a newcomer if you're patient.

HOW TO START

At the time of this writing, there were few regulations pertaining to who could call himself or herself an appraiser. But check thoroughly before hanging out a shingle, because that situation is in a state of flux.

Some agencies do offer voluntary certification for appraisers. The American Institute of Real Estate Appraisers (430 N. Michigan Ave., Chicago, IL 60611) offers such certification. Passing the exam is not easy, but the membership initials M.A.I. after your name are quite prestigious.

The pros advise that the first thing you'll want to do is get some experience working for other appraisers. They're listed in the Yellow Pages and are often receptive to hiring beginners.

Working for someone else, you can usually expect to make a reasonable hourly fee, but it varies greatly. An appraisal of a piece of residential property usually takes about two hours, and another two hours is typically needed to type up the report. A bank might pay $150 for an appraisal, but sometimes the figure is discounted to under $100 if the bank throws the appraisal firm a lot of business.

RESOURCES

If you're interested in appraisal, you might start by checking out some of the available references, including *The Appraisal of Real Estate*, published by the American Institute of Real Estate Appraisers.

REAL ESTATE INVESTOR

☐ Start-up costs: Several thousand dollars, but since the ultimate goal is to use other people's money, good credit is perhaps a better asset than a limited amount of cash.

☐ Estimated hours per week: 10 to 30

☐ Number of staffers needed for start-up (including founder): 1

Real estate is an excellent investment; no one will dispute that. Real estate is also a very time- and labor-intensive investment. Management time is high, and to make intelligent decisions, you must do a great deal of investigation into potential investments. Should you become a landlord, be forewarned that managing rental property requires a lot of time.

But the time and effort can be worth it, should you enter into this profitable part-time enterprise.

THE WORLD OF REAL ESTATE INVESTMENT

"Investment" in real estate may be as simple as buying your own home (the best basic investment anyone can make, really). But there are many ways to make your money work for you in real estate, some carrying high risk as well as potentially high profits.

Here are some of the more common real estate investment methods being practiced today:

- Investing in single-family homes. Author David J. Grzesiek maintains that single-family homes have outperformed all other types of real estate investments for years. In addition, he contends, single-family home investment is easy to control and easy to understand. Essentially, you buy a property and rent it out, getting some return from the rental and counting on the typical appreciation shown by single-family homes.
- Investing in realty partnerships. You enter a limited partnership with other investors in a certain property, say, an office building. You share in the profits and in some of the risks. Investments in limited partnerships usually start at about $20,000.
- Investing in land. This is tricky, because vacant lots do not always appreciate. But should you have some special knowledge of the neighborhood—for instance, you feel that the lot's zoning is going to change—you could reap a substantial profit.
- Investing on options. You offer a building owner $1,000 for a purchase option on his property for an agreed upon price, say, $75,000. This means that for a specified period, usually a year, you have the first right to buy the property if the owner decides to sell. Should the property appreciate considerably, you make the purchase and then you might immediately resell it, say, for $86,000. Your $1,000 option may bring you $10,000 in profit.
- Investing in rental property. Multiple-family homes and apartment buildings are usually good investments but have some risks and do require a great deal of management time. However, if you have some people skills, you can often make a hefty return on your part-time investment.

RESOURCES

There's no shortage of books on real estate investing, and no shortage of schemes, either. Use your best judgment. When something sounds too good to be true, it probably is. And when it seems unethical, it may very well be illegal. Keep your eyes open.

In the beginning, read everything you can put your hands on. Good for starters: *How You Can Become Financially Independent by Investing in Real Estate* by Albert J. Lowry (Simon & Schuster) and *Financial Independence Through Buying and Investing in Single-Family Homes* by David J. Grzesiek (Pelican). Columnist Robert J. Bruss has written a good, comprehensive start-up guide titled *Effective Real Estate Investing* (Regency Books). And for a good technical and legal desk reference, read through *The Dow Jones Irwin Guide to Property Ownership* (Dow Jones Irwin).

REAL ESTATE SALESPERSON

☐ Start-up costs: Real estate brokers generally incur considerable advertising and other start-up expenses, so several thousand dollars as an initial cushion is necessary. Working as a home-based freelancer for an already established broker or agent entails virtually no expense, except for educational fees to get your realty license. This is a much better way to start your business.

☐ Estimated hours per week: 8 to 16, most of those hours on weekends.

☐ Number of staffers needed for start-up (including founder): 1

The boom in real estate sales means big money for people who can master the techniques of selling property. Selling real estate is not particularly easy, but can be quite rewarding financially.

THE NATURE OF THE BUSINESS

Quite a few salespeople are part-time, and they often operate out of their homes. Real estate is typically sold on nights and weekends, but an increasing number of sales are being transacted during regular business hours, too.

You need a license to sell real estate. There are two general types of licenses: a salesperson's license and a broker's license. A salesperson works for a broker, and in most cases you can't be a broker until you've invested a certain amount of time in real estate sales. So what you'll probably do is to start out by getting a salesperson's license and working for a broker. Should you decide to go entirely on your own—which can be difficult and expensive—you could then apply for a broker's license. By the time you apply, you'll have gained some experience.

You obtain a license by passing an exam which is given periodically in various locations across your state. There are abundant prep courses, and they usually only cost $150 or $200.

HOW TO BE A FREELANCER

You usually can find many brokers willing to associate with you as a freelancer. After all, if you're taken on as an independent contractor the broker doesn't have to pay witholding taxes or get involved with other payroll intricacies.

What happens is this: The broker will usually supply you with names of people who have inquired about a home he or she has listed. Sometimes, you'll come into the broker's office and cover the phones, perhaps on the weekend. Either way, you'll escort potential buyers to the home in question and do your best to close the deal.

MONEY MATTERS

The broker and salesperson earn a commission on the total sale price of the house, usually between 6 and 8 percent. That commission is split between the broker and salesperson; the percentages vary widely. You might call six different brokers in town and literally get six different answers about the split. In some localities the ratio hovers around the 50/50 mark for brokers and salespeople, but in other areas of the country —California, for instance—very large brokerage companies may keep up to 80 percent of the commission. This may seem patently unfair, but remember that a broker who has an office, subscribes to a listing service, and advertises each house listed incurs enormous overhead.

In light of this, you might wish to remain a freelance salesperson and not cross over into the broker ranks. It's difficult to handle a whole operation on a part-time basis, but it can be done. Just make sure you get the experience first—don't risk a lot of money up front until you learn the vagaries of the business and the peculiarities of selling real estate in your community.

RESOURCES

Call brokers in town and ascertain their arrangements for working with salespeople. You can work with several brokers on a freelance basis, but it's generally considered good form to deal with one exclusively; since most houses are multiply listed, you'll be selling the same goods, anyway.

An interesting reference is *The Complete Professional Salesman* by Robert L. Shook (Harper & Row), also *The Great Salesperson* by the same author (Harper & Row).

RECORDING STUDIO RENTAL

☐ Start-up costs: Quite variable, depending on the equipment you buy, but $5,000 is a reasonable minimum. You can shave that figure if you're handy repairing old equipment.
☐ Estimated hours per week: 10 to 20
☐ Number of staffers needed for start-up (including founder): 1

A home recording studio can be surprisingly affordable, and with a little promotion and business sense, it can be profitable, too.

HOW YOU CAN PROFIT FROM A HOME RECORDING STUDIO

One obvious market is the growing number of bands who need demonstration tapes for prospective clients and sometimes for record companies. In order to produce a reasonably decent sound, a tape must be recorded with the components isolated—that is, a separate channel for the singer, a channel for the bass, and so on. The reason is that a really perfect tape has to be doctored a bit, and only a studio setting offers that opportunity. For example, if the singer was a little flat, the vocal track can be recut and the song remixed. Sax a little loud the first time? No problem, just turn down that channel on which the sax was recorded.

Another market for your studio is the growing number of people who produce slide shows, multimedia presentations, even radio commercials. (When a client buys a commercial to air on only one station, the radio station usually provides production facilities for free; but when an ad agency makes a commercial to run on a number of stations, the agency generally rents an independent studio.) Producers need multitrack recording facilities (a concept explained in a moment) to produce the complex audio track for a show or commercial.

A WORD ABOUT EQUIPMENT

Your recording studio will need these features:

- A multichannel mixing console. Such a console can record and play back several tracks on one tape, so that channels can be mixed and remixed. Consoles typically come in channel configurations of 4, 8, 16, and 32; they rise in complexity of operation and cost as the number of tracks increases.
- A multitrack tape deck. You need a deck that can record the multiple channels coming in. Four-track machines are relatively cheap, but the larger models can be breathtakingly expensive.
- A studio configuration suitable for recording. You need soundproofing to keep external noise out and, for the sake of your neighbors, internal noise in. It's also necessary, if you're recording rock music, to have an isolation booth for drums. A narration booth is handy for doing commercials or voice tracks; the drum booth and narration booth can be the same facility.
- Mikes, wires, and stands. High-quality studio mikes are quite expensive—some cost over $1,000 each—but you can generally get by with lower-quality mikes.

MARKETING

Notices in area music stores are good clientele-builders. So are ads in the so-called "alternative" weeklies and other lifestyle publications. If you're going to use the studio for production of commercials and slide shows, contact ad agencies and the public relations departments of local firms. Some firms have in-house AV departments but, contact them, too, because sometimes they don't have very sophisticated audio equipment.

PRICES

It's surprisingly difficult to charge top dollar for a studio, especially when you're dealing with rock musicians who may not have a lot of money. A fee of $25 to $40 an hour for music recording time is reasonable. You can generally charge more, perhaps as much as $45 to $50 an hour, for soundtracks and commercials. A very small studio, of course, will command a smaller price than a large and complex setup.

RESOURCES

There are three very good books that will provide an A to Z education on recording studios. Start with *How to Build a Small Budget Recording Studio from Scratch: With 12 Tested Designs* by F. Alton Everest (TAB Books). For details on recording techniques, check out *Audio in Media* by Stanley R. Alten (Wadsworth), a college textbook available in almost all large libraries. If you're going to get into the technical end of studio design and operations, pick up a copy of *The Recording Studio Handbook* by John M. Woram (Elar Publishing).

REFERRAL SERVICE

☐ Start-up costs: Highly variable.
☐ Estimated hours per week: 5 to 15
☐ Number of staffers needed for start-up (including founder): 1

Here's an idea with no ground rules. Tailor it to whatever situation you wish.

WHAT'S A REFERRAL SERVICE?

At its most basic, it's a service that refers and recommends something to interested clients. As an example, consider the business done by a Los Angeles referral service called H.O.M.E.S. Guild. According to a report in a recent issue of *Venture* magazine, the guild is highly successful; it enrolls recommended tradespeople—charging them dues ranging up to $2,000 a year—and gives their names to people who call the guild looking for a plumber, carpenter, or similar service. The guild will expel members who don't do good work; it also offers a seal of approval which guild members can use in their advertising.

SOME IDEAS

You might not be able to operate on the scale of H.O.M.E.S. Guild, which started as a home-based business and expanded into an office with several employees, but you can operate on a modest scale. Consider a referral service for

- Students and parents seeking tutors.
- Musicians looking for freelance studio assignments.
- Good places to entertain out-of-town guests. (This could be developed into concierge service, page 85.)

Focus on an area with which you're familiar and in which you perceive a need.

REMODELER _____

☐ Start-up costs: You'll usually need about $2,000 worth of tools. A van is also very useful.
☐ Estimated hours per week: 5 to 20
☐ Number of staffers needed for start-up (including founder): 1

With housing prices soaring, today's homeowner more often than not elects to fix, expand, or redo his or her current home rather than look for a new one. While remodeling can be a complex, full-time business, there are plenty of jobs you can handle in your spare time.

STRATEGIES _____

Remodeling involves more opportunities than you might at first consider. You can work out of your home-based business by

- Remodeling kitchens, bathrooms, and other rooms in the house. This route isn't particularly easy for the part-timers, since there are so many full-time pros in the business. But there's heavy demand, and you may be able to grab a piece of the local pie.
- Renovating buildings. Many people buy an old building, redo it in their spare time, and then sell it, rent it, or perhaps move into it. Granted, this can be a gamble, but real estate is about the safest way to gamble nowadays. A Chicago couple, for example, moved to Georgia in 1979 and purchased a century-old building. Using a modest investment and a heavy dose of elbow grease, they refurbished it, opening a deli on the ground floor. While there were some rocky times along the way, the building and the deli are now a success.
- Undertaking specialty renovations. Armed with book learning and some on-the-job experience picked up as he went along, a South Vietnamese

refugee was able to form a company specializing in historical restorations. He works in Savannah (an ideal spot for this type of work) and his company has grossed $3 million.

STARTING UP

You certainly don't have to enter the remodeling field on a grand scale; start small and learn as you go. If you opt for the bathroom–kitchen remodeling field, check with your city or town hall concerning the permits you'll need (there will probably be several). Next, find out what kind of deal you can get from supply houses for cabinets, lumber, and the like. Be aware that suppliers are reluctant to offer new contractors great discounts; it's only after you generate repeat business that you'll be taken seriously and offered the 40 to 60 percent wholesale discounts the big contractors get.

You can profitably advertise your business in the "business services offered" category of the local paper. Spread the word among friends and acquaintances.

RESOURCES

Do some reading. Of particular interest are Michael W. Litchfield's *Renovation: A Complete Guide* (Wiley) and Michael McClintock's *The Home How-to Sourcebook* (Scribner's).

RESEARCHER

☐ Start-up costs: Minimal
☐ Estimated hours per week: 5 to 20
☐ Number of staffers needed for start-up (including founder): 1

- What was the Wheeler Commission, and how did it affect the workings of American railroads?

- What was the critical reaction to *Moby Dick* when it was first published?
- How are delegates chosen for presidential conventions?

These are some of the questions that researchers have been paid to answer. If you have an intrinsic curiosity and a penchant for digging into books and records, researching could be a profitable part-time venture for you.

WHO NEEDS RESEARCHERS?

Writers, college professors, and certain businesspeople frequently need freelance help to dig up facts and present them concisely. Clients may not have the ability, the inclination, or the time to sift through tons of books, newspapers, and periodicals.

Incidentally, the scope of the researcher is now extending to computerized databases, although that kind of research is often highly business-oriented and takes on a different flavor than library work. (For information on computer research, see *Information Broker,* page 163.)

FINDING CLIENTS

It's not easy, but once you find a client you may have a long-term— and profitable—relationship. Some prospecting strategies used by successful researchers:

- Cold-calling on publishers. Many houses need people who can supply facts on a freelance basis, often for use in books by another author or in staff-produced works. Send a letter and describe your services. You probably won't be overwhelmed with responses, but since research is often a long-term assignment you won't want to take on too much too soon anyway.
- Cold-calling on local writers. Regularly read the book review section of your local paper; such sections almost always feature reviews of works by local authors. Authors usually have listed phone numbers; give them a call and describe your services.
- Advertising your services on university bulletin boards. Almost every university library has a bulletin board where researchers, typists, word processors, and the like advertise for clients. Hint: Distribute fliers to faculty offices.
- Advertising in writers' magazines, which frequently carry ads for researchers. If you have a special area of expertise, place ads in a journal or newspaper related to your field.

BUSINESS ASPECTS

Researchers do not make big money. A rate of $6 to $7 an hour seems fairly typical. However, the work is not unpleasant, and no one will be looking over your shoulder to put you back on track if you decide to browse a bit. Also, many researchers find that they can make significant progress in their own work by incidental facts and figures they turn up during work for others. (For example, a researcher hired to dig up facts and figures about World War II stumbled over some fascinating information on rocket scientists; that information served as the basis for a book in itself.)

Another benefit: If you keep copies of everything you research, you'll eventually encounter clients who want the same or similar information. Most researchers feel that it is reasonable to charge the standard rate—the rate charged the first time the research was done—for those second requests. Eventually you'll be able to do the research with blinding speed; you may wish to restructure your fee schedule as your expertise grows. You may be cutting your own profits by charging on a strict hourly method at this point.

RESOURCES

Anyone who discovers how to efficiently use standard library tools such as periodicals indexes, newspaper indexes (especially the *New York Times* index), and card catalogs will have a tremendous advantage over the uninitiated. And there's a simple way to learn the use of such research tools: Pick up a copy of Alden Todd's *Finding Facts Fast* (Ten Speed Press). It's probably the best guide ever written on finding information.

RESUME WRITER_____

☐ Start-up costs: Assuming you have the basic office equipment, only $100 to $200 for initial advertising. Word-processing equipment, of course, will add substantially to the total.
☐ Estimated hours per week: 8 to 14
☐ Number of staffers needed for start-up (including founder): 1

The resume has become an indispensable tool for modern job seekers. Just a few years ago, the resume was a simple recitation of jobs and degrees. But today it's a marketing tool that must compete with hundreds of others. Many people simply don't have the time, patience, or ability to create an effective resume. This dilemma has opened up something of a cottage industry for resume writers and counselors.

WHO QUALIFIES AS A RESUME WRITER? _____

It's not essential to have a background in personnel or employment counseling to help a client frame an effective resume. It is necessary, however, to be objective, to have good interviewing skills, and to be able to spell and punctuate with precision.

You can become an expert on resumes by reading the vast amount of material available (listed at the end of this section). These sources will familiarize you with the various formats and features of resumes. This puts you far ahead of the client who comes to you seeking help. (And after all, clients won't come to you in the first place if they feel confident about doing the job themselves.)

WHAT YOU'LL BE DOING _____

A resume writer must spend a moderate amount of time listening. Spend at least an hour with your client, asking about the client's strengths and weaknesses, related experience, how he or she wants to be placed in the job market, etc.

Eventually, of course, you'll organize those facts into a format that illuminates the client's most impressive achievements and skills. For example, a client with a great deal of practical experience and accomplishments will benefit from a resume that highlights results achieved on the job ("Boosted sales by 52 percent over a two-year period as managing director"). Your job is to succinctly express the client's accomplishments and qualifications in powerful and direct language. There will be cases where a client has few results and little experience, so it will be up to you to dig for what good points there are and stress them in writing.

FINDING CLIENTS

Small ads in daily papers work well. Simply advertising something to the effect of "Resumes—Effective and Confidential, Call . . ." will often bring a flood of responses.

Now, a problem arises. Where do you meet your customer? In many cases, a home office just won't be appropriate. You want to attract businesspeople who may be distrustful of your "homegrown" look. Meeting your clients at their places of work might not be appropriate either, as this is not the place where they want to discuss their job-hunting plans. Some resume writers report good results meeting in neutral territory—for lunch, perhaps—or arranging to visit the client's office after regular working hours. But be sure to ask if you can meet at clients' offices, though, because they may have a private office or may not care about workplace confidentiality.

SERVICES

Many resume writers take advantage of word processing (see page 306) to offer additional services, for instance, personalized cover letters. If you have the opportunity to offer this service, by all means do so. You can charge a small additional fee for this service.

You may also run interference for your client with printers, since many people want professionally typeset resumes. It is perfectly appropriate, in this case, to mark up the printing costs (15 percent or so) to compensate for your time and effort. Basically, however, your job is to objectively evaluate the client's strong points and put those features in writing. Don't lose sight of this objective in the effort to design glitzy pieces.

You can generally charge $10 to $15 an hour for the time you spend preparing a resume, and for the interview time, too. It is common for a resume to wind up costing the client about $100, plus the costs of duplication. Be sure not to charge a price too far out of line with other resume preparers, because prospective customers do shop around for this kind of work.

RESOURCES

As Yogi Berra eloquently stated, "You can observe a lot just by looking." Follow his advice and read up on the various resume strategies and styles. Start with *Resumes That Get Jobs,* edited by Jean Reed (Arco), *The Complete Resume Book and Job-Getter's Guide* by Dr. Juvenal L. Angel (Pocket Books), and *High Impact Resumes and Letters* by Ronald L. Krannich and William J. Banis (Impact Publications).

ROOMMATE REFERRAL SERVICE

- ☐ Start-up costs: About $1,500 for initial advertising and other business expenses, such as cards and stationery.
- ☐ Estimated hours per week: 10 to 20
- ☐ Number of staffers needed for start-up (including founder): 1

The price of housing in many major urban centers in the United States has left many people—even those upwardly mobile professionals we hear so much about—with no option but to share their living accommodations. You can take advantage of the housing crunch by offering a service that brings potential roommates together.

HOW IT'S DONE

Roommate services typically try to match up prospective apartment- or housemates according to their ages, occupations, and likes and dislikes.

Usually, some sort of questionnaire is administered. In addition to the more obvious factors, the questionnaire evaluates such items as

> hobbies
> pet peeves
> religious practices and preferences

Get the idea? You want to match people who share the same general outlook on life and therefore show the greatest chance of succeeding as compatible roommates. In addition to the general matchup questions, a roommate service will ask potential renters for character references, employment references, and references from former landlords.

One strategy involves a roommate service representative arranging a meeting between the parties and acting as mediator.

THE BUSINESS END

Some agencies charge the potential roommate a month's rent for a successful linkup; others charge a flat fee for referrals such as $60 for four referrals (with no other services, such as mediation, offered). In most cases, the service is offered for an existing apartment vacancy, although there's no reason why a simple matchup service (just between potential roommates) couldn't be offered.

HOW TO START

Do some careful checking with your local town or city hall to find out what, if any, restrictions apply to this type of service. In some cases you may have to comply with licensing laws that relate to real estate agents, but that could be no problem if you team up with a real estate professional. Give that idea some thought, as many successful roommate services are tied in with realty offices.

SALES: HOME PRODUCTS

☐ Start-up costs: Minimal
☐ Estimated hours per week: 5 to 20, more if you don't have a full-time regular job.
☐ Number of staffers needed for start-up (including founder): 1

There's something very intriguing about being your own boss, and direct sales of home products offers that opportunity. Since you don't have clients per se, you're not at their beck and call. And because there's no boss involved in the process, you set your own hours and work at your own pace.

OPPORTUNITY FOR EVERYONE

One notable advantage of selling home products is that it's among the most democratic of jobs. Since there's no old-boy network, the field offers unlimited and equal opportunity for everyone, including women and minorities. Bertha Simmons described her moonlighting success when interviewed for *Black Enterprise* magazine: "In 1983, when I was an assistant vice president at Security Pacific Bank in Los Angeles, I sold $43,000 worth of Avon products part time, thus earning $21,500 for myself."

BUT...

Don't forget that this type of money only comes from long hours of hard work. Ms. Simmons noted that she did so well because she sold all the time, everywhere: on her lunch hour and after church. So whatever

247

line you choose to sell—Amway, Avon, Shacklee, Mary Kay, Tupperware—remember that nothing comes easily. You have to go out and drum up sales, and you must be willing to constantly approach people with a sales pitch.

STARTING UP

The way you'll begin varies with the individual distributor, of course, but most will provide you with some training. Mary Kay Cosmetics, for example (yes, the ones with the pink Caddies), makes it a practice to initially pair up new salespeople with experienced sales associates.

Many home products, such as the ubiquitous burping food containers, are sold by the party system, whereby you invite friends and acquaintances to your home or travel to someone else's home. People who sell this way often contend that it's a much less nerve-racking type of sales pitch than the door-to-door cold call.

But cold call you will if you get into direct sales. Many representatives for various lines sell from the doorstep. Bear in mind that this is a tough way to make a living and often not as productive as marketing through parties, or to acquaintances at work, or through various other methods. Even the king of door-to-door sales, the Fuller Brush Company, is moving into retail sales and catalogs, although it still will keep its home sales, which reportedly produce over half the firm's revenues.

Operations differ widely among home products sales firms, but one factor applies to any avenue you investigate: be wary of any direct sales firm that seems determined to make you shell out a lot of money in the beginning. Major reputable firms can get you started for a modest investment or none at all. Carefully examine any deal that involves your sinking hundreds or thousands of dollars into training or inventories.

RESOURCES

The odds are in your favor should you care to investigate the home products field; there are many firms looking for sales reps, and they sincerely want and need people. Look up all the familiar names—Avon, Amway, etc.—in your phone book. The big companies and their distributors maintain listings across the nation. If you can't find a listing in your local phone book, visit the library and get the number from the phone book for a nearby, larger community.

Compare training programs and other opportunities the companies offer in your area.

SCHOLARSHIP, FINANCIAL AID, AND GRANT RESEARCH SERVICE_____

☐ Start-up costs: If you computerize, you'll probably need to invest in a minimum of $1,500 for a computer and a database program. Reference materials will cost another $200.
☐ Estimated hours per week: 5 to 15
☐ Number of staffers needed for start-up (including founder): 1

College administrators often get close to the point of tearing out their hair when potential students ignore the vast amount of financial aid and scholarships available. Much of this money goes unclaimed, essentially because people don't know how to go about searching for it. If you have an organized approach to research, you can capitalize on this market and help people finance their educations.

WHAT YOU'LL DO _____

There aren't a lot of scholarship, financial aid, and grant research services around, so you won't have much competition. This also means that you won't have an established demand for your service, so you'll have to start your promotion, billing, and profit-building practices from scratch.

Your product, however, can be quite appealing as it's not readily available. You'll scan all the available references and recommend appropriate avenues of funding for your client. You might suggest, for example, a group that provides scholarships to Nebraskans who are children of veterans killed in action. (Yes, that's for real.) Or a foundation that gives grants to women interested in pursuing careers in journalism.

You'll charge just for the information, you can't be held liable for whether or not the applicant receives the grant. Your fees will depend entirely on what the local market will bear, but it won't be out of line for you to attempt to get a $15-an-hour return on your search time. You should also charge for the time you spend interviewing the client. You'll want to know as much as you can about his or her background and special interests to find the most appropriate scholarships or grants.

HOW YOU'LL DO IT

Initially, you can scan the available references for scholarships, financial aid, and grants (some of which are listed below). If you have a good memory, you won't have much trouble remembering where to look.

However, your speed and the volume of work you can handle will be enhanced considerably if you use a computerized database. Database programs are available for almost all personal computers. These programs work by allowing you to "sort" on any particular detail. So if you enter the information properly, you would, for example, be able to search your material for scholarships available to

1. residents of New York state
2. people pursing a career in politics
3. minority groups

The beauty of a database is that you could sort for opportunities available to each of the above categories simply by entering the appropriate keyword ("NY," "POL," or "MIN") that you've programmed.

Find clients by advertising in local and college papers. College bulletin boards are also a good bet. Try contacting your local high school guidance office, too. Get them to invite you to give a short seminar to college-bound seniors who may call you later for more detailed information. Or consider a mailing to the homes of high school seniors in your area—their parents may be more interested in your services than the students are!

RESOURCES

Thumb through the banks of information available in bookstores or the reference section of the library. Good starters are *Peterson's National College Data Bank*, *Directory of Financial Aids for Women* by Gail Ann Schlacter (Reference Service Press), and *Peterson's College Money Handbook*. There are literally dozens of other directories of grant money and financial aid.

SECRETARIAL SERVICE _____

☐ Start-up costs: Varies according to what services you plan to offer, but the most basic setup will cost about $2,000.
☐ Estimated hours per week: 6 to 18
☐ Number of staffers needed for start-up (including founder): 1

The communications explosion means big business for people who can help others write memos or letters, do mailings, or pull together presentations. A secretarial service cashes in on the growth in written communications, and you can take several different avenues should you decide to moonlight in this business.

TYPES OF SERVICES YOU CAN OFFER _____

A secretarial service meshes very well with several other services described in this book. For example, you can offer resume writing (page 243), and word processing (page 306). In addition, you can provide

- Dictation and shorthand services. Take a letter? If you can, you'll find this skill marketable.
- Fill-in secretarial and receptionist services. You can set your home-based business up as an agency and fill the needs of area businesses; just be sure that you sign up your secretaries as independent contractors.
- General typing services. You can make a profit with a typewriter, as some types of documents just don't lend themselves to word processing. You'll find particular demand for old-fashioned typing services among firms that use many forms, such as insurance agencies.

NATURE OF THE BUSINESS _____

One advantage of running a part-time secretarial service is that the work, believe it or not, can be quite interesting. Dora Black, owner of the After 6 Secretarial Service in Fords, New Jersey, says that her business gives her a chance to use all the skills she's accumulated over the years. In an article written for the book *Women Working Home,* she noted, "The secretarial/resume writing business requires skills such as communication, writing, ingenuity, imagination, selling, time management, economics, finance, credit, psychology, and a smattering of knowledge about many occupations."

The last point is well taken, for if you can provide some specialized knowledge, your skills will be in great demand. Technical, scientific, medical, or legal skills—or at least a familiarity with the lexicon of those professions—are highly marketable.

MAKING CONTACT _____

And speaking of marketing, don't be reluctant to trumpet the arrival of your new secretarial service. In particular, notify area hotels; hotel guests frequently need secretarial work done, often after hours, and you can profitably fill their needs. Advertising in the classified sections of your local business-oriented publication may produce good results, too, if you indicate that you can handle a firm's overflow during peak demand period.

You'll probably be expected to quote an hourly fee, since most clients really won't have an idea of how long a particular job will take. A rate of $10 an hour is quite reasonable for most parts of the country.

RESOURCES _____

Check out *How to Start Your Own Secretarial Services Business at Home* by S.G. Kozlow (SK Publications) and *How to Start and Run a Successful Home Typing Business* by Peggy Glenn (Aames-Allen).

SEMINAR PLANNER/ PROMOTER _____

☐ Start-up costs: Minimal costs of mailing, fliers, cards, etc.
☐ Estimated hours per week: 2 to 3 for marketing purposes; a seminar a month entails 8 to 9 hours contact time.
☐ Number of staffers needed for start-up (including founder): 1

Developing and leading seminars can be highly profitable and can bolster your other business interests as well—if you know the right way to plan and promote the event.

Before outlining the procedure, let's look at the *wrong* way to put together a seminar:

* Pick a subject and then try to draw an audience.
* Run a lot of ads. Make sure you mention the word *seminar* as often as possible.
* Rent a conference room in an expensive downtown hotel. Add up your losses.

Not an attractive scenario, but one that occurs with great regularity. "There are about 200,000 workshops and seminars given each day in the United States," says marketing consultant and author Jeffrey Lant. "And most of the them don't make any money."

HOW TO BE SUCCESSFUL IN THE SEMINAR BUSINESS _____

But seminars *can* make money if you follow Lant's approach:

- First, sell the solution to a problem, not a discussion of one. Giving a seminar on preventing osteoporosis? Sell the idea of keeping your bones strong and healthy, not a seminar on osteoporosis.
- Go where the prospects are, don't wait for them to be drawn to you. Arrange to hold your osteoporosis seminar, for example, at an aerobics center where you're likely to find mostly women, the population segment most prone to the disease. You then have a built-in audience of those interested in health and fitness.
- Start small. Suppose, for example, you are a lawyer. You could start by giving seminars on no-fault divorce at a community college, which certainly would welcome your hands-on experience in the classroom. Contact a college in the area and arrange to give a seminar in your area of expertise. You'll make a little money, risk nothing, and learn how to be an effective seminar leader.

EXPANDING THE BUSINESS

Continuing with the example of a lawyer giving a seminar on no-fault divorce, let's assume you've given several seminars and you now want to start increasing your income. Now that you've made a name for yourself locally, you can begin charging more for your seminars and hold them for fellow professionals rather than people who attend seminars at community colleges. One way to make a little extra cash is to find a good book on the subject and include the book, at retail price, in the cost of the seminar. You can buy the book at a discount from the publisher, and therefore make as much as a 40 percent profit. With a little more experience, you could write a script and narrate an audiocassette to sell during your seminars. And, of course, each attendee at your seminar is a potential client for your practice.

You don't have to be a lawyer to benefit from seminars. As long as you know a subject well and feel that people would be interested in it, there's a good chance that a seminar could be a success. If you can promote other business interests as well, so much the better. For example, successful integration between seminar promotion and business interests could include

- A kennel owner giving a seminar on raising a gentle but effective watchdog.
- A computer store owner leading a seminar on desktop publishing for business.
- A financial planner offering advice on new tax laws.

There are infinite angles for integrating your business interests into the seminar field, and those business interests can relate to home-based moonlighting or your regular job. In any event, you can generate a good part-time income from seminars. Lant estimates that a well-organized person can earn between $500 and $1,000 per month for one day-long seminar accompanied by two or three weekly hours of marketing activity.

RESOURCES

Money Talks: The Complete Guide to Creating a Profitable Workshop or Seminar in Any Field can be ordered from Jeffrey Lant Associates (50 Follen St., Cambridge, MA 02138). In addition, be sure to attend some seminars; you'll learn a great deal from successful—and not-so-successful—seminar operators.

SHOPPING SERVICE ___

☐ Start-up costs: Minimal
☐ Estimated hours per week: 6 to 15
☐ Number of staffers needed for start-up (including founder): 1

Many people don't have time to shop—or simply hate shopping. And, of course, there are people who love shopping. If you fall into the latter category, you can earn a part-time income and enjoy yourself at the same time.

KINDS OF SERVICES YOU CAN OFFER

You'll have to make a compelling case to convince a client to pay for your shopping service. Service is the operative word here, so add a personal touch to your offerings. Consider shopping for

• Gifts. Many men feel that they are too busy or otherwise unprepared to buy gifts for their wives. Talk with the client about his wife and get an idea of what kind of person she is. Then pick out a proper and expressive gift (maybe the kind *you'd* like to get). Obviously, women executives would also welcome this service for gifts for relatives' birthdays, weddings, etc. Corporations might also pay you to select appropriate gifts for valued clients, or for employees for so many years of service.

- Wardrobe items and accessories. It's generally not practical to buy clothes for someone else, but you can offer a very good service buying scarves, hats, purses, belts, and other coordinated accessories. (Also see *Wardrobe Consultant*, page 297). Many people are unsure about the principles of wardrobe design, so if you are a clothing expert you can find a market for your services. You might also recommend items of clothing to complete the wardrobe, and with some types of apparel (such as blouses) you can buy the item for someone else if you know the proper size.
- Groceries. You can do plain-old food shopping, of course, but if you can offer your client the benefit of your expertise in picking nutritional, well-balanced combinations of foods, perhaps delivered with menu suggestions, so much the better.

With any sort of personal shopping, the key is finding out what the client needs—to save time? Advice on what to buy? Unusual or hard to find items?—and satisfying that need.

BILLING

Some shoppers charge a percentage of the total bill; one shopping service owner asks for 10 percent plus an hourly fee of $10. There are two problems with relying entirely on a percentage of the bill: you may wind up doing a lot of work for small profits if your client wants mostly cheap items, or your client may suspect you're buying the most expensive items in the store just to pad the bill.

Another option is to charge a flat price for the job, say, $15 for doing the weekly shopping. You must be sure, however, that the magnitude of the job stays relatively constant. The advantage of the flat fee approach is that you can combine jobs. If you're shopping for four customers at once, you can earn a hefty fee for a few hours of work.

Give some thought to charging a mileage fee if your shopping takes you far afield.

PROMOTION

Many of your jobs will probably come through acquaintances or acquaintances of acquaintances, so talk up the service. Ads in weekly papers may work well, and you could get some press coverage once your unusual service gets off the ground. Make up a flier describing your services; you can hand it out or mail it to likely prospects. Those prospects just might include harried customers emerging from a grocery store during 6 o'clock rush.

SPECIALTY FOODS BUSINESS

☐ Start-up costs: Anywhere from $200 on up.
☐ Estimated hours per week: 10 to 15
☐ Number of staffers needed for start-up (including founder): 1

A Syracuse woman found gold in French pastry. An Atlanta man turned a sideline into a successful business by making company logos out of chocolate. A New York woman does a booming business in Eastern European breads.

What these people found out is that there's a good and growing market for someone who does one special thing and does it very well.

HOMING IN ON YOUR SPECIALTY

It's this distinction that separates specialty food production from the general food business. You don't try to be everything to everybody; instead, you become the best in the business in your particular corner of the market.

And corner the market you will, if you can produce a unique product and put it in the hands of a buyer. That market is growing; one trade association estimates that the gourmet and specialty food industry grows by 20 percent yearly.

MARKETING

One successful home-based specialty food marketer offers the following two-step formula:

1. Come up with a product. It seems that no product is too bizarre for the modern epicure, but baked goods are among the simplest for a home-baser to produce. Be sure that it's *unique*. Chocolate chip cookies won't set the world on fire, but you might discover a market for your grandmother's Authentic Bavarian Christmas Pfeffernüsse.
2. Find clients who will buy in bulk. Gourmet shops and delis will be your best bets. Supermarkets are harder to crack. Be sure you can fill any order you take on. How do you reach these clients? Simple—take a batch from deli to deli and offer the owner a sample.

BUSINESS ASPECTS

Some deli owners are reluctant to buy from home-basers, but some are not. If you can convince a reluctant deli owner that you're completely in compliance with health codes you can overcome many of his or her objections. You should find out what laws and regulations apply to a food producer in your town or city. (See *Caterer,* page 62, for more information, as well as the resources listed at the end of this entry.)

How should you price the specialty foods you produce? Many people triple the price of the ingredients, but you may have to take a little less or a little more. You'll get less when selling large quantities to a food outlet, because the owner will want to buy at a price approximating wholesale; if he or she buys a large order, a deep discount will be expected. You may be able to get more than three times the price of ingredients if the article in question takes a great deal of work, such as fancy pastries.

RESOURCES

Specialty foods overlap into the field of catering, and there are a number of books of particular interest to caterers and specialty food producers. Try *Cater from Your Kitchen* by Marjorie P. Blanchard (Bobbs-Merrill) and *Cash from Your Kitchen: A Complete Guide to Catering from Your Home* by Catherine Harris (Henry Holt).

SPEECHWRITER _____

☐ Start-up costs: Approximately $500 for general typing and office equipment; or at least $1,000 for word processing gear, which is very useful in speechwriting.
☐ Estimated hours per week: 5 to 15
☐ Number of staffers needed for start-up (including founder): 1

Putting your own words in someone else's mouth may not do much for your ego, but it can certainly fatten your wallet. Speechwriting is a lucrative, if less than glamorous, task for a moonlighter who's facile with language. And if you have a good understanding of a certain field—politics, for example—you can develop a very good business with clients who may not have the time or the skill to persuasively translate their ideas onto paper.

WHY YOU CAN TURN A PROFIT _____

Speechwriting pays well because it's hard work. The trade-off is that simple. Demanding deadlines are almost always part of the job, as are continual criticism and constant revision of your work. To make matters worse, you may write a brilliant speech and get no credit for it whatsoever, nor can you tell anyone about its true authorship. Confidentiality is one of the basic tenets of the speechwriting business.

These conditions are precisely why you can charge $300 or more for a fifteen-minute speech—and that's just for starters. As you build your reputation, you can raise your price to three or four times that level. Unfortunately, your reputation must grow via the old-boy network; since you usually can't circulate copies of the speeches you've written, you generally have to rely on confidential recommendations among the movers and shakers who hire speechwriters.

THE CRAFT OF SPEECHWRITING ⸻⸻⸻⸻⸻

When someone needs a speech, they generally need more than a recitation of facts and figures. Instead, they need a galvanic piece that can entertain, inspire, and inform—all within the space of a few minutes. Frequently, detailed and highly accurate research is required. In addition, the speechwriter has the heavy burden of tailoring the work both to the audience and to the speaker.

Before you happily begin to write, ask yourself and the client a few basic questions: Is the audience likely to be large and restive? If so, you'll need to punch up the speech with a few well-chosen jokes and anecdotes. Does the speaker tend to stumble over his words? Then it's your job to use simple and flowing verbiage; tongue-twisting phrases will cost your client his or her dignity and may cost you your next assignment.

FINDING CLIENTS ⸻⸻⸻⸻⸻

Writing or calling local politicians or local political party headquarters is a good way to start. It's wise to try to cultivate your political jobs on only one side of the street, however: the Republican candidate is not likely to continue to engage your services if it's discovered you've been writing for the Democrats, too. Large corporations are often more lucrative markets for speechwriting than are political organizations; to crack a corporate market, write or call the public relations department or the executive who serves as the assistant to the chief executive officer.

If you get a bite, make an appointment and discuss the project. Don't forget to specify the fee and the schedule on which the fee is to be paid. Speechwriter Mike McCarville, who has penned over 400 speeches, recommends that you ask for 25 percent of the fee up front, 25 percent upon delivery of the first draft, and the remainder when the work is completed. Be particularly cautious about getting money up front when dealing with politicians. They and their sources of money are notoriously undependable.

PROFESSIONAL PRACTICE ⸻⸻⸻⸻⸻

These three hints can help you keep your clients happy and expand your business:

- Use a word processor. Speeches go through many revisions, and a little computerized help can save you lots of time.
- *Read* the speech to your client first, instead of immediately handing him or her a draft. A speech is meant to be spoken. Instead of giving your

client a draft, make him or her *listen* to it. This conveys the true impact of the speech and keeps the client from getting mired in picking over minor points like individual word choices.

- When the job's over, ask your client to recommend you to colleagues.

RESOURCES

Any of the public speaking books available in libraries and bookstores will give you an idea of the structure of a successful speech. In addition, you can learn about speechwriting technique by reading top speeches both to yourself and aloud; important works are reprinted in a periodical titled *Vital Speeches of the Day,* which is available in almost all libraries. Read and analyze these speeches for pacing and content. Also analyze how an experienced speechwriter writes for the ear, creating speeches that sound good, not merely read well.

SPORTS REFEREE

☐ Start-up costs: None except for uniform.
☐ Estimated hours per week: 4 to 15
☐ Number of staffers needed for start-up (including founder): 1

If you know the rules of a certain sport, can make quick decisions, and have a thick skin, you can pick up a sideline income as a sports referee. You can work freelance, based out of your home office, and the hours are ideal for a moonlighter.

WHO NEEDS REFEREES?

All the sports played in area high schools and colleges, and under the auspices of a local parks and recreation department have to be supervised by officials. Each sport has a referee society which trains and certifies officials; you can find out how to locate your local branch by calling your town or city parks and recreation department. Athletic departments of schools and colleges will also be able to give you guidance on locating the organizations.

WHO ARE REFEREES?

In most cases, sports referees are people who have played the sport in high school or college and want to continue their association with it. Refs and umpires come from all walks of life; they're teachers, coaches, insurance salespersons, construction workers. In general, as a ref, you should be in good physical shape, although you don't have to be able to match the athletes stride for stride to keep control of a game. Knowing the game, and understanding how to position yourself, is more important than being able to race from end to end of the court at blinding speed.

You need to know the rules, of course, but experienced refs are quick to point out that you must be able to apply the rules, meaning that at lower levels, such as Little League, you may not stick to the strict letter of the law.

FINDING WORK AS A REF

After you've been trained and certified, which usually involves several sessions of night classes, you can put your name in with the local sports organizations. (You'll find out more about this at the class.) Demand is highest for such sports as soccer and field hockey, by the way. More established sports, such as football and baseball, have a better supply of aficionados interested in refereeing or umpiring.

RATES

Prices vary according to the level of the game and the standard rates in your part of the country. A high school basketball game will probably pay in the neighborhood of $45. A baseball varsity game may net you $36; a Babe Ruth game $16. A college football game can bring in $50.

STEREO AND VCR CONSULTANT _____

☐ Start-up costs: None except for classified advertising.
☐ Estimated hours per week: 5 to 10
☐ Number of staffers needed for start-up (including founder): 1

Here's a novel idea you can try at virtually no cost or risk.

New technology—VCRs, digital recording, etc.—has made buying and setting up home entertainment devices a real hassle for the uninitiated. If you know a lot about home entertainment equipment and are handy with wires and connectors, you can make some part-time income by helping people select and set up their equipment.

WHAT YOU'LL DO _____

Stereo and VCR consultants often advertise in the "business services" section of weekly papers. The more local the advertising, the better, since people have a preference for dealing with neighbors. Besides, you probably won't want to travel great distances for a house call. Your ad might read:

Need help setting up your VCR? Want some expert assistance in getting the best response from your new stereo system? Need advice sorting out the specs in the ads? Call Jim—555-1212.

A fee of $20 an hour is a reasonable price for a house call. Some jobs may take several hours, so ask some detailed questions about the job during the first phone call. That way you'll be able to allocate your time most efficiently.

KINDS OF SERVICES

Here are some of the services you can offer:

- Setting up VCRs. Not an easy job, especially when a cable hookup is involved. You need to make the right series of connections in order to feed the signals in the correct sequence to allow recording off the cable, for example.
- Evaluating equipment purchases. If, for example, your client wants an expensive graphic equalizer, and has a collection of old jazz recordings, you'll help decide which equalizer would do the best job restoring some of the lost fidelity. If the collection is modern music on compact disc, however, you'll probably recommend not buying the equalizer.
- Getting the best sound from a stereo system. Such simple tricks as raising the speakers six inches off the floor, which significantly improves the "sparkle" of the sound, is the kind of suggestion an expert would make to a client to get the most from the equipment.

RESOURCES

TAB Books publishes a useful line of guides for anyone interested in this kind of consulting. Of particular use will be *Maintaining and Repairing Videocassette Recorders* by Robert L. Goodman and *Successful Sound System Operation* by F. Alton Everest. Your best bet for staying abreast of home entertainment trends are magazines devoted to the field. Try *Stereo Review* (P.O. Box 2771, Boulder, CO 80302) and *Video Times* (3841 W. Oakton, Skokie, IL 60076).

STUDIO MUSICIAN

☐ Start-up costs: Assuming you already have an instrument, you'll incur only the basic costs of self-marketing, such as business cards and resumes.
☐ Estimated hours per week: 3 to 10
☐ Number of staffers needed for start-up (including founder): 1

The availability of relatively inexpensive professional-quality recording equipment has brought about a proliferation of studios throughout the country. Today, ad jingles, soundtracks, even limited-edition albums are being produced in almost every city and quite a few small towns. If you're a capable musician, you can tap into this trend.

OPPORTUNITIES

The foremost opportunity available to you will probably be advertising slogans, known as *jingles,* or, when the music is in the background, *beds*. Ad agencies and production houses need reliable musicians who can work in a tightly controlled environment to produce what must be a precise job. You may work as a singer, or you might back up the vocalist on guitar, drums, or virtually any musical instrument.

Demo tapes also present you with an opportunity for work. Demos are usually done by a vocalist who's seeking work, and the vocalist typically hires a group of musicians to back him or her up during the recording session.

Cutting albums or sound tracks is difficult work to obtain. It's often done only in large cities and under union contract. (And if you're a union musician, you obviously don't need to read this section.) But some albums are cut in small cities, even small towns, so don't be afraid to go after this work.

MARKETING

Recording studios are listed in the Yellow Pages. It's a good idea to visit the local library and check the phone books of nearby cities, too; you'll want to contact as many studios as you can reasonably serve.

Send the studios a copy of your resume and, if you have it, a cassette tape demonstrating some of your work. Also, drop a resume to area advertising agencies; sometimes they'll have a hand in booking, too.

Prices vary widely, but, in general, studio work pays well. Even in a small city you should expect between $10 and $15 an hour, more when you become established.

RESOURCES

Some additional marketing tips and other music opportunities are highlighted in a very good book for the working freelance musician entitled *Making Money Making Music* by James Dearing (Writers Digest).

SWIMMING POOL MAINTENANCE SERVICE _____

☐ Start-up costs: Under $500 for the basic equipment. You can use a car, but a truck is much more convenient.
☐ Estimated hours per week: 10 to 20
☐ Number of staffers needed for start-up (including founder): 1

The best aspect of a pool service is that the work is regular. People generally don't hire a pool cleaner for a one-time-only job; they want him or her on a regular basis, usually once a week. Other jobs that come up, such as minor repairs and opening and closing of pools, are gravy.

WHAT YOU'LL DO _____

Basically, a pool service cleans pools and keeps the mechanical parts of the pool in operating order. You'll skim off the top waters with a vacuum device (which is part of the owner's pool installation), check the chemical balance, and maintain the filter. Many pool owners request a complete cleaning of the pool, which means draining it and scrubbing the sides and bottom with an acid compound.

Pump motors can and do break down, and many pool service people fix those motors on a regular basis.

WHAT YOU'LL NEED _____

You can start with just a pool skimmer, some brushes, and a box of standard hand tools. As the business grows, you may want to have an inventory of gaskets and motor parts, as well as a generous supply of pool chemicals.

WHAT YOU CAN CHARGE

Here, it's largely a matter of what the competition charges. In the western part of the United States, for example, the prices for services are substantially lower than in the Northeast, which may reflect the fact that the pool season is shorter in the Northeast and therefore pool services need to charge a higher rate. In any event, you can usually get at least $10 for a visit, including a skim and a check of chemicals; anything you do beyond that is extra. Opening and closing pools is very profitable; in some areas of the country you can get about $215 for opening or closing a pool.

If you supply chemicals, which you probably will do, you can mark them up about 40 percent over the price you pay from the wholesaler.

LOCATING CLIENTS

Use ads in weekly papers. Have some professional-looking business cards printed up. And don't be afraid to stop in at the homes of swimming pool owners to offer your services.

RESOURCES

Dan Ramsey's *Trouble-Free Swimming Pools* (TAB Books) is written for the pool owner, but it tells you just about anything you'll need to know about cleaning and maintaining a pool. In addition, ask questions of the wholesalers who sell pool supplies. They want to keep you in business—and buying their supplies—so they'll usually bend over backwards to help you out.

TAILORING AND CLOTHING DESIGN____

☐ Start-up costs: $1,000 minimum
☐ Estimated hours per week: 10 to 20
☐ Number of staffers needed for start-up (including founder): 1

Tailoring is an ideal home-based job. The equipment is not tremendously expensive or bulky, and even if you own only a sewing machine and an iron, you can set yourself up in business. In addition, you might be able to eventually expand into marketing your own designs for particular pieces of clothing.

TAILORING: THE BASICS ____

In technical terms, tailoring means custom-making a garment from a pattern. Clothing design extends to creating the pattern and making the garment from scratch. Practically speaking, anyone who wants to do tailoring or clothing design from the home will also wind up doing a great deal of mending and alterations (alterations are also frequently thought of as "tailoring," too).

This is time-consuming, close work. Tailoring a suit could take a week of almost full-time work; if you're so inclined, you could probably clear $400 in profit for this type of job—if you have the time. Simple mending and alteration is less involved and can generally return a $10 an hour profit. Clothing design is a crapshoot in some cases, but it can become highly profitable if your designs catch on. A pair of Florida entrepreneurs stitched together some swimsuits which caught the fancy of an investor. Today they have 125 employees and net $250,000 a year.

WHAT YOU'LL DO

Realistically, though, you're better off starting small. To keep your business humming, you'll want to be well-versed in the types of patterns currently popular and to offer reliable, timely service to your clients. In addition, you'll offer quick fixes on zippers (easy when you have some experience, tough when you don't) and will take in and let out various items of clothing. This last chore can be surprisingly difficult, because to alter some items—men's jackets, for instance—you almost literally have to take the entire garment apart and restructure it.

MARKETING

Word of mouth is a good way to get started. Offer to mend a friend's suit. If your work is good, he or she will tell others about it. Also advertise in your local newspaper. Put up a small sign if zoning regulations allow. (Check on this as well as on union regulations as they pertain to home-based garment work.) Leave your business card in sewing supply stores and dry cleaners who do not offer mending and alteration services.

RESOURCES

Read the wide variety of sewing magazines you'll find in the sewing shops. *The Vogue Sewing Book* (Harper & Row) is a good reference.

TAX PREPARER

☐ Start-up costs: For bottom-level service, nothing other than basic business and promotional costs. But computers are an increasingly important part of the business. Computer software capable of calculating tax items can cost from $200 to $2,000, depending on complexity, and computers to run that software will cost upwards of $1,000.
☐ Estimated hours per week: 3 to 20, more during peak tax season.
☐ Number of staffers needed for start-up (including founder): 1

There's a gray area regarding who can prepare taxes for a profit. According to the Council of Better Business Bureaus, anyone can hang out a shingle as a tax preparer. However, experts in the field of taxation note that if you cross the line into other services, such as offering accounting, you'll need to be a certified public accountant (CPA), which is not something you can become easily. So before starting out as a tax preparer, check with your state Bureau of Accountancy to determine where the line is drawn in your area between tax preparation and accounting services.

THE JOB

In most states you don't need formal qualifications, but you do need to know what you're doing. A serious screwup can cause major problems for a client and for you. There's always the possibility that you could be sued if the mistake represented gross malfeasance.

You can approach the job in a number of ways. You can get a part-time job for one of the major tax return preparation firms; the pay is not great and you won't be working at home, but it's a start, and you'll have access to advice and supervision. There is some night work available, so a person with a nine-to-five job may find some opportunities locally. The big advantage of taking this route is that a 70-hour training course is usually required, invaluable training and experience if you eventually want to go out on your own.

If you're confident that you can handle the work, you can hang out a shingle (figuratively; check with zoning ordinances before you do it literally) and prepare returns at home. With the new tax laws, you'd be wise to stick to the simpler 1040 forms and some of the related schedules. Most people who do this type of work charge about $25 an hour, with a $25 minimum.

PROFESSIONAL GROWTH

If you're interested in establishing some formal credentials, give some thought to becoming an enrolled agent. Enrolled agents are one of three professionals (the others being lawyers and CPAs) who can represent clients before the Internal Revenue Service. Tax preparers cannot provide this kind of representation and are not expected to. Becoming an enrolled agent isn't easy—in fact, passing the test is very difficult—but you don't need a college degree or specified professional experience to take the test. So if you have a broad background in taxation, give it some thought. For more information, write to the National Association of Enrolled Agents (6000 Executive Blvd., Suite 205, Rockville, MD 20852).

TEACHER _____

- ☐ Start-up costs: None except for any special equipment or modifications you may have to make on your home.
- ☐ Estimated hours per week: 6 to 12
- ☐ Number of staffers needed for start-up (including founder): 1

If you have a certain skill or knowledge, there's a good chance some-one else will want to learn it. Several entries in this book specifically address the teaching of certain skills, such as *Music Teacher* (page 191) and *Crafts Teacher* (page 92). But there are many other options; think about what you have to offer and explore the potential market.

ONE EXAMPLE _____

Consider, for example, the case of a police officer who had developed a proficiency in karate. He converted his garage into a gym. The only extensive modification needed was putting down a wooden floor and in-stalling baseboard heaters.

He then advertised in the classified section of local papers and was able to fill two evening classes with 10 students per class at $10 each. Soon a Saturday class for children was filled, entirely by word of mouth.

Regular classes are like money in the bank because you can project growth and revenues. In addition, if the home-based teaching business becomes large enough, you can turn it over to an assistant, paying him or her and pocketing a profit for yourself.

KINDS OF OPPORTUNITIES _____

What you can teach depends, obviously, on your skills and on your ability to convey that skill to other people. Where you teach also depends

on whether you need a special facility or if you can set up a class anywhere. Give some thought to these ideas, many of which might be adaptable to you:

- Public speaking. Here's a course you could teach at home, in clients'
  meeting rooms, or as a seminar. Everyone is interested in more effective speaking, and a course like this is a natural, *particularly if you
  slant it toward business speaking*. One Stow, Massachusetts, business-
  woman takes her business speaking courses directly to high-tech firms
  in the Boston area. Her business is thriving and highly profitable.
- Writing. Many emerging executives memorized the material in their
  technical courses but slept through Freshman Comp. Suddenly, they
  find that their jobs require them to communicate ideas and information
  in a coherent style. A number of entrepreneurs are offering on-site
  courses to teach more effective business writing. If you have strong
  verbal skills, you can probably find a market for them.
- Home improvement skills. Adult education classes dealing with such
  subjects as wallpapering are almost always full. That's an example of
  one skill that people will always want to learn—and one that's very
  difficult to pick up from books. You could teach in a classroom or offer
  your services to help a homeowner put up his or her wallpaper and learn
  the skill at the same time.

    Other skills you might teach include remodeling, painting, and land-
scaping. (If these ideas strike you as being farfetched, take a look at the
classifieds in your local paper and notice how many other people are
teaching home improvement skills.)

WHAT TO WATCH OUT FOR

One of the first decisions you'll have to make is whether to teach at
home or to offer your services at another location. Aside from zoning and
insurance factors, teaching at home can be difficult because of the trauma
of having your home invaded by 20 strangers. Give that some serious
thought.

When you're teaching business seminars, such as writing and speaking, also keep in mind that you'll be expected to come up with some
bottom-line justification for your efforts. Businesspeople want some proof
that attendees write or speak better after finishing your expensive course.
Be prepared to offer documentation if you want referrals or another contract.

TELEPHONE SALES AND RESEARCH _____

☐ Start-up costs: None
☐ Estimated hours per week: 10 to 20
☐ Number of staffers needed for start-up (including founder): 1

A few years ago, some accountants got together and figured out that the average price of a personal industrial sales call was as high as $300—whether the salesperson made the sale or not. That reality fueled a boom in telemarketing, a field you can enter from your home.

WHAT'S INVOLVED? _____

A research firm specializing in telemarketing offered a good definition of the art and science of selling by telephone: Telemarketing "brings a trained and prepared human being into a tightly controlled dialogue with another human being who has been carefully selected for contact."

The key words are *tightly controlled* and *carefully selected*. A good telemarketer knows how to pick and choose his or her words carefully in order to elicit the most positive response, and works from a narrow list of prospects. As an example relating to choice of words, research shows that a friendly question at the beginning of the conversation—"How are you tonight?"—gets the respondent into the talking mood and opens up more opportunity for the person making the sale.

FINDING WORK _____

Many telemarketing firms and research firms hire people to work from home. You can sell just about anything by telephone, and this includes products you, personally, are selling. Don't just think in terms of telemarketing for someone else; you can quite easily market your own stock of goods, such as home products and cosmetics. Anything's fair game. A Vermont telemarketing company sells books—so many books that it moves an estimated 95 percent of one publisher's out-of-bookstore sales.

If you do sell for someone else, you'll probably be looking at a maximum rate of return somewhere in the neighborhood of $10 an hour. Yes, some people do make more, but home-based telemarketing is not something you can count on to make you rich. If you do research, you'll probably make closer to $6 an hour, but often productivity bonuses can raise the figure somewhat.

Please note that it's dirty pool to disguise yourself as a researcher and then try to sell something. This makes people suspicious of legitimate researchers and hinders serious social research, something which is very important to everyone.

To find work selling for someone else, just look in the help wanted section of your local paper. Ads for telemarketing jobs are always abundant. But if you're interested in telemarketing, do give some thought to selling in a way that's more directly profitable to you; see if you can match telemarketing with some other ideas in this book that pique your interest.

RESOURCES ⎯⎯⎯⎯⎯⎯⎯⎯⎯⎯⎯⎯⎯⎯⎯⎯⎯⎯⎯

Joe Girard and Stanley H. Brown's book, *You Can Sell Anybody Anything* (Warner Books), gives an excellent introduction and overview. Also, check out James D. Porterfield's *Selling on the Phone: A Self-Teaching Guide* (Wiley).

TELEVISION PRODUCER FOR BUSINESS AND INDUSTRY _____

☐ Start-up costs: Assuming no equipment is purchased initially, allow about $1,500 for first-time rentals and deposits.
☐ Estimated hours per week: 5 to 15
☐ Number of staffers needed for start-up (including founder) 1. You must have a team of at least 2 or 3 for most assignments.

Within the last fifteen years or so, video has become a standard training tool in industry and education; television professionals today produce many videotapes for closed-circuit presentation to workers and students. Also, the taped television presentation, shown to clients, is emerging as a promotional tool in business and industry. Millions of training and public relations dollars are waiting to be tapped by savvy businesspeople with the know-how to create a promotional or instructional tape.

THE MOONLIGHTING MARKET _____

Promotional and instructional videos are the best fields for a freelancer. These categories call for less technical sophistication and hardware investment than do television commercials or fully produced programs intended for broadcast or telecast. Leave those supercompetitive markets to the full-time pros. Instead, think about selling directly to medium-size businesses (big firms often have their own in-house video setup). Here are some ideas that have been successful for various freelance producers:

- Training tapes for new employees in a restaurant, demonstrating food preparation and serving procedures. One 10-minute program was produced because restaurants in general and the client's establishment in particular have a very high rate of personnel turnover. Playing the tape for new employees on a video cassette recorder substitutes for dedicating an assistant manager to several hours' worth of touring and training once or twice a week.

- A promotional tape for an auto parts recycling business. The owner of this multimillion-dollar business wanted to communicate the idea that his establishment is no "junkyard." Instead, it's a computerized, modern business where anyone can shop for a part and have his order filled quickly by a polite clerk. This tape was shown to prospective clients and also at a large auto show.

In both cases, the individuals working on the tapes—the writer, cameraman, producer, and editor—each cleared between $500 and $1,000 in profit from two weekends of work.

SETTING UP A PRODUCTION TEAM

The secret to profitable TV moonlighting is to assemble a group of talented people looking for some additional income. You can rent equipment and editing time; if you put your team together carefully, it's also possible to find a freelancer with access to a camera and tape deck through his or her regular job, who can check the gear out on weekends. While many organizations quite justifiably frown on their employees' freelancing with company gear, it is common practice. In fact, some corporate video specialists regard access to equipment as one of the perks of the profession.

In any event, you'll find out about the equipment situation when you assemble the team. To get started, you need someone with at least a basic knowledge of TV production. Make some phone calls. Contact communications faculty at local colleges (always eager for work), video production people now working for major local companies (just call up and ask for the video department), and production people at local TV and cable stations (ask for the production department). Introduce yourself, mention that you're interested in putting together some freelance jobs, and ask the person on the other end if he or she is interested or has a colleague who might be.

Lest you feel presumptuous placing yourself in the role of producer, remember that any job has to have an organizer and a motivator who sells the idea to a client in the first place. That, basically, is the definition of a producer. And you'll find that even the most experienced TV pro will listen to an energetic newcomer to the field who can put together a profitable project.

As you gain experience, you'll get to know more about the various aspects of TV production; perhaps you have some of that knowledge now. In any event, the goal is to assemble a team who can

- Conceive an idea.
- Sell the idea to a client and secure a contract.
- Write a television script.
- Operate the television camera (a difficult job which definitely requires experience).
- Edit the tapes, usually on a ¾-inch editing system with two tape decks.

Experienced TV people can usually do more than one of the above jobs, so you might need only two people, depending on what you are able to do yourself.

FINDING JOBS

As a freelance producer, you quickly will come to know a great many people interested in the production business—a lot of jobs will come your way by word of mouth. A crack cameraman might mention that a local factory needs a tape demonstrating the workings of a new machine, or a small college needs a tape to show during recruitment. The cameraman will be happy to share this information with you because he can't do the job himself; and unless you, the producer, can assemble a team and pitch the client, he won't get a piece of the action.

Pricing these jobs is tricky, but essentially it's a matter of estimating the number of hours needed for the task and factoring in the hourly wage expectation of each team member, as well as the cost of the equipment. You may want to build in an on-top profit—10 percent, perhaps—to the person who negotiates the contract and makes the sale (that's you).

While you may wish to invest in equipment someday, rental is the best first option. Be aware that as a producer and perhaps writer you can literally rent an entire camera crew complete with gear; just call any of the firms listed under "Television Films—Producers and Distributors" or "Video Production Services" in the Yellow Pages. They won't come cheap, but you're not paying the final bill; just make sure that when everyone else is paid you've reaped a fair profit.

RESOURCES

One advantage of going into the TV business is that there are many excellent books to show you the basics. *Television Production Handbook* by Herbert Zettl (Wadsworth) is a masterpiece. You can find it in almost any large library, or you can order a copy through a local bookstore. To learn all about planning, budgeting, and scripting a business video, check out Diane M. Gayeski's *Corporate and Instructional Video: Design and Production* (Prentice-Hall). Also, consider a subscription to *Videography* magazine (50 W. 23rd St., New York, NY 10010), which gives the low-down on all the latest trends in corporate video.

TELEVISION REPAIRER_____

☐ Start-up costs: $8,000 and up, possibly less if you can jury-rig and/or repair old test equipment.
☐ Estimated hours per week: 6 to 15
☐ Number of staffers needed for start-up (including founder): 1

A good repairman (or woman) is hard to find. You can capitalize on this problem if you can provide fast, honest TV repair out of your home.

OPPORTUNITIES FOR THE HOME-BASED REPAIRER _____

There aren't very many TV repair people working out of their homes today; this kind of work takes an independent breed (rapidly vanishing) and has been made more difficult by the supersophistication of modern sets. However, the decline of the independent repairer, both home-based and in the small shop, has also created opportunity for the real hustler who works hard and produces good results.

In short, if you are very knowledgeable about TV repair, or can make yourself a true expert, you'll have plenty of business. Here's what you will need to do:

• Become officially qualified to repair television sets in your locality. There are widely differing regulations regarding TV repair, but a typical scenario involves a written test and a practical, hands-on exam.

- Obtain the full complement of test equipment. You'll need an oscilloscope, various meters, soldering equipment, and new special devices for removing microchips. You'll also need a generous assortment of standard hand tools.
- Assemble the inventory of replacement parts you'll need. Your inventory depends on the type of set(s) you intend to service; in any event, you'll have to have parts on hand because customers just won't tolerate long delays while you wait for orders.

BUILDING A MARKET

You have two types of potential clients:

1. The general public
2. Service centers for retailers

The general public, of course, will bring you any and every type of set. You can do a good business with the public, but you'll need broad knowledge and a good parts inventory. Retailers and retail service centers frequently will feed you a great deal of business for a particular type of set. (Not all retail repair centers do repairs in-house; they often send the repairs out to people like you.)

You can market to the general public with small ads in local papers or, if your zoning permits, with a sign outside your house. Reach stores by contacting their service manager. Ask if they have repair work they can farm out to you and stress your capability in handling the particular brand(s) they sell.

PRICING YOUR SERVICES

If you're good, you can easily command $35 an hour. In certain cities and for certain services, you can make even more.

RESOURCES

TAB Books publishes a line of guides dealing with television and electronics repair. The most basic is the *Beginner's Guide to TV Repair* by Homer L. Davidson. Also of use are *How to Test Almost Everything Electronic* by Jack Darr and Delton T. Horn, and *How to Troubleshoot and Repair Electronic Circuits* by Robert L. Goodman. Also, seriously consider the idea of working part-time for another TV repair shop before starting out on your own; the experience will be quite valuable.

TOUR GUIDE _____

☐ Start-up costs: Negligible
☐ Estimated hours per week: 3 to 8 for local tours, much higher for out-of-town trips.
☐ Number of staffers needed for start-up (including founder): 1

Being a tour guide is, to (badly) paraphrase Dickens, the best of jobs and the worst of jobs. At best, the job involves trips to interesting and exciting places. At worst, the tour guide must deal with cranky clients, lost luggage, and a host of logistical foul-ups.

OPPORTUNITIES FOR TOUR GUIDES _____

One opportunity particularly attractive to moonlighters who live in large cities is working as a city guide for bus companies. Bus firms in cities such as New York, San Francisco, and Toronto frequently hire locals to escort groups around the city and to local attractions. Anyone with a good knowledge of the terrain and sharp verbal skills can do this type of work.

Travel agencies frequently need tour guides for short trips. For example, if you live in New York and your work schedule allows you to take an occasional full day off, you may find some opportunities escorting a group of gamblers to Atlantic City.

Longer trips are usually difficult for a moonlighter, but part-timers can and do go overseas on escorted vacations. You will be particularly in demand should you be

- A teacher or professor with a specific knowledge of the language and culture of the destination.
- A native of the country in question.

MARKETING YOURSELF

Call travel agencies in your area and discuss your ambitions. Local travel agents can inform you of any local opportunities and will have an encyclopedic knowledge of which national travel firms might need your particular skills. Also, check with local bus companies. Travel schools offer courses related to working as a tour guide, but be aware that you don't have to attend a school to do the work. By the way, your local community college or adult education center may offer travel-related courses.

ONE MORE OPTION

What about setting up a tour of your own city? You might work as a tour packager (page 282) or simply conduct a walking tour of local historical sites. If you have a good store of knowledge concerning local history, you might be able to fill a weekly walking tour of 10 people at $10 or $15 a head. Be creative; think in terms of "The Historic North End," or "The Sites of Three Famous Revolutionary War Battles."

MONEY AND THE LACK OF IT

Tour guides don't make a lot of money. A fee of $6 to $8 an hour is usually considered quite good for many types of tour duties. Tour guides do receive tips, but you can't count on it. Sometimes, tour companies will recommend in their literature that a long-trip tour guide receive a certain tip—say, $5 per day per person—but that doesn't always materialize. You may receive a dollar or two per person for a day-long bus trip, but then again, you may not.

Although you'll never get rich, the work is varied, and you'll meet many interesting people along the way.

TOUR PACKAGER _____

☐ Start-up costs: Figure $1,000 to cover expenses, which will be reimbursed.
☐ Estimated hours per week: 5 to 8, but longer if and when you accompany tours.
☐ Number of staffers needed for start-up (including founder): 1, but it's a good possibility for a husband-and-wife team effort.

A tour packager comes up with an intriguing travel idea, finds people to fill up a trip, and builds in enough profit to at least pay for his travel and sometimes to make a cash profit. The work is ideal for people who love to travel and are looking for a home-based moonlighting opportunity.

ENTERING THE TRAVEL WORLD _____

There aren't many travel opportunities that lend themselves to home work. You pretty much can rule out starting a travel agency because it can't, by convention, be home-based. But even though you can't book flights and tour packages the way a travel agent can, you can work directly with the sales departments of some airlines and you always have the opportunity to book your tour through an established travel agent.

HOW PACKAGING WORKS _____

Suppose you're a native of Ireland and you want to organize a tour to Dublin, your hometown. Here's one way you might do it:

- Contact likely prospects in your community. They might be members of the Hibernians, or the fire department's fraternal organization. You determine if they would be interested in a guided tour; if so, you get a commitment from them.

- Work with travel providers to get the best bargain. You won't get the same discounts as a travel agency, but airlines and hotels are always willing to bargain if they have a large guaranteed group. You must make all the arrangements, remember, and that includes hotels and ground transportation. Ideally, you'll charge members of your tour group a price that covers the costs and provides a fair fee for your services.
- You might choose to work through a travel agency, which will do the scut work. There's less of a chance that you'll turn a profit on the deal when working through an agency, but you can still arrange to travel for free. As a general guideline, you can usually travel free on an overseas flight if you book 25 people; on a cruise you'll usually have to book 10 cabins.

AN EASIER ROUTE

Consider starting small. Organizing something like a fall foliage tour to a country inn 100 miles away is a reasonable and decently profitable option. Contract with a bus company for a vehicle and driver and set up a luncheon deal with the country inn. Now, it's a simple matter of arithmetic: set a fee for the tickets, and sell as many as needed to cover the expenses and your services. If you've gotten some commitments in advance you won't be taking such a risk. To set reasonable prices, check with tour agencies and find out what they charge for similar trips.

In sum, the secret to this or any other travel package is to *identify a likely group*. The local senior citizens' organization, for instance, might be a natural for the fall foliage trip. Similarly, the historical society would probably be good customers for a bus trip to Civil War battle sites. Think specific. You're not a travel agency, so you cannot and should not try to compete for business from the general public.

TRANSLATOR _____

☐ Start-up costs: Negligible other than mailing and telephone costs, and perhaps association memberships.
☐ Estimated hours per week: 5 to 15, although major blocks of time are often required for rush projects.
☐ Number of staffers needed for start-up (including founder): 1

Figuratively speaking, the world is becoming a smaller place every day. Modern businesses frequently deal with foreign suppliers or sell their goods in foreign markets. Publishers, for example, have found foreign markets quite profitable. And government agencies and certain private concerns need an in-depth understanding of the news and views of the non-English-speaking world.

THE TRANSLATOR'S JOB MARKET _____

It's obvious that much international business must be transacted in a foreign language; so someone facile in Japanese, German, French, Italian, Chinese, or just about any language can earn part-time income. If you have a good understanding of a language and its subtleties, there's a reasonable chance you can find an outlet for your skills translating correspondence, books, magazines, and technical papers. Remember, though, *you must also be very fluent in English,* because the people who pay for translations into English want insightful and expressive interpretations of the foreign work.

FINDING CLIENTS _____

Experienced translators report that it is somewhat difficult to find work initially in this field. However, once you've established a toehold, satisfied clients will steer regular work your way. How do you prospect for those jobs? You can contact some potential clients by sending resumes to

- Local firms conducting international business. Try asking the local chamber of commerce for ideas on which firms to approach.
- Firms that conduct international business in a specialty with which you're familiar. (This double-whammy significantly increases your chances of getting an assignment.) One successful translator uses the tactic of preparing a translation in the field of chemistry and mailing that sample translation—both the English and foreign version—to chemical companies.
- Government agencies. The federal government uses many translation services. It helps to live in or around Washington, but that's not absolutely necessary.

In addition, don't overlook the possibility of doing part-time or freelance work for translation agencies. Look for them in the Yellow Pages under "Translators & Interpreters." You'll probably earn a lower fee than you would getting a job on your own, but until you build a reputation, agency work may be your best—and perhaps only—option.

FEES AND SERVICES

Fees are quite variable. The American Translators Association notes that one indication of fee structures for translators is the schedule the U.S. State Department uses to pay freelance translators:

General material	$70 per thousand words
Semi-technical material	$75 per thousand words
Technical material	$80 per thousand words

Income from interpreting (that is, translating spoken presentations at the site of the event and repeating the speaker's words in another language) can be quite lucrative. One Japanese–English interpreter reported that he frequently has earned more than $200 a day. He cautions, however, that interpreting is exhausting and difficult work, and you'll earn every penny of your fee.

RESOURCES

You can find out more about the field of translation and interpreting by contacting professional groups, which include the American Translators Association (109 Croton Ave., Ossining, NY 10562).

TREE SERVICE _____

☐ Start-up costs: At the bare minimum, you'll need a pickup truck and a chain saw, preferably a small saw for use while climbing and a larger one for felling trees. A small saw can cost about $200, with a large one ranging up to $800. Other equipment can be quite expensive. Should you elect to add a stump grinder, you can pay $20,000. A chipper costs from $10,000 to $16,000. It often pays to rent these larger items on a per-job basis.
☐ Estimated hours per week: 10 to 20
☐ Number of staffers needed for start-up (including founder): 1, if you stick to small jobs.

A GROWING OPPORTUNITY _____

The world's tree supply may be dwindling, but there are still plenty of trees around that need care. But the number of specialists who can prune, cut down, or nurse trees back to health shrinks dramatically every year. There's a steady demand for people to do tree work, from simple pruning, to clearing woodlots, to felling huge trees in dense residential areas.

WHAT YOU'LL DO _____

Unless you're a real expert, you probably won't want to attempt felling a tree in a densely populated area. In the words of one tree service owner, "A dummy with a chain saw can do an awful lot of damage in a short time." But you can do the simpler jobs, such as woodlot clearing, and there's no reason why you can't drop trees if you know the technique and have the right insurance.

Tree specialists often make $8 to $15 an hour. If they have a heavy investment in equipment, fees rise proportionately.

WHAT YOU'LL NEED

Insurance is essential; you can't operate without it. The cost will vary from location to location, but be forewarned that the cost can be substantial. In most locations you don't need a special license other than a standard permit for doing business, but do check local regulations. Many tree specialists are certified arborists; you can become certified in most states by taking a one-day test. Check with your secretary of state.

RESOURCES

One advantage of this business is that it's relatively easy to get on-the-job training. Existing tree services are usually desperate for help. The job is hot, dirty, and sometimes dangerous, so there aren't too many applicants. If the prospect of this type of work doesn't bother you, take on a part-time job with someone else's tree service so you can learn all about trees and the tree business. You can also pick up some useful hints from the books *Trees for Every Purpose* by Joseph Hudak (McGraw-Hill) and *Trees, Shrubs and Lawns* by Donald M. Hastings (Taylor Publications).

TUTOR

☐ Start-up costs: Very low; classified ads are the only real expense.
☐ Estimated hours per week: 4 to 10
☐ Number of staffers needed for start-up (including founder): 1

A couple of decades ago, we learned that Johnny couldn't read. More recently, we found that he was lousy at science and math, too. Today's headlines seem to indicate that Johnny can't do much of anything.

This, indeed, is a sad state of affairs, but it's a veritable gold mine for a moonlighting tutor.

TUTORING TIPS

One experienced tutor is quick to point out that tutoring is not the same as teaching. Even an excellent teacher can be a poor tutor, and vice versa. Tutoring, you see, is helping a student solve a problem by himself. It's not so much a matter of imparting information as it is instinctively and systematically guiding the student through a learning process.

TUTORING MARKETS

You can tutor on several different levels and in various settings. Two sources of part-time tutoring jobs are.

- Jobs in area schools and colleges. Check your community colleges first, which often have resource centers for remedial writing and math. While most of the staff jobs are during the day, some are at night.

  Be aware that college tutoring work is not particularly hard, but it can be frustrating. Teachers who refer students for tutoring sometimes expect quicker results than a tutor can deliver, and quite frankly the students are not always enthusiastic about the situation. College tutoring also may not pay well; a community college may pay only $5 to $6 an hour for a tutor.

  In most cases, you need a bachelor's degree in a related subject to tutor on the college level.

  Incidentally, you'll be much more marketable as a tutor if you speak another language, particularly Spanish.
- Private tutoring. You can help students in your home or in their homes; the first option seems more popular. Usually, tutoring is done in private, but occasionally it is done in small group situations.

  Tutoring can be done in any field, but writing appears to be the subject most in demand. Math is second, followed by history and science.

  There are no rigid qualifications for home-based tutoring, but parents will be reassured if you have teaching experience and the appropriate college degree.

PLUSES AND MINUSES

Tutoring is slow, steady work. "Breakthroughs" are only made after long periods of work. To be perfectly honest, you'll usually be working with slower students, and often with students who regard the tutoring as a form of punishment for poor performance in class.

But some will be well motivated, and their parents certainly will appreciate any progress the student makes. Just remember that it's a long haul.

One other caveat: Be sure *you* can do the work. Helping a high school senior with calculus doesn't make sense if you yourself got only average grades in the subject as a college freshman 20 years ago.

HOW TO MARKET YOUR SERVICES

If you want to tutor at a small college, send a resume to the English or math department. You'll be interviewed if your resume strikes a responsive chord. Now, be forewarned that you may be interviewed by someone who speaks educationalese instead of English. You'll most likely be asked, "What instructional paradigms do you prefer for instilling knowledge of linguistic skills?" rather than, "How would you go about helping this kid speak up in class?" Take a cue from the Boy Scouts and be prepared.

Private tutors get most of their work from ads in daily and weekly newspapers, and then from the resulting word of mouth. Schoolteachers often seem reluctant to recommend particular private tutors to students or students' families. Should you be proficient in college-level subjects, put up a notice in the college library.

VENDING MACHINE OWNER/REPAIRER

☐ Start-up costs: If you plan to buy machines, the initial investment can be quite heavy—up to $4,000 for one coffee-dispensing machine. There are other opportunities in vending that involve little or no start-up costs.

☐ Estimated hours per week: 5 to 25

☐ Number of staffers needed for start-up (including founder): 1

Vending is not a quick way to get rich, despite what you may have heard. If, however, you can make a substantial first investment and have good contacts, vending can pay off handsomely. Smaller investments can provide you with more modest returns.

VENDING BASICS

Vending is worth checking into if you're willing to invest time and money. The time investment involves learning the ropes, since this is too risky a business to venture into blindly.

You can get into vending with an investment of as little as $100 a machine for those little gum-containing globes you see in grocery stores. Of course, you'll harvest only pocket money from them unless you manage to do a high-volume business.

You have to make arrangements with a property owner to place your vending machine. Often, that involves paying the owner a commission (usually less than 10 percent) on your gross sales. In some cases, you'll be charged no commission; on occasion when you provide a badly needed service, such as vending machines for a factory cafeteria, the business will actually pay you.

SOME OTHER OPPORTUNITIES

Don't rule out big-budget vending, but do learn about the business before you make any investment. You can get part-time jobs at a number of levels, and you'll gain exposure and see what the climate is like locally. One freelance opportunity is in vending machine repair (a handy skill if you someday plan to own your own machines).

RESOURCES

The National Automatic Merchandising Association (20 N. Wacker Dr., Chicago, IL 60606) offers a correspondence course in vending machine repair. The association also provides information about the vending business.

VIDEOTAPING SERVICE_____

☐ Start-up costs: About $2,000 minimum.
☐ Estimated hours per week: 6 to 15
☐ Number of staffers needed for start-up (including founder): 1

The technological advances in video have made home video truly affordable, and those who have an artistic eye and a steady hand can cash in on the trend by starting a videotaping service.

THE NEW VIDEO _____

By "home video," or "consumer video," we mean the type of gear sold to individual consumers who plan to use it for personal use, not for production of a program to be aired over a broadcast outlet. It's this type of gear you'll use to start a videotaping service. You can buy professional-standard gear, but it is *much* more expensive. Should you be interested in producing professional-quality video productions for business and industry (see *Television Producer for Business and Industry* page 275) you'll want to use professional gear, which you can rent.

You can use consumer-quality gear to run a videotaping service from your home, taping events such as weddings, graduations, and parties. Weddings are a particularly popular video offering nowadays, since more and more couples have access to a home video cassette recorder (VCR).

EQUIPMENT _____

What's involved in consumer video? For starters, you'll need a camera and a VCR; some units combine the two into a device known as a camcorder. Cameras vary widely in price and function, and in the selection process much depends on the particular tastes and requirements of the prospective user. Recorders for consumer video use ½-inch (the width of the tape) cassettes, almost always in the format known as VHS.

Consumer-style editing gear is also available; but if editing is necessary (i.e., rearranging the sequence of shots), most videotaping pros advise renting editing time from a local studio. If you have a listing of where the shots are located on tape (recorded by the counter numbers on the VCR) and a well-organized shot-sheet, you can edit a reasonably complex wedding video in an hour, at a cost of perhaps $30 to $50. You can rent a lot of editing time before you incur anywhere near the costs of owning your own editing equipment.

FINDING CLIENTS

Many videotaping services concentrate on weddings. If you're so inclined, you can find out who's getting married and cold-call on prospects simply by reading the engagement announcements in the local newspaper. Classified ads in daily and weekly papers are quite productive, and some videotaping service owners report good results from large Yellow Pages display ads.

You can also advertise the following services to clients: videotaping of valuables for insurance purposes, video yearbooks to be sold on cassette at local high schools, tapes of parties, and recordings of speeches of local politicians.

But back to basics for a second: You'll have to have a tape to show prospective clients, and there's no way around this requirement. Your best bet is to offer to tape a wedding for free, giving the bride and groom a copy of the tape in return for allowing you to use it as a marketing tool.

FIGURING COSTS

Overhead in any business involving high-tech gear is high, so you must adjust your fees accordingly. Unfortunately, there's a built-in ceiling on how much you can charge, which is the going rate in your town; customers looking for this kind of service do shop around. Prices vary widely, and there often is no discernible reason for the fluctuations among going rates. Call around and find out what other services charge for various functions and set your rate accordingly.

Be certain that you can charge a decent rate in your community before investing heavily. Remember, your overhead for equipment, transportation, repairs, tape, and studio rental time might be as high as $25 to $35 an hour once everything is added up, so carefully evaluate the prospects for turning a reasonable profit.

RESOURCES

Any good video person knows equipment and technique inside out, so study up in advance or you'll be swamped by the competition. As a first step, pick up a copy of *How to Make Movies with Your Video Camera* by Stuart Dollin (Putnam/Perigee). It's probably the best book ever written about consumer video and techniques, and contains a highly detailed chapter on how to shoot a wedding. Also of use is Ted Schwarz's *How to Make Money with Your Video Camera* (Prentice-Hall).

VINYL REPAIR SERVICE

☐ Start-up costs: You can get rolling for under $1,500. A truck is useful but not essential.
☐ Estimated hours per week: 10 to 20
☐ Number of staffers needed for start-up (including founder): 1

It doesn't take a genius to notice that there's an awful lot of torn and tattered vinyl around. Just take a careful look at the condition of the seating next time you go out to dinner. And those seats are expensive! It's much more attractive to a restaurateur to have those rips and nicks repaired than to order new chairs and booths.

If you're handy, you can tap into this market, and several other markets, for vinyl repair.

WHAT YOU'LL DO

Most repair jobs are done on-site. You insert a fabric backing behind the rip and attach it with a special glue. You then fill the hole with a vinyl compound. The difficult part of the task is to match the color exactly. You accomplish this by using a series of dyes, adding small amounts of the appropriate colors until you achieve a match. This isn't easy, but you can become remarkably adept at it with practice.

The final step involves heating the repair and sealing it with a rubberized template that matches the texture of the particular vinyl.

With practice you can produce surprisingly good results, but as one veteran of the business points out, you can't completely disguise all the scars. This sometimes becomes a point of contention between repairer and customer, so be forewarned.

POSSIBLE MARKETS FOR YOUR SERVICE

Restaurants are a good place to start. You can drop in, leave some of your business cards, and possibly wind up with a major contract. (If you pick up some basic upholstery skills, you can increase your marketability. Also, if you can truck the chairs back to your home and do the work there you may gain favor with the restaurant manager.)

Contact automobile repair shops; they sometimes contract out interior or vinyl top repair work. A newspaper ad can drum up some casual business, too.

HOW MUCH CAN YOU MAKE?

You can usually generate peak income in high-volume jobs, such as fixing all of the restaurant's chairs and booths. Fixing a cigarette hole can fetch $5 to $10; repairing a significant rip will net between $30 and $40. You can do quite a few of these jobs in the space of several hours, and experienced hands say you can pocket between $15 and $30 an hour.

RESOURCES

Most of the business start-ups in vinyl repair are available through mail order. Check the ads for vinyl repair start-up kits in various business magazines. *Entrepreneur* magazine (2311 Pontius Ave., Los Angeles, CA 90064) offers a start-up manual.

WALLPAPERER _____

☐ Start-up costs: Minimal
☐ Estimated hours per week: 5 to 12
☐ Number of staffers needed for start-up (including founder): 1

Wallpapering is a well-kept secret, both in terms of how to do it and how much money you can make running a home-based part-time wallpapering service. Inexperienced people just don't like to hang their own paper because they're afraid (often with good reason) that the results will be disastrous. As a result, they frequently hire outside help.

WHAT YOU'LL NEED _____

The beauty of a wallpapering business is that you can start it with just a few dollars. All you'll really need are

A yardstick
Several big sponges
Good scissors and a cutting instrument
A bucket
A plastic dipping bin (available where wallpaper is sold, for a minimal cost; sometimes the store will even give it to you)
If paper is not prepasted, you'll need a paste brush and paste

WHAT YOU'LL DO _____

Wallpapering is tricky, but virtually anyone can master it with practice. The most trying part of the operation is matching up the pattern, especially around corners. For example, if your paper has an umbrella pattern, and half the umbrella is at the end of the paper, you must overlap in such a way as to carry the pattern over uninterrupted.

That's really not so difficult, but it can get tricky in an old house with uneven corners. You'll find that dropping a plumb line is helpful (using a weight held from a string to determine the true vertical). Another tricky operation is cutting around many corners in rooms with several surfaces, such as bathrooms. Here, you'll need to learn by doing.

FINDING CLIENTS

Small ads in local papers, especially weeklies, work quite well. Word of mouth is also effective. You might also make up a flier and slip it under the doors in newly finished or recently renovated apartment buildings.

HOW TO FIGURE YOUR CHARGES

Many paperhangers charge $15 a roll hung for standard rooms; a roll has two individual sheets (or "drops," as they're known in the trade). The cost of the paper itself is borne directly by the client. Papering a typical bedroom would earn you about $150. You can usually charge $20 a roll for complex rooms such as bathrooms and kitchens.

RESOURCES

Take an adult education course in wallpapering. It's among the most popular of all adult ed courses. Learning to paper hands-on is important, because the tricks of the trade often can't be picked up from books. You could also have a knowledgeable friend teach you.

WARDROBE CONSULTANT _____

☐ Start-up costs: Except for basic promotional items such as business cards, costs are negligible. Of course, you do have to be well-dressed yourself, and that costs money.
☐ Estimated hours per week: 3 to 8
☐ Number of staffers needed for start-up (including founder): 1

If you have a natural flair for picking colors, styles, and designs, you probably don't realize how much other people don't know and how insecure they are about the way they dress. Many people may not know the fine points of dressing for the business world. All they know is that they occasionally hear not-too-flattering remarks about their paisley shirts and plaid jackets, and they are frustrated by having to play a game in which they don't know the rules.

WHY PEOPLE NEED YOUR HELP _____

It's no secret that choice of clothing affects a person's success in business. John Malloy, author of *Dress for Success,* conducted experiments which demonstrated that a person wearing clothes that projected the right image (a beige raincoat, for instance, as opposed to a black raincoat) was treated better by secretaries, or admitted to see an executive more frequently, than was his less appropriately attired counterpart.

It's also quite obvious that a person's taste in clothing affects other people's perceptions of him or her. What is your reaction to someone who wears mixed plaids and white socks? Case closed.

WHAT YOU CAN DO

An image consultant helps people choose clothes that suit their profession and status and make them look as attractive as possible. Your advice can assist your clients in their efforts to advance their professional standing. You'll evaluate the client's image, the client's *intended* image, and the current state of his or her wardrobe. Then you'll recommend changes. This business could also be combined with *Color Consultant* (page 74).

Market your services to executives, both male and female. Should you be unsure how to reach them, contact your local chamber of commerce; they can almost always provide lists of local firms and their leaders. If you don't have any luck there, ask a reference librarian for assistance.

MARKETING A WARDROBE CONSULTANT'S SERVICE

One way to advertise your service is to place a classified ad in one of the local publications geared to businesspeople; specifically, offer prospective clients assistance in dressing in a manner both tasteful and appropriate for their business. Another marketing idea is to leave your business cards at clothing stores. You might be successful with this tactic if you agree to refer clients to those stores.

PRICING

You'll probably want to offer an initial blanket consultation, which includes an evaluation of the current wardrobe, recommendations on what to buy in order to improve and update the wardrobe, and advice on certain clothes that will:

- Accentuate the good points of the client's appearance.
- Hide figure problems.
- Produce what executives like to call a "power image."

Some consultants also go shopping with the client. Price is largely a matter of what the market will bear. Some image consultants charge $150 for a consultation; others charge much more than that. Just be sure that your prices are reasonable enough that the client will call you for a return engagement when it's clothes-buying time again.

Remember, it's not your job to turn each client into a fashion plate. Your goal is not to dress a portly businessman in the clothes featured in the latest edition of *Gentleman's Quarterly;* he'll look like an idiot, and so, by extension, will you. Concentrate on building an *appropriate* wardrobe.

RESOURCES

John Malloy's classic *Dress for Success* (Warner Books) is a carefully researched and beautifully presented book full of information that will never go out of date. *The Professional Image* by Susan Bixler (Putnam) offers a total program of wardrobe advice for men and women. You can use the knowledge from these and other books in your practice, but it's really essential that you have a knack for wardrobe planning, which is something you probably either have or you never will. (And if you don't, of course, you hire a consultant.)

WATCH AND CLOCK REPAIRER

☐ Start-up costs: Anywhere from about $2,000 for basic clock repair to $25,000 for sophisticated watch repair. Items you'll need include a cleaning machine, testing devices, and a wide assortment of hand tools.
☐ Estimated hours per week: 12 to 25
☐ Number of staffers needed for start-up (including founder): 1

Watch and clock repair is, by some estimates, a dying profession. We live in a throwaway world, and more often than not a consumer with a malfunctioning watch or clock will simply toss it and buy a new one. This factor also has resulted in a shortage of watch and clock repairers, so you might find yourself a profitable part-time niche if you're patient and mechanically oriented.

THE FUNDAMENTALS

Many watch repairers work for jewelry stores that frequently farm out to freelancers. Watch and clock repairers also secure business through newspaper and Yellow Pages ads.

It's not particularly easy to learn the trade. You can attend a watch repair school (there are many scattered across the country) or, as is more commonly done these days, learn the business by apprenticing to a craftsman now in business.

THE BUSINESS

You can usually charge $50 to $60 to repair an expensive watch, and a clock can sometimes fetch even more. If you're very good, you can fix several watches within three or four hours, but problems do arise and can slow you down considerably. That's one reason why experienced craftspeople usually work on six watches at a time. Should they encounter a difficult problem, they move on and approach the tough repair job when they've had some time away from it. (Of course, you also work on a number of watches because it's necessary to monitor a device to be sure that it is keeping the correct time; you won't work efficiently if you fix one watch, wait, check it again, wait, and then move on to another watch.)

RESOURCES

Call watch and clock repairers in your area and ask if they're looking for an apprentice. Should you desire formal training, check out the American Watchmakers Institute and its publication, *Horological Times* (3700 Harrison Ave., Cincinnati, OH 45211). A good reference book is Henry Gordon Harris's *Handbook of Watch and Clock Repairs* (Harper & Row).

WEDDING MUSICIAN

☐ Start-up costs: No major costs other than instruments and sheet music. Sets of sheet music can run several hundred dollars per person.
☐ Estimated hours per week: 6 to 8
☐ Number of staffers needed for start-up (including founder): 4 to 6

A versatile musician can make a steady income in the booming wedding reception biz, either as part of someone else's combo or as head of his or her own. It's a perfect moonlighting job, since gigs are outside the typical working day, and the job itself offers a refreshing break from daily duties.

THE NATURE OF THE BUSINESS

This is not to imply that playing weddings is all fun and games. It is very hard work and sometimes involves some unpleasant situations. Here are some of the things that make wedding musicians tear out their hair:

- An audience that does not like their style of music. Wedding bands are generally hired by the bride and groom—young people who often like loud rock music. Weddings are *attended* by the families of the bride and groom, who usually hate loud rock music. The wedding combo is then in the unusual position of being asked to turn it down and turn it up at the same time.
- An audience that does a lot of drinking. Weddings get rowdy, and disturbances are common. More than one wedding band has had to play through a brawl and/or put up with drunken hecklers.
- Having to play plain-vanilla music. Musicians who want to engage in experimental improvisation need not apply to the wedding business.

REQUIREMENTS

If you can put up with the above, you'll probably make a good wedding musician if you play accurately and reliably. Most wedding combos use collections of sheet music known as fake books, which consist of popular tunes and old standards arranged for a typical instrumentation. Fake books are available in music stores, as are a variety of other combo instrumentations. (Hint: You can save time and find a big selection if you go to a large, well-stocked music store. A drive to a nearby city will be worth it if that's where the larger stores are located.)

Instrumentation may vary, but usually a wedding combo is composed of a singer, guitar, keyboard, reed, percussion, and base. Most musicians are pretty versatile, so some doubling is probable (vocal and guitar or vocal and keyboard are typical).

FINDING CLIENTS

Some wedding bands market themselves through an agent (usually listed under "Entertainment Bureaus" in the Yellow Pages). An agent secures bookings for a cut of the fee. But eventually most of a combo's work will come through referral. After all, you'll usually be playing before several hundred people at each wedding, and that quickly supplies a healthy network of potential customers. Be sure that you leave an adequate supply of business cards with the bride and groom, and give cards to anyone who asks about your services during the reception. Be certain, too, that the name of your combo is prominently visible somewhere on stage.

MONEY MATTERS

The low end for playing at a reception nowadays is about $400; bands with name recognition can garner considerably more. Reception gigs usually last about three or four hours. Be sure to specify up front how long you will be expected to play and how many breaks you'll receive. The typical arrangement is 45 minutes on and 15 minutes off, or 40 on and 20 off.

WINDOW AND SCREEN REPAIRER

☐ Start-up costs: Usually under $300.
☐ Estimated hours per week: 5 to 15
☐ Number of staffers needed for start-up (including founder): 1

The nice thing about windows and screens—from your standpoint, anyway—is that they occasionally need expert repair. Cutting a screen or installing a pane of glass is not something the weekend do-it-yourselfer does very well (or cares to spend the weekend on), as a rule. If you can master these tasks, you can generate some good part-time income.

TOOLS OF THE TRADE

You'll need a wide variety of tools, but none of them is very expensive. Your shopping list includes several putty knives (straight and bent blades), good heavy chisels for digging out putty, a screen roller (a sort of heavy-duty pizza cutter used on screening), trimming knives, screwdrivers, and a small pry bar. Tools for more advanced functions include a torch for burning out putty, a plexiglass and glass cutter, and a long, heavy straightedge for cutting glass. An electric putty heater and point gun are luxuries, but very handy ones.

To drum up business, place an ad in your local paper. Word of mouth among your friends and acquaintances will also generate quite a few inquiries.

Shoot for $10 an hour in labor costs. A typical job of scraping, reputtying, and replacing a pane in a wooden storm window (usually consisting of two 28-inch square panes) can be done in a half hour. Materials for the task might cost about $8.50. So, for a typical job you'll only have to charge $13.50, meaning that homeowners will see a good value and call you back for more work.

HOW TO GET STARTED

It's important that you really are skilled in doing this kind of work before you attempt to charge for it. Window and screen repair is not something that can be easily learned from books, although how-to books can serve as worthwhile references. It can also be very tedious work for the beginner. There are some aspects of window and screen repair an experienced hand must demonstrate; for example, glass makes a certain sound when it's cut properly, and you can't learn that from a book. If you want to pick up the skills, try adult education classes or get a part-time job at a window repair company.

One other warning before you go into the business: It's wise to see the job first before giving an estimate. Old windows may have unusual construction, which may lengthen the job considerably.

WOODWORKER _____

☐ Start-up costs: Varies, depending on the type of work you plan to do. A basic workshop can be set up for under $1,000.
☐ Estimated hours per week: 10 to 20, highest before peak demand seasons such as Christmas.
☐ Number of staffers needed for start-up (including founder): 1

Beautiful woodwork will always find enthusiastic buyers. We're drawn to wood and wood products, perhaps because wood is such a basic part of our environment. For some, appreciation for fine woods creates a lifelong hobby—a hobby that can also turn a decent profit.

HOW WOODWORKING PRODUCTS ARE SOLD _____

Consider the example of a Venice, California, artist and woodworker who showed one of his ornamental wood designs to the proprietor of an art gallery. The proprietor bought all 27 samples. Encouraged by the quick sale, the woodworker sent slides of the ornaments to a Los Angeles museum gift shop. The reply came quickly: Send us 63 dozen. Eventually, another order was placed for 85 dozen.

Some woodworking products sell equally well when marketed directly to consumers. *Forbes* magazine recently profiled a Maryland entrepreneur who sells do-it-yourself kits for assembling antique furniture reproductions by mail order. According to *Forbes*, what started as a sideline now probably clears over $1 million a year.

THE HOME SHOP _____

Woodworking takes some experience and expertise, although newcomers can sometimes crack the specialty and gift store market. On the low end of the woodworking skill scale are such items as

Cutout Christmas ornaments
Nameplates
Bookends and other small pieces

A skilled woodworker with the right equipment can turn out such big-ticket items as

Cabinets
Tables
Statuary and other artwork

Obviously, the level of work you attempt depends on your skills and to an extent your equipment. Good woodworking tools do not come cheaply. A 15-inch planer can set you back about $800. A 14-inch band saw will cost close to $300, as will a decent 10-inch table saw.

FINDING YOUR NICHE

For small novelty pieces, show samples to local merchants or mail slides to large outlets. Shoot a number of slides showing different varieties and views of your product. Be sure to ship the slides in clear plastic sheets, available in any camera store.

Gift and specialty stores in your area are promising potential customers. Call on the shop owners when they aren't busy and show samples of your work. Be prepared to dicker: Merchants will want to get your products at a low enough price so that they can mark them up at least 20 percent. You, of course, want enough for the product so that you can make a decent profit. Sometimes, stores will take your merchandise on consignment, although purchasing an order outright is more common.

Pricing depends on the type of product you're selling and where. Simple items—those requiring little labor—can be marked up two or three times the cost of materials. For instance, you might want to sell each pine duck for double what it cost you for the wood, glue, and stain. More complex jobs, common in woodworking, might be pegged to the hourly rate you want to earn. Scout out as many stores as possible in your area and find out what they sell similar works for; that will give you an indication of your ballpark charge per item and the hourly rate you may be able to obtain.

Experienced moonlighting woodworkers point out that anyone considering taking orders should seriously evaluate the time factor. Getting an order for 90 dozen Christmas ornaments is exciting, but spending eight hours a night chained to a band saw may not ultimately be worth it to you. Be realistic about the time you want to commit to your new business.

Also, don't be afraid to get family members in on the act. Enterprising woodworkers know that Henry Ford really did have a better idea when he instituted mass production. A few motivated volunteers in an assembly line can speed things along exponentially.

RESOURCES

There are countless books on woodworking. One of the best is *Making Country Furniture* by Richard A. Lyons (Prentice-Hall). Even if you don't want to make furniture, you'll benefit from the sound general business advice in the book.

Fine Woodworking (Taunton Press, P.O. Box 355, 52 Church Hill Rd., Newton, CT 06470) is an excellent periodical for the more advanced hobbyist. It contains practical articles of particular interest to the home woodworker, such as "Improvising a Spray Booth." If you can locate the September/October 1986 issue of the magazine in your library (or back-order it from the magazine), you'll come across a list of regional woodworking guilds, organizations that pool their skills and talents. Such idea-pooling is also one function of the various national woodworking organizations, such as the Woodworking Association of North America (P.O. Box 706, Plymouth, NH 03264).

WORD PROCESSOR

☐ Start-up costs: A minimum of $2,000 for a word processor, software, and printer, much higher for more sophisticated equipment.
☐ Estimated hours per week: 10 to 20
☐ Number of staffers needed for start-up (including founder): 1

Communication via the written word continues to grow at a staggering rate. This trend represents a good opportunity for those who can produce a neat and accurate page and are comfortable with computer technology.

AN EXPLODING MARKET

Computer-aided typing, which is all word processing really is, has become a virtual necessity for many segments of the population. For example, graduate students preparing dissertations or theses must make many revisions in their texts. Doing this the old-fashioned way—typing, retyping, and typing again—takes much more time than simply entering the changes into the word processor and having the machine print out a clean, revised copy.

In the increasingly competitive job market, it's de rigueur to send a personalized letter of application along with a resume (see *Resume Writer*, page 243). This can be a troublesome task for the applicant with a standard typewriter, but it's a snap for a word-processing expert armed with the right equipment and software.

Most of those people who need word processors regularly or on occasion can't afford one or simply don't want to learn how to use one. That's where you come in. With the right equipment and know-how, you can easily earn $20 to $25 an hour. You'll usually want to charge a per-page rate that adds up to this hourly total, perhaps $1.25 to $1.50 per page. You'll have to charge more for highly complex pages, such as statistical charts and summaries.

START-UP

Initially, you need to make a rather considerable investment of both time and money. Here's what you'll need:

- The word-processing machinery itself. You have two choices: a personal computer suited to word processing or a machine that does nothing but word processing (known as a "dedicated word processor"). Among experienced word-processing pros the concensus seems to be that a personal computer is by far the better bargain because the range of applications is much broader and the equipment itself is usually lower-priced, but you may get better service and support with a dedicated word processor. You also need a printer that produces letter-quality characters. The cheaper dot-matrix printers can't be used in word processing, although newer and more expensive models produce beautiful copy. So-called daisy-wheel printers (which use a daisy-shaped printing element) produce characters identical to a typewriter's, but they print more slowly. Speed is a big consideration, for obvious reasons.
- Word-processing software. Basically, your program tells your computer how to perform the task at hand, such as reformatting a paragraph,

moving a block of text from one location to another, or searching the entire document for a word you may have misspelled. Popular software includes such trademarked entries as WordStar, Perfect Writer, and Peachtext. Word-processing packages can cost about $400, but in some cases they are included in the purchase price of a computer. All programs don't work with all computers, so buying a bundled system (software included as part of the computer purchase deal) can be a good idea. Be sure to try the program in the store before making any purchase.

BUSINESS PRACTICE

You can solicit customers by placing ads in newspapers and business publications. Circulars posted in the libraries of local universities are also quite helpful.

When dealing with customers, be sure to find out exactly what is expected for a particular job and to agree on the fee. Some word-processing professionals insist on a deposit or some other form of up-front payment.

A good idea if you are working with students: Obtain copies of various manuals and stylebooks that give instructions on proper formats for various academic papers. The popular series of manuals by Kate Turabian, available in any bookstore, is a good start, as is the stylebook of the Modern Language Association. Once you know proper academic format and build a reputation, repeat business from both students and faculty can be quite healthy. You can also solicit business from commercial firms; some will farm out reports and such to you. Write letters to area businesses describing your services, and consider an ad in a local business-oriented publication.

RESOURCES

Read the computer magazines. Learn as much as you can about the latest hardware and software on the market. Bookstores carry rack after rack of books dealing specifically with the use of various word-processing programs. For more information on the business end of word processing, visit the local library and peruse the titles dealing with word processing as a business (look under the heading "Word Processing"). One of the best is Gary S. Belkin's *How to Start and Run Your Own Word Processing Business* (Wiley).

BIBLIOGRAPHY _____

Works that apply to a specific topic described in this book are cited at the end of the entry. The following are general-interest resources of use to anyone establishing a moonlighting business at home. Please note that the material listed is only a small selection of the available information of interest to home-based moonlighters.

ACCOUNTING, FINANCE, AND TAXES _____

Cornish, Clive G. *Basic Accounting for the Small Business*. Blue Ridge Summit, PA: TAB Books, 1981.

McQuown, Judith H. *Inc. Yourself: How to Profit by Setting Up Your Own Corporation*. New York: Warner Books, 1981.

Morse, Wayne and Harold P. Roth. *Cost Accounting: Processing, Evaluating and Using Cost Data*, 3rd ed. Reading, MA: Addison-Wesley, 1981.

U.S. Internal Revenue Service. Publications of Interest include:
 #334, Tax Guide for Small Business
 #533, Self-Employment Tax
 #587, Business Use of Your Home
Contact your local IRS office for ordering information.

BUSINESS PLANS _____

McLaughlin, Harold J. *Building Your Business Plan: A Step-by-Step Approach*. New York: Wiley, 1985.

Williams, Edward E., and Salvatore E. Manzo. *Business Planning for the Entrepreneur*. New York: Van Nostrand Reinhold, 1983.

U.S. Small Business Administration. *Business Plan for Small Business Firms*. (See ordering information under Public Relations listing in this bibliography.)

ENTREPRENEURSHIP

Baumback, Clifford M., and Joseph R. Mancuso. *Entrepreneurship and Venture Management*. Englewood Cliffs, NJ: Prentice-Hall, 1975.

Revel, Chase. *184 Businesses Anyone Can Start and Make a Lot of Money*. New York: Bantam, 1984.

_____. *168 More Businesses Anyone Can Start and Make a Lot of Money*. New York: Bantam, 1987.

White, Richard M., Jr. *The Entrepreneur's Manual: Business Start-ups, Spinoffs, and Innovative Management*. Radnor, PA: Chilton, 1977.

MAGAZINES OF SPECIAL INTEREST TO THE HOME-BASED MOONLIGHTER

Entrepreneur. 2311 Pontius Ave., Los Angeles, CA 90064. Publishes a series of start-up manuals for various businesses.

In Business. Box 323, 18 S. 7th St., Emmaus, PA 18049.

Venture. 521 Fifth Ave., New York, NY 10175.

NEWSLETTERS DEALING WITH SPECIFIC ISSUES RELEVANT TO HOME-BASED MOONLIGHTERS

Home Business News. 1791-D Rolling Hills Dr., P.O. Box 443, Twinsburg, OH 44087.

National Home Business Report. P.O. Box 2137, Naperville, IL 60566.

PUBLIC RELATIONS AND ADVERTISING FOR SMALL BUSINESS

Benoit, Philip and Carl Hausman. *Do Your Own Public Relations*. Blue Ridge Summit, PA: TAB Books, 1983.

Dean, Sandra L. *How to Advertise: A Handbook for Small Business*. Wilmington, DE: Enterprise Publishing, 1983.

U.S. Small Business Administration. *Plan Your Advertising Budget*. Publication # MA 4.018. To order any SBA publication, write SBA, P.O. Box 1534, Ft. Worth, TX 76119. Ask for order forms 115A and 115B; the order forms are free. BA publications are sent for a small processing fee.

WORKING AT HOME

Behr, Marion, and Wendy Lazar. *Women Working Home: The Homebased Business Guide & Directory*. Distributed by Rodale Press, Emmaus, PA.

Bohigian, Valerie. *How to Make Your Home-Based Business Grow: Getting Bigger Profits from Your Product*. New York: New American Library, 1984.

——————. *Real Money from Home*. New York: New American Library, 1987.

Davidson, Peter. *Earn Money at Home*. New York: McGraw-Hill, 1982.

Edwards, Paul and Sarah Edwards. *Working From Home: Everything You Need to Know About Living and Working Under the Same Roof*. New York: J. P. Tarcher, 1987.

National Small Business United. 1155 15th St., N.W., Suite 710, Washington, DC 20005. Publishes *Enterprise USA* monthly.

MISCELLANEOUS ASSOCIATIONS OF PARTICULAR INTEREST TO HOME-BASED MOONLIGHTERS

Homebased Businesswomen's Network. 5 Cedar Hill Rd., Salem, MA 01970.

National Alliance of Homebased Businesswomen. P.O. Box 306, Midland Park, NJ 07432.

National Association for the Self-Employed. 2316 Gravel Rd., Fort Worth, TX 76118.

CATALOG OF BUSINESS SERVICES

Readers of this book can obtain a free copy of the *Sure-Fire Business Success Catalog,* a catalog of services and goods of particular interest to home-based moonlighters, by writing: Jeffrey Lant Associates, Inc., 50 Follen St., Suite 507, Cambridge, MA 02138.

THE PHENOMENAL
NATIONAL BESTSELLERS
FROM TRACY KIDDER

A·M·O·N·G
SCHOOLCHILDREN

71089-7/$9.95 US/$11.95 Can

For an entire year Tracy Kidder lived among twenty school-children and their indomitable, compassionate teacher—sharing their joys, their catastrophes, and their small but essential triumphs.

71115-X/$9.95 US/$11.95 Can

Tracy Kidder's "true life-adventure is the story of Data General Corporation's race to design and build the Eagle, a brand new 32-bit supermini computer, in the course of just a year and a half…compelling entertainment."

Washington Post Book World

HOUSE

71114-1/$9.95 US/$11.95 Can

With all the excitement and drama of a great novel, Kidder now takes us to the heart of the American dream—into the intimate lives of a family building their first house.